FINALLY.......

THE HOW TO OF FORGIVENESS

A Three-Tier Approach to Dry Your Tears

Dr. Joan Weathersbee Ellason

DEDICATION

Dedicated to my son,

Chad Weathersbee Ellason

The Joy of My Life

Finally…….The How To of Forgiveness

A Three-Tier Approach to Dry Your Tears

Dr. Joan Weathersbee Ellason

Copyright © 2020 Oasis Workshops with Dr. Joan Weathersbee Ellason
Cover design by pro_design37

Formatting design by Aslamkhan116

Copyright Notices:

Some scripture quotations taken from the (NASB®) New American Standard Bible®, Copyright © 1960, 1971, 1977, 1995, 2020 by The Lockman Foundation. Used by permission. All rights reserved. www.lockman.org.

Some scripture quotations are taken from the *Holy Bible*, New Living Translation, copyright © 1996, 2004, 2015 by Tyndale House Foundation. Used by permission of Tyndale House Publishers, Inc., Carol Stream, Illinois 60188. All rights reserved.

Some scriptures taken from the New King James Version®, Copyright © 1982 by Thomas Nelson. Used by permission. All rights reserved.

Some scriptures taken from THE HOLY BIBLE, NEW INTERNATIONAL VERSION® NIV® Copyright © 1973, 1978, 1984, by International Bible Society®, 2011 by-Biblica Inc®. Used by permission. All rights reserved worldwide.

Some scriptures taken from *The Authorized (King James) Version. Rights in the Authorized Version in the United Kingdom are vested in the Crown. Reproduced by permission of the Crown's patentee, Cambridge University Press.*

Some scripture quotations taken from the Amplified® Bible (AMP), Copyright © 2015 by The Lockman Foundation. Used by permission. www.Lockman.org.

Some scripture quotations are from the ESV® Bible (The Holy Bible, English Standard Version®), copyright © 2001 by Crossway, a publishing ministry of Good News Publishers. Used by permission. All rights reserved.

All Rights Reserved.

All rights reserved. No part of this publication may be reproduced, distributed, or transmitted in any form or by any means, including photocopying, recording, or other electronic or mechanical methods without the prior written permission from the author, except in the case of brief quotations embodied in critical reviews and certain non-commercial uses permitted by copyright law.

Permission is granted to the original purchaser to reproduce the pages in Appendix A, containing the additional exercises and guided imageries, Tables 1 – 7 and Figure A graphic, for educational, ministry, and client care purposes.

The information given in this book should not be treated as a substitute for professional medical or clinical advice; always consult a medical or clinical practitioner. Any use of information in this book is at the reader's discretion and risk. Neither the author nor the publisher can be held responsible for any loss, claim, or damage arising out of the use, or misuse, of the suggestions made, the failure to take medical or clinical advice, or for any material on third-party websites.

First Printing: 2020

ISBN: 978-1-7357627-7-7

LCCN: 2020920695

Dr. Joan Weathersbee Ellason

Address: 1809 K Avenue, Suite 1,

Plano Texas 75074, U.S.A.

(469) 831-4548

Email: DrJWE@outlook.com

www.DrJoanWeathersbee.com

Dr. Joan Weathersbee Ellason is available to provide Workshops on Forgiveness or other topics.

For booking information Call or text (469) 831-4548 or email: DrJWE@outlook.com,

include WORKSHOP in the subject line.

Disclaimer

The stories described in this book are from personal accounts, according to the recollections and reported personal experiences of contributors, whose names and identifying details have been changed for their protection and privacy.

Joan Weathersbee Ellason, PhD, LPC

Dr. Joan Weathersbee Ellason brings a powerful and unique approach to healing in her workshops. Integrating over four decades of experience, she combines educational, clinical, spiritual, and musical training into a creative symphony of inspiration that brings a breath of fresh air. She helps people move beyond emotional challenges with her blended approach of insights and experiential techniques from a Christian perspective that can rejuvenate the soul.

With a career devoting her energies to learning effective methods of treatment, Dr. Weathersbee Ellason has helped many clients rise above life's difficulties. In the 1980s, she began helping survivors of trauma on a voluntary basis. From that point, she went on to obtain a bachelor's degree at Angelo State University, a master's degree at Texas Woman's University, and a doctorate degree at the University of Texas. She has poured countless hours and energy into publishing hope through scientific, psychological, and psychiatric journal articles with Dr. Colin A. Ross, MD, and other trauma experts. These publications include the *American Journal of Psychiatry*, the *Journal of Nervous and Mental Disease*, and the *American Journal of Pastoral Counseling*. She has served in private practice as a Licensed Professional Counselor since 1994.

As a Christian, Joan has volunteered to serve in music ministry for churches through the years and has also served as lead female music soloist for the Texas Air National Guard. She now brings the culmination of these talents and training into her workshops in such a way that can propel the listener into a deeply personal transformation. Her workshops include "Who Takes Care of the Care-taker?" "Developing Your Potential," and "The How-To of Forgiveness."

For workshop and presentation requests, contact Dr. Joan Weathersbee Ellason at email DrJWE@outlook.com, or you may call or text her at 469-831-4548. For emails, please indicate WORKSHOP in the subject line and provide your contact information, including your phone number. Feel free to visit her

website:www.DrJoanWeathersbee.com.

Table of Contents

Part I: INTRODUCTION 1

Chapter 1: What You May Already Know . . . Or Not 8

Chapter 2: What You Need to Know . . . *Oh, Yes You Do*.. 31

    Myth #1 – The Authority Myth 33

    Myth 2 – The Amnesia Myth.. 40

    Myth 3 – The Kiss and Makeup Myth............................. 44

    Myth 4 – The Miracle Myth 47

    Myth 5 – The Omniscience Myth.................................... 49

    Myth 6 – The Self-Deception Myth................................. 52

    Myth 7 – The Omnipotence Myth 55

    Myths 8 – The Martyrdom Myth..................................... 56

    Myth 9 – The Bliss Myth.. 59

    Myth 10 – The Conclusion-Delusion Myth.................... 64

    Moving from Mythology to Reality 69

Chapter 3: Necessary Tools and How to Use Them 83

Part II: Now, On With the HOW 103

Chapter 4: Tier I: How to Grieve 109

Chapter 5: Tier II: The Cognitive Shift.................................136

Chapter 6: Exercises: How to Turn Your Trauma into Triumph 188

Chapter 7: Tier III: A Higher Order Perspective Existence (H.O.P.E.) 234

    Bullet Proof, Powerful, and Beyond............................. 234

Appendix A: Additional Exercises and Guided Imageries..287

REFERENCES 295

SUGGESTED READINGS AND RESOURCES............302

Inspirational lectures and Teachings 306

ACKNOWLEDGMENTS...307

LIST OF TABLES AND FIGURES

Figure A: What Was Poured Into You? How Do You Want to Filter the Love Offered to You Now?...................................... 75

Figure B: Emotional Pain Scale (Subjective) 194

Figure C: Emotional Repair Dimension (Subjective)......... 200

Table 1: Ten Myths of Forgiveness 76

Table 2: The Grieving Process of Forgiveness Work 116

Table 3: Examples of Taking Care of Yourself Through Positive Thought and Action 130

Table 4: Situations for Alternative Ways of Thinking........ 157

Table 5: Three Resource Pathways 168

Table 6: The Cognitive Shift.. 186

Table 7: Walking Invincibly: Higher Order Perspective Existence (H.O.P.E.)... 273

Part I
INTRODUCTION

―――――∽―――――

Jamie collapsed onto the floor shaking and trembling. Amidst the screams and tears – "Why! Why does this keep happening all over again? I forgave already, and here it is again. Here I am triggered as if I never forgave them at all!" The pain came roaring back up like a hurricane, hijacking all focus, concentration, and the ability to function. The perpetrator, though, seemed utterly unscathed. Jamie had unexpectedly bumped into them, and they seemed to be going along just fine – happy-go-lucky as if they had done nothing wrong. Where is their pain?! They hurt me, and I have to work ten times as hard to get over it while they seem care-free. Where is the justice?!

This book is written to show you the how-to of forgiveness by intertwining many practical, clinical, and spiritual perspectives. It is written from a Christian viewpoint because it was the author who personally found such concepts to be restorative. All readers from all walks and faiths are welcomed to explore the tools and exercises in this book and apply them according to what works personally.

These pages are written by a licensed professional counselor with a doctorate degree in psychology who has applied many of these concepts in private practice as well as in personal life. While formal education is valuable and doctoral training is rigorous, true-life experience is irreplaceable. Often, life experience is a *trial by fire*, surpassing the traditional academic education, expanding the insight, and providing a deeper boot camp level of forgiveness training.

The purpose of this book is to provide you with a combination of clinical, spiritual, and practical training with true-life examples and some general situations to show you how to rise above some of your own difficulties. All three levels of the process taught are designed to help you reach a level of forgiveness that goes beyond a mere head-level decision (which I refer to as a cerebral level of forgiveness). The purpose of this book is to give you specific and tangible tools that you can apply and adapt to your own unique situation, helping you to achieve a deeper level of emotional freedom.

How This Book is Different from Other Teachings

Most of us stop at the cerebral level of forgiveness, which involves merely reciting words to the offender, such as, "I forgive you" or "I release you." Even though I believe that we are doing our best to be obedient and God recognizes our sincere effort in our heart of hearts, the pain often comes roaring back to the surface unexpectedly when we thought that we had forgiven them once and for all. I believe that if you have only accomplished the cerebral level of forgiveness, you have sincerely obeyed God in your heart. If you find that the issue keeps coming back up and you are triggered with guilt from the remaining resentment or just triggered in general, read further. This book is written so that you can gain relief at a deeper level and achieve a higher level of emotional freedom.

Before going further, there are several writers who have provided excellent work on forgiveness, who are worth acknowledging. Many of their writings are listed among the suggested readings at the end of this book. Colin Tipping[i] has provided in-depth psychological and theoretical applications to learning how to forgive others. Joyce Meyer offers insightful writings from deep biblical foundations.[ii] This book is not a replacement for any of the work already accomplished. It is an addition that translates the clinical, behavioral health, and spiritual into a tangible, day-by-day application.

The chapters that follow are designed to go beyond the current literature on forgiveness while acknowledging the validity of the writings already in existence. Many respectable religious writings give wonderful teachings on *why* we should forgive. Scientific and clinical literature provides very detailed descriptions of the physiological mechanisms that come into play when we remain in an emotional state of distress due to unforgiveness. If you are looking for a scholarly rendition of the neuro pathways and biochemical processes involved in emotional stress, you may enjoy reading Caroline Leaf's book, *Switch on Your Brain: The Keys to Peak Happiness, Thinking, and Health*.[iii] The present book gets right down to the mechanics of *how* to do the forgiveness itself. I have applied many of the spiritual and behavioral aspects of this version of the how-to of forgiveness successfully in my personal life and private practice. These concepts have helped many clients learn how to soar with new freedom.

Stories and Examples in this Book

Throughout this book, there will be true-life examples described from contributors who offered to share their own stories. Names and many details have been changed to protect identities and shield recognizability. Also, other examples are generalized types of offense with which many readers may have dealt. Transgression, in general, may range in severity from person to person. What is trivial to one person may be devastating to another. Therefore, the samples written here have a broad range of severity, and the true stories applied here have been provided with permission. The generosity of the contributors may provide examples with which you may relate.

How to Use this Book

First of all, understand that any event that you experience and perceive as traumatic in your life, even though it may seem small to someone else, still merits the full attention to forgiveness work for you. One or more of the three levels of forgiveness work described in this book (Tier I, II, or III) may apply to your needs. Become familiar with all three of them as we often need all of them at one time or another. Apply the tools in this book to fit your specific needs with consideration of the possibility that you may need to engage the help of a professional as you embark on this journey.

While this book reviews perspectives that you may have already studied, it is recommended that you do not skip any of the chapters, as you may discover a deeper perspective than you received before. Furthermore, each chapter builds upon the other and provides a better understanding of the exercises that follow. This will enhance your preparation and the safeguards required to do the work of forgiveness.

This book is divided into two major sections. Part I covers essential concepts and tools that you will need in order to do the work, and Part II takes you through the three-tier approach. These three levels of forgiveness build upon each other and are often intertwined. The first two chapters are designed to provide an efficient overview. Peruse the subheadings in these segments to see if you notice any new information or perspectives that you may not have considered before. Forgiveness may not be exactly what you think it is. The third chapter provides crucial elements to help you prepare for any difficult work ahead.

After reading Part I, you may be better prepared to embark

upon the actual journey of forgiving in Part II. Here, you will see specific, detailed, and tangible techniques, including cognitive tools and practical spiritual perspectives. This is not a one-size-fits-all method for forgiving. There may be some tools that work for others that do not work for you. Take your time to examine the range of options as a buffet of tools and choices from which to select strategies that may personally work for you.

IMPORTANT: Please Read the next Section Before Going Further in this Book

Before starting the exercises in chapter six of this book, consider your own subjective level of pain for you in any situation that needs work. Pain varies in perceived intensity between individuals and across situations. Five people can experience the same event differently. What is trivial to one person may be excruciating to another. Therefore, do not assume that because a particular event did not impact someone else, that you should have the same level of tolerance. Be honest with yourself about how much you are hurting and respect that reality. There is no shame in pain.

There is no shame in pain.

Assess your own personal level of emotional pain, with zero representing the least amount of pain and ten representing the greatest amount of pain. This is a measure of your own personal perception of the amount of emotional pain that you feel regarding a hurtful experience. This construct was originally used for the measurement of physical pain.[iv] It has subsequently been found to be valuable in the measure of psychological pain for effective tracking of emotional pain in trauma work.[v]

Using a scale of zero to ten, with zero representing no emotional pain and ten representing the most extreme level of emotional impact, discern your subjective level of pain on this scale. If an accurately perceived level of emotional pain is at one or no higher than three, you can likely process many of these tools without the help of a professional or supportive guide. If your emotional pain level ranges from four to five, you may be able to process some of these steps with a trustworthy confidant or supportive friend. For painful experiences perceived as having higher than a level of five, I recommend that you bring this book to a competent therapist of your choice so that you do not process your pain alone. Often our forgiveness work needs the aid of a competent, trained professional. Also, be patient with yourself, as some of the exercises in this book may need to be read in segments because many emotional wounds take time to heal.

You may find licensed therapists listed on your insurance plan or through your pastor. The concepts in this book are derived from established theories, including gestalt therapy,[vi] and inner child work,[vii] as well as cognitive therapy.[viii] While reaching out to a therapist, you can ask whether they are familiar with these approaches. A therapist does not have to be a scholar on the origins of these theories; however, it is helpful for them to be trained in these techniques. Beyond professional expertise, you may also want to see if the prospective therapist is a match for you in your spiritual beliefs. Yes, it is perfectly all right to interview a potential therapist briefly. You can ask the above questions within a short phone call.

Finally, the following prayer is intended to support you in your search for a higher, freer level of recovery.

God, I thank you that you are the ultimate Healer and that you never leave any of us nor forsake us. Please speak through the pages of this book <u>to every single person who reads them</u> and open their spiritual eyes in the specific areas that they need. Please guide each one through the pages of this book to a positive outcome and help them reach the level of hope that is life-giving, freeing, and triumphant.

Thank You for the abundant blessings, healing, and freedom that you can deliver to everyone through this book. In Jesus' Name, Amen

Enjoy......

Chapter 1

What You May Already Know . . . Or Not

We've heard it over and over again:

We must forgive . . . Unforgiveness is unhealthy . . . It is toxic . . .
We have to forgive, or else God will not forgive us . . .
Holding resentment only hurts ourselves . . .
I know, I know, I know, on and on and on it goes . . .
Blah Blah Blah.

If you are one of the many people who have heard it all before, this book is designed for you. There are plenty of teachings on *why* we *should* forgive and what it does to us if we do not. Even so, you and I can always benefit from some reminders of what we already know; therefore, it is recommended that you still at least peruse this chapter in search of one more possible nugget of truth.

The concept and benefits of forgiveness have been outlined in religious teachings, the social sciences, and the medical field. Forgiveness can be multidirectional, including forgiveness for a friend or partner, the forgiveness of oneself, forgiveness of a deity such as God, or forgiveness of a situation. Whether it is targeted at a person (including oneself), deity, or thing – it is necessary.

Often, forgiveness can be granted without any expectation of the restoration of justice. This itself would seem very unfair. However, it is far more unjust for the victimized person to have to delay their healing contingent upon the perpetrator's act of conscience. How long might it take for the offender to know that they have done something wrong and make amends or rectify the situation? Some damage is not reparable, and sometimes it may seem too late because the offender has passed away. Even in an ideal situation where the offender does apologize, express remorse, and make amends, the task of removing the wound from our soul may still remain and the recompense may not seem adequate.

Sincere Intentions and Cerebral Level of Forgiveness

Were you taught that you must forgive immediately? In the midst of your pain and anger, did you do that right away out of obedience? Did you proclaim that you forgave the person right then and there, only to feel guilty later when the original pain and anger re-emerged? First of all, you are to be commended for your sincere act of morality and good intention. In my past experience, when I would immediately say, "I forgive you," I would have the same thing happen. In my heart of hearts, I truly wanted to forgive that person and let go of the bitterness, so I would proclaim the forgiveness in obedience, yet discover that the pain would rear its ugly head once again down the road. This is what I call cerebral forgiveness, meaning that it is processed in your head only without filtering down into your soul, heart, and spirit. In reality, you and I may have been merely stuffing our feelings. What happens with cerebral forgiveness, is the potential for the pain to fester somewhere in the unconscious mind or erupt somewhere else in the body, leading to emotional or physical symptoms.

I genuinely believe that many sincere Christians often stop short at the cerebral level of forgiveness, verbalizing the words "I forgive you," yet unconsciously stuff their emotions deep inside of their soul. This involves emotions going underground, metaphorically. If these emotions are merely stuffed, they have a way of rising again to the surface. Do you find that you have said, "I forgive you," and then later, out of the blue, those unwanted feelings come roaring back with a vengeance? A dear former LPC colleague of mine, the late Mark Felber (1961 – 2019), referred to this as an emotional tsunami.[ix]

Oh No – What if I have not really forgiven? Don't worry. Read on.

Now, before you take the deep dive into self-condemnation, thinking that you have not forgiven at all, pause a moment. First and foremost, I am not discounting the cerebral (head-level) level of forgiveness, because I believe that God takes our sincere efforts and completes them with His Grace and Power. For instance, if we put forth a tiny grain of faith with an effort that is the size of a mustard seed, God will bring it into harvest. Where we are weak, He is strong through us (2 Corinthians 12:9-11 NKJV). I believe the teachings of forgiveness in this manner are valid and that God perfects us in our weakness. Undue self-condemnation,[x] which I refer to as false guilt, can send us into an unnecessary tailspin. God already knew from the very beginning that at our best, we are weak, and that is why Jesus paid in advance for our sins.

The teaching of praying for those who persecute us is also a valid part of forgiveness. This book is designed to show you how to change your thinking and perceptions in such a way that makes it easier to do so. Your acts of obedient forgiveness can become deeper, with more authenticity, and increasingly automatic as you grow and apply the tools outlined in later chapters. We are to continue increasing in stature and virtue, bearing more fruit as we grow and moving beyond our first primary state of spiritual immaturity (Hebrews 6:1, 1 Corinthians 13:11, Colossians 1:9-10 NKJV).

Cerebrally forgiving is a respectable first step. If you find that a resurgence of the anger follows later, it merely means that there may still be some unresolved pain to process. There is a deeper, more complete level of forgiving that follows in the pages ahead, including the highest level of forgiveness that we all in our hearts long to be able to achieve. The more immediate sections describe reasons why learning how to forgive more thoroughly may be well worth your time as you embark upon this amazing journey. The next pages describe several reasons to learn a deeper level of forgiveness than that of the cerebral.

Emotional Reasons for a Deeper Level of Forgiveness Than the Cerebral

Emotions contain energy. When that energy includes anger, and it does not have a place to go, it will tend to be turned inward toward the mind, body, soul, and spirit. Anger is also a secondary emotion, which means that anger generally has a root emotion at its core involving pain, such as hurt, fear, disappointment, or sadness. With no known appropriate place to direct this unresolved emotional energy, the pain goes underground, and rather than being outwardly explosive, it becomes inwardly implosive, impacting our mental and physical health. One may agree that if a person refuses to forgive, they are choosing to remain in a state of anger (and pain) toward the perpetrator, the situation, God, or themselves. As this unresolved anger begins to overburden them, they can become infected with depressive symptoms, anxiety, or medical problems. Maybe this is a crucial reason that scripture tells us, "Be angry, and do not sin: Do not let the sun go down on your wrath" (Ephesians 4:26 NKJV). I also, therefore, interpret this scripture as telling us to refrain from letting our unresolved anger become stuffed into our body, mind, or spirit because it can make us sick.

Caroline Leaf describes a brilliant dichotomy of our emotions in her work.[xi] She divides all emotions into two groups: 1. Fear-based, and 2. Faith-based (which I like to call Hope-based). The positive emotions are in the Faith (or Hope) category, such as joy, thankfulness, anticipation, and enthusiasm. The negative one (the Fear-based category) is considered to include, not surprisingly, fear and anxiety, plus anger, resentment, and rage, to name a few. If you have been severely hurt, it may be more challenging to generate positive, faith and hope based emotions. Positive emotions involve a level of trust that may be difficult if you have been hurt frequently or your trust has been broken. Being able to trust that there will be a hopeful outcome may require a measure of healing first. If you have been disappointed often in your life, hope may be difficult. The good news is that there are tools you can learn that can bring you relief. Furthermore, the world does not necessarily have to be a trustworthy place for you to heal and achieve this level of freedom and peace.

Noticing how our emotions involve energy, remember a time when you were feeling a positive emotion versus a negative emotion. Notice how differently your body and energy level felt in comparison of the two different states. You may recognize that positive emotions promote a feeling of freedom and peace, while negative emotions create tension with a sense of bondage and constraint.

It makes sense that the emotion of anger falls in the category of fear, according to Leaf's paradigm.[xii] When a person is feeling any form of anger, whether it be mild irritation or extreme rage, they go into a state of fight or flight. If mildly annoyed or irritated, you may tell the perpetrator to stop (fight) or find a way to remove yourself from the situation (flight). When severely abused, hurt, or devastated, the natural response we have, in addition to many other emotions, is anger - whether we acknowledge it or not.

The emotional reasons to forgive are broadly encompassing. When holding on to unfinished business, unresolved pain and anger steal our time, our focus, and our much needed emotional and physical energy. It also crowds out the room in our hearts, where we could otherwise recognize the abundant blessings that God wants to give us.

Physical Reasons for a Deeper Level of Forgiveness Than the Cerebral

Unresolved emotions not only weigh us down emotionally, but they also manifest in our physical body. If we remain in a state of unforgiveness, we are stuffing these emotions into our bodies, creating a state of ongoing stress. When we are in a state of stress, we naturally move into a state of fight or flight, designed only to take care of an immediate threat. If this state is prolonged, we drain all our resources toward continual defense and protection from the threat. The unresolved pain and anger do not get discharged out of the body but instead become internalized and, when prolonged, can cause our health to deteriorate from overexposure to the stress hormones and chemicals that are continually released. Thus, unforgiveness can cause us a prolonged stress response that can impact our bodily organs.

Although not every medical case is caused by emotional stress, a substantial number of them can be traced to stress with unforgiveness as the culprit. If we have established that emotionally stuffed unforgiveness does cause stress, it is essential to know that there are several physical conditions found to be associated with stress. Author R. Morgan Griffin, in his 2018 article *10 Health Problems Related to Stress That You Can Fix*,[xiii] identified 10 physical conditions related to stress. Among these are heart disease due to increased blood pressure and increased cholesterol and triglycerides into the bloodstream, and the exacerbation of asthma. Research has found that high cortisol levels seem to increase the amount of fat stored in the abdomen, which leads to a plethora of health issues. Studies also show us that stress appears to increase glucose levels in people who have type 2 diabetes. Stress can also trigger headaches and some migraines, and gastrointestinal problems, including heartburn, GERD, and irritable bowel syndrome. Stress has been related to medical depression and symptoms of panic and anxiety. This same article also cites findings that stress in rats progresses Alzheimer's disease and that reducing stress levels seems to slow its progression in humans. In several studies,[xiv] accelerated aging has been found to occur at the DNA level in groups identified as stressed. Furthermore, stressed participants showed a 63% higher rate of premature death than their comparison non-stressed cohorts.

If we mistakenly believe that we have forgiven the person or situation totally, yet we have stuffed the anger and negative energy into our bodies, this hurts us more than it hurts them. What a great epitome of injustice! *We* are the ones who become sick, while the perpetrator of our pain remains clueless about the gravity of their actions and unscathed.

It is important to mention here that some physical conditions occur from environmental toxins, inheritance, and purely physical causes and are not related to stress. Nevertheless, keeping our emotions clear from unresolved anger may equip us with an extra physical line of defense in our immune system.

Mental Health Reasons for a Deeper Level of Forgiveness Than the Cerebral

If it is true that merely forgiving at the cerebral level (from our head only) may involve suppressing the trauma, it can cause us further pain by remaining toxic inside of our souls. It awaits to resurface at a later, most inopportune time. Furthermore, we use an enormous amount of physical and emotional energy to suppress the unfinished business of our unresolved pain and anger. While we continue to push the pain down, denying that it is there, forgiving only at a surface level, distracting ourselves away, or avoiding the issue, much of our energy is being hijacked.

It is natural to want to avoid giving our attention to hurtful and painful information. The American Psychiatric Association suggests several natural symptoms that can occur after a traumatic experience.[xv] Avoidance of remembering or thinking about the traumatic event is one of the key symptoms. Amnesia, for part or all of the event, may rob the person of their confidence. Also, among these symptoms are sleep disturbance, intrusive recollections of the traumatic event, emotional detachment from loved ones, a sense of having a shortened future, distractibility, difficulty concentrating, hypervigilance (excessive watchfulness), hyperarousal (physiological startle response), nightmares, and sometimes flashbacks (perception of reliving the event although it is over).

More recently, symptoms involving negative cognitions (thoughts, perceptions, beliefs) have been added as a symptom category that is not only associated but is essentially required to cinch a diagnosis of post-traumatic stress disorder (PTSD). Some examples of negative cognitions can include gloom-and-doom thinking, doubt, negative self-perceptions, or self-blame. These are natural responses to unresolved emotional trauma, which can often take over the person's emotional, social, or professional life.

Stuffing emotional pain can also lead to extended sadness and depressed mood, excessive tearfulness, loss of joy in life, appetite increase or decrease, and feelings of excessive guilt or worthlessness. It can definitely steal your emotional energy. Stuffing emotional pain for too long can also drain your physical energy, either through dragging your energy down (psychomotor retardation), revving your energy up too high with excessive restlessness or irritability (psychomotor agitation), and make you feel exhausted regardless of having enough sleep. A person may also experience anxiety or even panic attacks because of stuffed and unresolved emotional pain or anger. Colin A. Ross, MD, has advanced his Trauma Model, which is an insightful theory about the relationship of trauma to subsequent emotional symptoms.[xvi] All human beings across the planet tend to respond to physical calamity similarly, with physical and medical symptoms that are proportionate to the level of physical impact incurred. If you have a fairly mild physical accident, your symptoms are expected to be relatively mild. If you have a very serious automobile accident, you will likely suffer more than just a bruise or a scratch. The same is true for emotional trauma. If you perceive the offense you experience as mild, it may only take you a few moments to move past it, and you can, therefore, truly say, "I forgive you" and have it never surface again. If you experience a very deeply hurtful event or devastation, expecting yourself just to get up, brush it off, recite a forgiveness phrase, and move on as it nothing has happened, it would be like expecting yourself to walk away from a five-car collision, completely unscathed. The valuable point here is for you to be patient with yourself if you are experiencing difficult sadness or increased anxiety.

A second point of valid importance is to also refrain from giving yourself a diagnosis based upon what you are reading in this book. For a specific diagnosis, several of these symptoms must co-occur in a particular pattern, have a particular duration, and severely impact the individual's life, so just having a number of these experiences does not necessarily indicate that you have clinical depression or PTSD. The main point is for you to know how much impact that unresolved anger and unforgiveness can have on your life.

Whether brought on by stress, inheritance, or both, if any of the symptoms listed above are interfering with your life, it is recommended that you see a trained professional for a full assessment. It is a good idea to first rule out anything medical that might be going on and, if not medical, explore the emotional. Many people can benefit just by having someone to talk to, and some situations may require the addition of medication. A wealth of tools can be discovered by consulting a competent health care professional.

It is immensely important to deal with unresolved anger or pain; because if left unchecked, it can steal our present quality of life as well as our dreams, destiny, freedom, and future. Regardless of whether you meet the full criteria for any of the mentioned diagnoses, if you look at these items above, it may be clear that any *one* of these symptoms is enough to be an inconvenience in your life. You have a God-given purpose and destiny in this life, and it is not helpful to you nor to anyone else if your energy is tied up in unresolved pain that has gone underground where it is blocking your dreams. This is not what God wants for us. The Lord clearly said:

John 10:10 (NIV)

"The thief comes only to steal and kill and destroy; I have come that they may have life, and have it to the full."

Spiritual Reasons for a Deeper Level of Forgiveness Than the Cerebral

In this next section, there are a number of robust scriptures about reasons to forgive those who hurt us. This section is not designed to induce fear or guilt. According to Scripture, we are saved by grace through faith in Jesus Christ (Ephesians 2: 8-9, Acts 16: 30-31, John 5:24, Revelation 3:20 NKJV). As you read through these next pages, remember that the entire reason that

Christ came to give His life for us is that God knew from the beginning that none of us would ever be able to obey the Scriptures without mistakes. We are all a work in progress, so as you read the next section, recognize this as the level toward which we are to strive. I believe the tools that follow in this book can equip you to move closer to a higher level of forgiveness that can increase your spiritual stature and emotional freedom. After you have mastered many of these approaches, Chapter Seven is a possible example of what it may look like to reach the highest level of forgiveness and emotional freedom.

Now, you may be very well versed in Scripture that tells us that we must forgive. We are to be patient with others and forgive them as God has forgiven us through Jesus Christ (Ephesians 4:32; Colossians 3:13 KJV). We are to forgive repeatedly. Jesus stated that if someone sins against us, we are to forgive them "seventy times seven" (Matthew 18:22 KJV), and even if someone continues to mess up and repeatedly comes back to us to apologize each time, we are to continue to forgive them (Luke 17:4 NIV).

We are to make amends whenever possible before we are able to bless anyone or glorify God effectively. In Matthew 5:23-24 (NIV) Christ says, "Therefore, if you are offering your gift at the altar and there remember that your brother or sister has something against you, leave your gift there in front of the altar. First, go and be reconciled to them; then come and offer your gift."

Do we just passively allow others to walk all over us (or someone we love) without speaking up or doing anything about it? On the contrary, it *is* biblically acceptable to confront a person in their transgression. "Be on your guard! If your brother sins, rebuke him; and if he repents, forgive him" (Luke 17:3 NASB). But we are commanded to be persistent in the forgiveness, "And if he sins against you seven times a day, and returns to you seven times, saying, 'I repent,' forgive him" (Luke 17:4 NASB).

Apparently, this forgiving business is extremely important to God because, in more than one place, the Bible tells us that we hurt ourselves spiritually if we hold onto resentment. "Whenever you stand praying, forgive, if you have anything against anyone, so that your Father who is in heaven, will also forgive you your transgressions" (Mark 11:25 NASB). Matthew 6:14-15 (NASB) states, "For if you forgive others for their transgressions, your heavenly Father will also forgive you." It continues, "But if you do not forgive others, then your Father will not forgive your transgressions" (Matthew 6:15 NASB).

Jesus goes further in Matthew 5:21 (NKJV), saying, "You have heard that it was said to those of old, 'You shall not murder, and whoever murders will be in danger of the judgment.' But I say to you that whoever is angry with his brother without a cause shall be in danger of the judgment." In 1 John 3:15 (NKJV), it is stated, "Whoever hates his brother is a murderer, and you know that no murderer has eternal life abiding in him." This makes a strong argument for the spiritual reasons to learn how to deal with our unresolved anger and pain by making an effort to forgive. It also speaks to the life-destroying nature of unforgiveness, which can be palpable physically, emotionally, and spiritually.

I believe that many of us, as Christians, have tried to forgive out of due diligence and sincerity to please God, yet it has not gone any deeper than a dutiful cerebral level. Without knowing what else to do, we suppress the rest of the pain, stuffing it back down repeatedly. When we do all that, we know how to obey the scriptures; I believe that God sees our sincere effort through the eyes of mercy. Nevertheless, without learning how to take our forgiveness to a deeper level, the remaining pain is stuffed inside, leaving us in torment. I am confident that God does not want any of us to live in torment. He wants us to be spiritually healthy.

I also interpret the last part of 1 John 3:15 (NKJV) in clinical terms. If you carry hate in your heart toward someone (including toward yourself), you literally annihilate and wipe out all life and life-giving energy from your heart and soul. This loss can manifest in decreased energy, loss of joy, and eventually disease. Do you recall a time when you may have hated someone? Do you remember how toxic and negative that emotion felt in your spirit and your body?

The Interweaving of Spirit and Body

It is interesting how science catches up with God's wisdom that has already been stated in scripture. God has already indicated that when we are in a state of chronic anger, it is not good for us emotionally, physically, or spiritually. Science then later discovered that when we hold onto anger, we are in a state of stress, where our body goes into a state of flight or fight. As mentioned above, stress hormones are sent through our bodies. Cortisol, among them, causes severe wear and tear on our organs, which, if prolonged enough, causes a host of diseases and, ultimately, death. We can be a sincere Christian, saved by grace, trying to walk with Christ - yet literally be like the walking dead. The verse says, "Eternal life does not abide in him" (1 John 3:15 NKJV). Life not abiding in him seems to fit with the medical research briefly mentioned above, indicating the idea that stress (for this case, caused by anger and unforgiveness stuffed inward) can lead to a diminished quality of life (poor health) and shortened life (accelerated aging or premature death), as described above. This makes sense emotionally, as the life that God puts in us gets squeezed and purged out each time we dwell on the hate or reminisce once again about the retaliation we wish we had inflicted. This causes emotional suffering for us and hijacks our focus from fruitful activity and abundant living. Instead of walking in victory, these pent-up emotions become toxic and wreak havoc on our health. We do literally drink poison through our own toxic chemicals (i.e., an internal overload of cortisol, etc.) while trying to avenge ourselves. Joyce Meyer, one of the world's leading practical Bible teachers and founder of Joyce Meyer Ministries, describes this as us drinking poison – trying to get back at them.[xvii]

Even if we think that we can scheme or plan the perpetrator's deserved punishment, we cannot instigate a penalty better than the Creator and Ruler of the universe can. God's words are the following: "Vengeance is mine, I will repay" (Romans 12:19 ESV) and "It is mine to avenge; I will repay. In due time their foot will slip; their day of disaster is near and their doom rushes upon them." (Deuteronomy 32:35 NIV). This is a very real, tangible promise. In Zachariah 9:12 (NIV), we are told to remain as a prisoner of hope, and God will give us a double portion of what we have lost. Frankly, I went over forty decades of my life as a devout Christian without being taught scriptures such as Zachariah 9:12 and Isaiah 61:7. Isaiah 30:18 (NIV) states, "Yet the Lord longs to be gracious to you; therefore He will rise up to show you compassion. For the Lord is a God of justice. Blessed are all who wait for him!"

Years ago, I sought refuge for a civil matter from a civil court judge. Being raised in a good Christian family, I had an innocent, trusting view of the world and our legal system. Not only did the judge fail to render the legally justified intervention I sought, but the low-dollar attorney that I modestly could afford to pay had also strung me along, wasting my time, energy, and trust. After this case resulted in devastation beyond belief, I gave it to God and turned my energies toward doing what I believed He wanted me to do on this earth. I handed over to God the parts that I could not fix. Sometime after that misfortune, while going about my day, the memory re-emerged in my mind. Rather than allowing myself to get derailed by emotion, I said the simplest, shortest prayer that took only a few seconds of my time. I asked, "God, would you please remove him from the bench?" Then I did not give it another thought. Sometime later, I discovered that an unknown attorney came forward and ran against him for his judicial position on the bench - and defeated him. For the first time ever heard of in my county for any judge, this judge had been removed from the bench. At some point later, I also found out that the attorney who had wasted my money and strung me along to nowhere had lost his license to practice. I had not lifted a finger and had just gone about minding my business. All of this occurred during my complete obliviousness as I focused on what I *could do* on this planet and not on revenge. This is a *far more* consequence than I had the power to do on my own. Would you rather continue trying to right a wrong situation beyond your control with your limited energy and strength, or would you instead allow God to do what He does best in His powerful omnipotence?

During my period of giving it to God, I had put my energies toward fruitfulness. This advanced my professional standing, relational connection, and financial strength, allowing my energies to become a flow of blessing to those around me. At the same time, God took care of those who had hurt my family and me. Remember, God is your Father, protector, defender, and *true* refuge[xviii] in 10,000 more ways than what we can do by ourselves alone. Learn to trust God.

Another Way to Go

In Matthew 5 (NJV), Jesus details some strategies for peacemaking and refraining from undue conflict. He encourages us to reconcile with others (Matthew 5:23 NIV). Specifically, He states, "Settle matters quickly with your adversary who is taking you to court. Do it while you are still together on the way, or your adversary may hand you over to the judge, and the judge may hand you over to the officer, and you may be thrown into prison." (Matthew 5:25 NIV). This does not necessarily mean that we are to cave in if the cause we are pursuing is important. Further sections discuss boundaries and options for standing your ground.

In future chapters, we will examine how to let go of unresolved pain and transform your emotional and spiritual life.

Without information on *how* to forgive, we are often left with guilt, frustration, or condemnation, which leads to even *more* stress – right? Furthermore, guilt, frustration, and condemnation all fall under the category of unhelpful fear-based emotions, according to Caroline Leaf's work. Remember that "God hath not given us a spirit of fear, but of power and of love and of a sound mind" (2 Timothy 1:7 KJV).

How Do I Know If I Have Forgiven?

Now, a last-minute check to see where you are in your forgiveness process. R.T. Kendall provides a very rigorous litmus test to determine whether or not one has *completely* forgiven another person who has wronged them. His earlier presentation, when he was a guest on the late John Paul Jackson's program, is paraphrased below with his book referenced here[xix] along with some of my own comments.

> 1. You will no longer feel the need to tell people what the person did to you. He gives two exceptions to this rule. It is often necessary and therapeutic to confide in someone who is trustworthy and wise. The second exception is for the sake of protecting others, for instance, warning other potential victims or testifying in court.

In my opinion, there is a third exception to this rule. There are sometimes reasons to tell your story for the purpose of helping someone else. In this case, your intention is to help someone understand what you did to survive and recover from the event. What makes this instance an exception is that there is no malice nor vindictive intent, because the identity of the person who hurt you is not relevant to the story, nor do you care to spend any energy exposing their guilt. What happened is now between that person and God, and it no longer steals your energy nor ability to be focused on the present here-and-now.

2. You will no longer want them to feel afraid of you or what you might do to them in revenge.
3. You no longer want them to feel guilty or down on themselves because of what they have done.
4. You can allow them in, RT Kendall's words, to *save face*.xx

There is a biblical example demonstrated in Genesis 9:23. It occurred after Noah with his family and several species of birds and animals had stayed continually in the Ark while it had rained for forty days and forty nights (Genesis 7:12 NIV). If you read further you will notice that they were unable to leave the ark for an additional period of many months due to lack of dry land before the ark eventually came to rest on the mountains of Ararat.

After they were finally able to step out on dry ground, Noah planted a vineyard and consumed some of the wine, and had become drunk. One of his sons found him naked inside his tent. All of this was not acceptable behavior. But Shem and Japheth took a garment and laid it across their shoulders. Then they walked in backward and covered their father's naked body. Their faces were turned the other way so that they would not see their father naked.

Forgiveness can be extended without enabling or excusing unacceptable behavior; for example, "love covers over a multitude of sins" (1 Peter 4:8 NIV). One might ask, why did Noah become drunk in the first place? There is no excuse, but perhaps there is perspective. Genesis 8:3 states that after the ark had lodged on Mount Ararat, it took 150 days for the water to go down, with an additional 40 plus 7, plus another 7 days before there was evidence of enough dry ground for Noah and his entourage to set foot back onto the earth safely. They were all cooped up in the ark with every family member, animal, and creature for an extreme number of months that I am sure seemed like an eternity. There was no electronic entertainment, no Wi-Fi internet connection, and no modern plumbing.

In more modern times, the year 2020 did not start out well. The first quarter of the year required a nationwide shut-down and a stay at home advisement, due to a pandemic from the COVID-19 virus that had been released early that year. Many people across the world during the COVID-19 pandemic became overwrought with cabin fever, some only after a month and a half of self-isolation. That year witnessed massive episodes of social unrest across our nation. Also, initially, basic products such as toilet tissue and cleansers became scarce.

Being cooped up with only a part of your family may pale in comparison with being shut in with all of your family plus the entire animal species of the planet, as in Noah's ordeal. Let me just say that compared to today, an absence of toilet paper was likely the *least* of their worries. Is it possible that after a number of months, the people in the Ark were *climbing the walls*? While reading through this book, you may come to see that there is often a backstory behind the surface of situations that you and I encounter.

Now, returning to R.T. Kendall's item number one, recall that this does not mean that you turn a blind eye or cover for someone who may continue in their wrong-doing, eventually allowing the perpetrator to hurt more people. There are times to speak up, yet while doing so, you can apply some compassion, as item five describes below.

5. You have a desire to protect them. For example, you prefer to spare them from shame and embarrassment. This just means that you are able to extend mercy to them.
6. Kendall's words are, "You have to keep doing it" (the forgiveness). What this means is that your forgiveness to them for the past infraction is permanent. Ideally,

you no longer have the need to bring it back up and chew on it again and again. You no longer feel the need to rehearse visions of how you could take revenge or get back at them. You are free from having it resurface in your mind. Alternatively, there may very well be times in which the offender repeats their actions, requiring repeated acts of forgiveness.
7. You pray for them. This is actually the most powerful part of forgiveness. You will see as you read further, the reason for this act of prayer. Clearly, people who cause harm to others have issues of one kind or another. Before we can get to this powerful act of prayer, we may need to go through the *process*.

Many sermons direct us to pray for those who have hurt us and to also bless them (Romans 12:14 NIV). The closer we walk with God, and the more we allow Him to fill us with His Holy Spirit, the more our nature, mind, and spirit will change into the likeness of Him. This is a direct spiritual route to forgiveness that has the power to surpasses much of the clinical work and can be achieved, the more we heal and grow closer to God. I believe that, while we strive for this level of forgiveness, we often need to walk through a healing process, as well.

Sometimes we may believe that we have instantly gotten over a hurt or infraction because of our closeness to God. Other times, however, this may turn out to be an exercise that does not go any deeper than the surface or cerebral (head level). Also, there are some situations that are so devastating that it requires a process. Sometimes we may pray for the perpetrator out of obedience and obligation, with mixed emotions, possibly cringing or tightlipped, all the while wanting to truly let go of the pain and forgive immediately. I believe that on some level, while doing the act of obedience, our heart may vacillate back and forth from anger to release and then back again to anger. To this end, we may be stuffing some of the pain and anger, suppressing it, and finding it later rise to the surface in an unexpected emotional outburst (explosive) or physiological illness (implosive) that we did not see coming. So, no matter how spiritual we are, recognize that it is only Christ who has mastered forgiveness perfectly. Recognize that no matter the level of spiritual stature, you and I are human and will have times when we need to go through the process of healing.

Through both training and personal experience, I have discovered tools that can help us arrive at the state of letting go more thoroughly so that we really have an emotional shift and a spiritual release that is deeper and more permanent than just the surface, cerebral level alone. The benefits of learning how to forgive at this level can bring much emotional freedom, unleashing you to powerfully soar into your destiny that God has created for you.

What If I Do not Pass the Litmus Test of Forgiveness?

If you find any of the items in the *litmus test of forgiveness* above to be challenging, it is highly likely that you may be *stuffing* at least some of your feelings instead of getting rid of all of them. Forgiveness is a choice, as Joyce Meyer wisely asserts.[xxi] Most of the cases of forgiveness I have witnessed, while working in therapeutic groups, have involved making that choice to forgive. Still, in many cases, it merely remains at the surface, cerebral level, recited only from the head, and fails to reach the deeper level of the heart. When it does not resonate in the heart and soul, it can keep coming up again, haunting us with regurgitated pain, then subsequent guilt because we thought we had forgiven. We are now convicted of it again, still finding our energy held hostage to the old hurt, disappointment, and anger we thought we had released. We so often stop at conviction and miss the steps that lead to freedom and power.

I believe that this happens with many Christians who sincerely try to forgive, but sometimes there are reasons why the pain and emotions keep coming back up repeatedly. Before you allow yourself to indulge in unproductive guilt for the times that this has happened to you, it is essential for you to know some of the reasons that this occurs. One is a possibility that your recurring thoughts about the event are a natural symptom of trauma that any human being would experience. One of the classic symptoms of posttraumatic stress (mentioned above) include recurrent recollections of the event. Even if you do not meet the full criteria for PTSD, it is possible to have a few of the symptoms. It is possible that your repeated mental rehearsal of the event is <u>not</u> sin, it is a symptom. It is the brain's natural response to trauma. Often the intervention of a trained professional to walk alongside you through your healing process can be priceless.

Another reason that forgiveness sometimes involves a process is that many infractions require the steps of grief work. These steps take time. If you believe that you are not passing the litmus test above, don't be hard on yourself. Forgiveness is not reached immediately for many events, especially devastating ones. We will go further into these processes on how to grieve in a later chapter.

Many teachings on forgiveness fail to walk the person through the mechanics of how to effectively relieve pain, build inner strength, and above all, rise above the situation. Many of us already have the conviction that forgiveness is needed, yet we need the building blocks. The best teachings on forgiveness may provide *conviction without construction*. What good does it do to learn that we are wrong about something without learning what is needed to repair it? This book provides the construction within a three-tier approach, explaining three levels of process that can be both sequential and intertwined.

In my opinion:

>*For Conviction to be fruitful, it needs to include*
>*Construction and*
>*Construction often involves Process.*

Although the established teachings are crucial because we need to be reminded that we *must* forgive, they seem to omit many practical instructions on how to actually *do* the forgiveness. One strategy taught in a lot of sermons is to pray for the person who has hurt you. This is definitely valid, scriptural, and recommended. For many of us who struggle with that approach, I believe that God bridges the gap between our weaknesses and His strength. Even if we pray for them merely at an obligatory level, God does work a miracle in our hearts by building upon our act of obedience.

Joyce Meyer,[xxii] within a wealth of information, states that "Forgiveness is not how you feel. It is how you treat someone." Many authors declare that forgiveness is a choice. I believe that we can go beyond the level of choice and respectful obedience and move into a deeper level, releasing the trauma from our soul.

The Essence of this Book

The approaches here in this book are to provide some of the stepping stones that I have learned in my own walk. The teachings in this chapter can also show you more about why hurtful people do need prayer. Perhaps sharing some of these stepping stones may empower you to walk on water with Jesus much sooner and with less sinking again and again.

The next section describes what forgiveness *is* and *is not*. Then a framework of tools will be provided to help you prepare for the work ahead. Subsequent sections will help you learn more about the grieving process for devastating events, with instruction on ways to change negative thinking and perception into more helpful cognitive perspectives. Cognition refers to everything in our perception, thoughts, beliefs, interpretation, and outlook. This can become more automatic the more it is practiced. I call this the Cognitive Shift. Finally, as you build upon these skills, a level of continual forgiveness can be approached, where you are not offended as easily by events that occur here on planet earth. This Level I call H.O.P.E. because it involves a Higher Order Perspective Existence, an emotional, mental, and spiritual place in which to live and exist on a continual basis. This is a higher plain of existence where we are less easily impacted.

The following chapters on the *how* of forgiveness are taken from both academic and personal education that I consider to surpass my formal training. Difficulties that you walk through in life can turn out to become a high training ground, making you stronger, taller, and more invincible than before, from the negativity that may be thrown at you in life. While we may refer to this personal education as trials in life, I like to call it God's Ph.D. program. The difference between an academic program and personal life training experience is that in personal training, the following realities apply:

1. You do not owe anything for tuition nor have student loans,
2. You do not have to compete against other candidates for admission to the program. Usually, no one is competing to get in to these types of experiences, yet everyone is included in the learning opportunity,
3. If you don't pass the lesson the first time, you get to repeat it as many times as necessary to learn it (better to pass it early),
4. This type of learning can continue to pay you going forward with many emotional, physical, and spiritual blessings throughout your entire life, and
5. Your learning successes can spill over into others, making you into a profound blessing everywhere you go.

Chapter 2

What You *Need* to Know
... *Oh, Yes You Do*

Ivan and Ailith

Ivan and Ailith were madly in love. High school sweethearts, they were inseparable. Now married for 25 years and committing to another 25 together, it happened shortly after their wedding anniversary. For years, their motto was forgive and forget every issue and conflict that arose. Ailith was a homemaker, and Ivan worked hard to provide for the family, often taking on additional jobs to make ends meet. Through the years, when Ailith was upset at Ivan, she would call him up in the middle of his workday and just chew him out. He would take it in stride. He seemed so patient, so soft-spoken - rarely raising his voice. This went on for years as they would kiss and make up each night and forgive and forget. This marital system seemed to work smoothly. They were both in the prime of their life, flourishing and raising their children. One day, while Ivan was alone one night, Ivan unexpectedly had a fatal heart attack leaving behind a sparsely educated and unemployed wife to raise their three young children alone.

Not only is it imperative to learn how to forgive, it can also be critical to understanding what it is and what it is not in order to make sure to achieve it. Forgiveness has been considerably misunderstood across time. Many believe that it is an immediate act of letting the person off the hook with no further consequence or discussion. Frankly, many of the definitions of forgiveness just don't do it for me. The early Webster's Encyclopedic Unabridged Dictionary of the English Language[xxiii] defines the word forgive as "to grant a free pardon for or remission of an offense or debt; absolve, to give up all claim on account of; to cease to feel resentment against, to grant a free pardon, or to pardon an offense or offender." Pardon also is defined as a kind indulgence, as in forgiveness of an offense. Would this then mean that we are supposed to just forget about it? Are we to suppress our emotions and expect the offender to have no consequence for their actions? If so, then round and round we go. These definitions are long-standing and have been authoritative; however, they may be incomplete. Sometimes the offender does need to repay the debt or experience a consequence for their actions. It may be helpful to know, however, that the job of imposing that consequence does not necessarily have to fall upon our shoulders.

Do we genuinely understand what forgiveness is? A wise colleague of mine, Dr. Linda Marten Ph.D., LPC-S,[xxiv] defined it best: "Forgiveness is giving up your right for revenge." The difference here is that we can give up *our* right for revenge, but the consequence can still hold. I like this definition because it allows us to maintain the opinion that the person did commit a wrong and that a consequence may definitely be necessary; however, the delivery of that consequence does not have to be our job. You and I get to be free from the energy-draining burden of worrying about what, when, or how that inevitable consequence will be dispensed. Also, I like the wise words by Andy Stanley: "Forgiveness allows you to leverage the lessons of the past without lugging around the luggage of the past."[xxv]

Forgiveness Is . . . or Isn't?

Forgiveness is a term that has been mis-conceptualized far too long. Before we can understand what forgiveness is, we need to know what it is not. Therefore, let's take a look at what forgiveness *is not*. The following pages describe several common myths parading around as truth – *false truth*. For each, I have provided a new label to further illuminate our much-needed clarification.

Myths of Forgiveness

The misconceptions listed here include both clinical and spiritual perspectives. The contents ahead, including the attached table, describing ten common myths, some of which are typically explained in clinical and pastoral work,[xxvi] and three more that I have added. For each, I have expounded and given a memorable title. Scripture is applied with a few personal stories sprinkled throughout for application.

Myth #1 – The Authority Myth

I will be letting them off the hook.

Here is the reason that this is a myth. The reason that my forgiveness of the perpetrator does not let them off the hook if I forgive them is that I am not God. That person is merely being forgiven by a fellow human (me). Do you think that when we forgive that individual, God then just suddenly drops His head and shoulders in helplessness with His hands tied behind His back? Can you imagine our single act of forgiving that person rendering the Creator of the Universe helpless? Furthermore, can you imagine that the perpetrator's natural consequence becomes immediately and forever eradicated? That would have to mean that God suddenly drops His hands and says, "Well, I can't do anything about that because [insert your name] just now forgave them." Good news! You and I are not that powerful and, if it has not yet become abundantly clear, the universe does not beckon to our every wish and command. In one sense, I want to say, *Thank God for that* because I am pretty sure that I cannot run the world very well on my own. Our act of letting go of our perceived right for revenge does not cancel the natural consequences that God has already set up in the universe and for that perpetrator.

Galatians 6:7 (NIV)

"Do not be deceived: God cannot be mocked. A man reaps what he sows."

Romans 12:19 (NIV)

"Do not take revenge, my dear friends, but leave room for God's wrath,

for it is written: 'It is mine to avenge; I will repay,' says the Lord."

Moreover, God, being omniscient, knows every dimension of why that person committed the act, and He knows the exact amount of punishment, learning, and mercy that is the perfect fit for that individual. If we let go of our angst, we simply alleviate ourselves from emotional wear, tear, and strain to our minds, bodies, and spirits.

Keeping our energy focused on taking revenge for ourselves can destroy us while they continue to walk around oblivious and clueless. It is infinitely better to let God be God and to focus our energies on the exciting life that God wants to give us.

We may also believe that if we forgive someone who has hurt a loved one, we may be dishonoring the victim or inadvertently condoning their victimization. This is not the case. As mentioned above and in the next sections, there are appropriate times and methods to take action on behalf of the victim.

Timing

Does God just swoop down and immediately smite them? He has been known to act immediately, but more often; His timing is not our timing. I have lived long enough to witness that God's recompense *is indeed **real**, and He is **truly faithful**.* His method of recompense can also be different from our idea of restoration and justice, but I can guarantee you that God's ideas and methods are better than what you and I can think up together. His ways and thoughts are much higher than ours (Isaiah 55:8-9 NKJV), and He will come through for us (Psalm 37:1-5 NKJV).

Hebrews 10:23 (ESV)

"Let us hold fast the confession of our hope without wavering, for he who promised is faithful."

Justice

It is morally, clinically, and spiritually acceptable to pursue justice. In many cases, the perpetrator may harm someone again if they are not held accountable. Furthermore, God is a God of justice. To describe this feature in His character, there are a large number of verses in the Bible that use the word Justice, indicating that Justice is very important to God.[xxvii]

You can take a stand to pursue justice while in a state of forgiveness simultaneously. An example would be a calm and emotionally neutral person taking the appropriate steps to file a report to the correct organization, perhaps after dealing with the initial pain. One can sometimes find closure because they have placed the perpetrator into the hand of the proper authorities. Do we operate like robots or automatons, completely emotionless? No. You will see in chapter four the consideration that many events require time to grieve and heal.

The decision to press charges or confront in some other manner is a case by case discernment process. Sometimes the stakes are too high to press legal charges against a sociopath who might harm the whistle-blower or their family in retaliation. Other cases may involve a perpetrator who is highly skilled in deception to the point that the lawsuit may fail or backfire, wasting the victim's time, hard-earned money, and emotional energy. So, within each separate case, ask whether going after them is your job, the legal domain's job, or entirely God's department. Listen to scripture, the leading of the Holy Spirit, and seek wise counsel.

The bottom line is that when you forgive, you do not cause the person to get away scot-free. Natural consequences have been set up from the beginning of time. God assures us: "Do not be deceived: God is not mocked, for whatever one sows, that will he also reap" (Galatians 6:7 ESV). This truth is not only anchored in Christian beliefs. This credence has also been endorsed in the universal law of cause and effect, which states that every single action in the universe produces a reaction no matter what.[xxviii] It is true that the offender does not get away without being impacted by the natural consequences of their actions.

A Psalm of David

Psalm 37:1-4 (NIV)

"Do not fret because of those who are evil

or be envious of those who do wrong;

for like the grass they will soon wither,

like green plants they will soon die away.

Trust in the LORD and do good;

dwell in the land and enjoy safe pasture.

Take delight in the LORD,

and he will give you the desires of your heart."

Also, Psalm 33:13-22 states that God sits on the throne and looks down, sees our pain, loves us with unfailing love, and is our help and shield. These verses may comfort you to know that God *sees* you, He acutely knows your pain, and He does not sit idle on your behalf.

Confrontation

There are times for appropriate confrontation. Scripture describes an example of confrontation with an option for bringing in support when it is met with conflict or resistance, as described here: "If your brother sins, go and show him his fault in private; if he listens *and* pays attention to you, you have won back your brother. But if he does not listen, take along with you one or two others, so that every word may be confirmed by the testimony of two witnesses. If he pays no attention to them [refusing to listen and obey], tell it to the church; and if he refuses to listen even to the church, let him be to you as a Gentile (unbeliever) and a tax collector" (Matthew 18:15-17 AMP).

Whether to confront or not and the actions to choose in the confrontation require discernment and prayer. Again, seek scripture, the leading of the Holy Spirit, and wise counsel. If given the advice of an attorney or a highly educated therapist, still go back to God and first see whether you feel a peace that this is the right course of action to take. Attorneys, therapists, pastors, counselors, and psychiatrists are all human beings and can sometimes misguide their clients.

There have been times when *expert advice* and even *legal advice* have created more chaos than no advice at all. There is an informative movie called *Divorce Corp*, directed by Joseph Sorge, released on January 10, 2014. It gives real-life accounts of families that are torn apart by bad advice from lawyers. This movie documents cases showing malicious actions of some attorneys who attempt to increase the hostility between the parties in order to increase their profits. In this documentary, the attorneys were shown to create distrust and animosity between their parties, thus racking up more and more billable time. This is highly unethical, and not all professionals behave in this manner, but it has been documented. While I repeatedly encourage you to utilize expert resources, I also encourage you to use discernment and prayer in your selection of the professional, as well.

Use discernment also in your choice of method of confrontation. The decision tree of how to seek justice, whether through direct communication, the use of the court system, engagement of law enforcement, purely divine intervention, or a combination of these, requires wisdom and forethought. There are times to make a police report, press charges, or file a lawsuit. It is a reality that some organizations are corrupt, and unfortunately, may only become motivated to cease from wrongdoing through the language of fines and penalties that impact their pocketbook - the only route to their heart. Check with wise counsel and always consult God in prayer for guidance on confrontation because there are indeed times to take action.

> **"The only thing necessary for the triumph of evil is for good men to do nothing." Edmund Burke**xxix

Christians are not meant to be wimpy, passive doormats. The method of dealing with injustice can take many forms. Handing the whole situation over to God can sometimes be the most powerful thing to do and does not represent weakness. Regardless of your chosen method, pursuing justice can be conducted while simultaneously in a state of forgiveness and peace, as you take an appropriate stand for prevention and protection. Just know that God has plenty of motivation and power to ensure that justice will prevail, with or without our help.

Romans 12:19 (AMP)

"Beloved, never avenge yourselves, but leave the way open for God's wrath [and His judicial righteousness]; for it is written [in Scripture],

"vengeance is mine, I will repay," says the Lord.

2 Corinthians 3:6 (NIV)

"He has made us competent as ministers of a new covenant--not of the letter but of the Spirit; for the letter kills, but the Spirit gives life. ....."

Galatians 5:25 (KJV)

"If we live in the Spirit, let us also walk by the Spirit."

Myth 2 – The Amnesia Myth

I should forget what they have done.

Remember Ivan and Ailith, with the motto, *forgive and forget*? Some people believe that you have not forgiven the person until you have erased it from your mind, created a clean slate for them, and have begun to behave as if the incident never happened. This myth can be costly on several levels. For one, you may just be stuffing your pain, which will eventually affect your health, and secondly, you may need to retain the knowledge of that person's actions and limitations.

The problems that this myth can create are far-reaching. What if the person continues to exploit you or does harm to those you love? What if your partner has cheated on you in several affairs? What if the harm done to you was intentional? What about the case of chronic lying? This myth can not only hurt your health; it can hurt your life.

Derek and Jacqueline

Jacqueline reached into the dryer and found a skimpy pair of hot pink underwear that she did not recognize amongst Derek's laundry after he returned from one of his flying trips. She turned to Derek with the undergarment in hand, and his eyes suddenly grew big like saucers. Seeing his distress, she immediately dismissed it as something that must have been random. He had professed his faithfulness emphatically to her many times before, and she trusted him implicitly. She loved and believed in him so wholeheartedly that whenever she was a passenger on a plane that he was flying, she had absolutely no fear. She believed that when he was flying the plane, all was safe. Even when, during one trip, the other pilot had caused the aircraft to hit severe turbulence and drop so abruptly that the passengers' beverages hit the ceiling of the cabin, she had hardly flinched. She believed that if he was in the cockpit, all was safe. She believed every word Derek said and trusted him completely. She trusted him with her life.

Forgiveness does not require blind trust after it has been broken. If someone has let you down in the past, this is merely information that they are capable of making that mistake and will need to make changes to prevent it from happening again. This applies to any type of relationship and broken trust. What if they repeat the same mistake? Is that rude for you to tell them honestly how you feel or to make changes in the relationship? Should you worry about hurting their feelings if you need to set new boundaries with them? It is scriptural to set a boundary between you and someone you do not trust. John 2:23-25 (NIV) states, "Now while he was in Jerusalem at the Passover Festival, many people saw the signs he was performing and believed in his name. But Jesus would not entrust himself to them, for he knew all people. He did not need any testimony about mankind, for he knew what was in each person." You are not morally nor spiritually wrong in setting a boundary physically, emotionally, or spiritually whenever you need to protect yourself or someone else.

It is often important to retain information in your memory about a situation or a person's potential to harm you. This information is needed to guide you on how to set new boundaries appropriately. For instance, in the event of infidelity, to totally forget could be devastating to the faithful spouse who runs the risk of contracting a sexually transmitted disease, some of which can be horrendous or even fatal.[xxx][xxxi] The concerned parent, where their child's peers have been a bad influence, needs to retain those facts in their memory to protect their child. Suppose someone is not emotionally, physically, or spiritually safe to be around. In that case, you *do* need to remember what they have done in order to remain aware of their limitations and potential for future harm. By trying to forget and move forward as if nothing happened, you may be enabling that person to continue in their bad behavior.

About Boundaries

Boundaries involve parameters, limits, and borders within which to maintain protection and balance. There are several types of boundaries, including physical, emotional, and spiritual parameters. Physical boundaries can range from limited contact with a person to no contact at all. Emotional and spiritual boundaries can involve choosing to love a person from a distance or with limited interaction, where you politely end a phone conversation if it begins to become abusive. You may choose to only pray for a person who has shown violence at face-to-face encounters. Another form of setting a physical boundary is to say no to financial bribes and manipulations. The level and type of boundary that you choose to set can be navigated with wisdom and discernment.

It is abundantly clear that we are allowed to set boundaries. Jesus set boundaries frequently. In the wilderness, when Jesus said *no* to Satan and told him to leave, Jesus was setting firm boundaries. When he went up on the mountain to be alone with God to recharge his spirit, he was setting boundaries even while being pursued by demanding and needy crowds. There are times when you need a moment to recharge regardless of the imminent demands of those around you, and by Christ's example, it is permitted. At times, Jesus refused to answer questions of religious hypocrites when knowing that their hearts were not sincerely wanting the answers. His most profound setting of a boundary was to protect us from the Evil One, through Jesus' crucifixion and resurrection, defeating death once and for all.

The Creator has provided you with boundaries from the very beginning. Your very first stage of inception and development was when you were the weakest while inside the womb. Here, you were wrapped in the strongest of boundaries. When you were born, you came with a thick layer of skin to physically protect your vital organs. Babies also have a generous layer of subcutaneous tissue (body fat) for more protection. As we grow, we can add increased muscle mass to our frames for further protection and strength. From the beginning, emotional and mental boundaries are present because others cannot read our thoughts. Recall a time when an infant could not stop crying, and the exasperated parent was at their wit's end trying to figure out the need that was in the infant's mind. Spiritual boundaries come in the form of free will given to us, where God does not force you to obey Him. Through free will, God is respecting our boundaries. Spiritually dark forces cannot force you either; however, they might deceptively attempt to convince you that they can.

Boundaries also need to be applied with balance and sagacity. Too much or too little boundary presents a problem. For instance, we wonder why horrible things happen here on this earth. I believe that this is the human exploitation of the free will boundary. There are definite consequences; however, as submitted later in this book, that are sure to come in time. The point is that you are allowed to set boundaries. You can say *no* when you don't feel comfortable in a situation. You can remove yourself from re-exposure to a negative encounter. For a more thorough description of boundaries, Cloud and Townsend provide a great teaching on the subject.[xxxii] You can also consult an expert for guidance on how, when, and types of boundaries to set in your life. Forgiveness is not forgetting nor letting the person avoid the consequences of their actions.

If you say no to exploitation, do you feel guilty? Do you think that you are selfish? What about the person who refuses to listen to your protests? Are *they* not being selfish? If you allow mistreatment of yourself to continue, you are participating by enabling that person's negative behavior to continue. Do you now feel even *more guilty* because I just said that you might be enabling the perpetrator?

Let me reiterate a fundamental term. It is called *false guilt*. Many people do not realize that they do not have to allow the relationship to stay the same, and they do not have to continue participating in the same unhealthy dynamic. False guilt is not healthy guilt. It is just that – false. The perpetrator's behavior is not your fault, even if they believe you provoked them. They have many alternative options from which to choose in response to your actions. Their choice of response is not your responsibility. The fact that they were able to wrong you simply means that you are on life's continual learning curve and that you did not cause the perpetrator to hurt you.

Saying no to someone is not selfish. Ill-intentioned people may rely on the hope that you will believe that saying no is selfish so that they can manipulate you. Furthermore, a person who tries to make you feel guilty for setting that boundary may likely be the one who is selfish. Knowing what boundaries are and applying them will become very useful for dealing with the next myth.

Myth 3 – The Kiss and Makeup Myth

I have to maintain the exact same relationship with them as if nothing happened.

There are some individuals whose behaviors, and in some cases, characterological disturbances, almost guarantee that they will hurt you again. You do not have to allow them subsequent access to your belongings, money, house, child, heart, body, nor any part of your life. You have no obligation to accommodate a person who has violated or mistreated you.

After an infraction, the relationship often needs to change. Many transgressions, big or small, lead to natural consequences. It is an understandable natural consequence that you may not be able to trust that person again right away (or ever). The relationship will likely need to go through a revision of boundaries, actions devoted to repairing, or even a change in status. Resuming the same status quo prevents the necessary opportunity for improvement, learning, healing, and growth.

Often setting boundaries is very tricky. Sometimes the offender is in a position of authority over you and you may be in a complicated situation.

Monique's Story

Monique grew up in high socioeconomic standing and culture. Her family was devoutly religious and academically prestigious.

Her parents met at an upstanding bible college, and her father went on to be a renowned scientist. Her father carried himself with pride, and everywhere he went, people looked up to him as brilliant and charming. Her mother was seen as meek, submissive, and loving toward her children.

Monique's father had a strong standing in the community. He was extraordinarily gifted and brilliant as a researcher. He discovered life-saving techniques that exalted him into the public eye.

How fortunate to be born and raised in such a family, one would think. Most families of this kind would be a great blessing and opportunity for a child, but another side of the story existed for this particular family. While both parents had been raised with solid moral doctrine, somewhere, a cancerous root had been planted within Monique's father.

Monique's father had two different sides to his personality. One was the jovial, friendly person who presented to the outside world as a wonderful man, and the other was the one who morphed into a monster behind closed doors. This dynamic is not a stranger to many families, with one family member or another having severe issues.

This hidden side of him became a deep, dark family secret, and woe to the person who even dared to question him for fear of making him look bad. The mother was afraid to speak up to him, for he dealt harshly with anyone who challenged him.

Throughout her life, Monique's father berated her, shaming her mercilessly in front of others. He would control her almost every move. With any hint of her emergence into self-confidence, he would immediately eviscerate her until her spirit was broken.

Then there were random nights throughout her youth when, in the middle of the night, she would be right in the midst of deep sleep, abruptly jolted awake, discovering the weight of his body on top of hers. She knew to never dare to tell him no, or the tirades or worse, would ensue. All she knew to do was the same thing she did during those berating sessions – freeze until it was over.

Monique, therefore, grew up with significant challenges involving her self-worth, sense of safety, and her perception of God as the 'Father.' Trust remained broken as her mother had been physically assaulted at any attempt to protect her. Her mother feared him -they all feared him. These were days when women did not have as much earning power as men; thus, her mother knew of no way to take care of the family if she were to leave him.

What happened to create such a monster? There is no excuse. Her father, who had tried so fiercely to break her, was already a broken man himself. Only God knew what crept into the deep dark secrets of his heart and wounded soul. This was a family that desperately needed help from outside sources, yet who would dare expose him? Everyone in the outside world loved him, and he was heralded as such a great man. There seemed to be nowhere to go. No escape. No refuge.

Dysfunction is no stranger to people in high places. It is no stranger to the renowned, highly educated, nor to the moral and religious or Christian groups. Even the best families can find themselves under the attack of evil influence. Many a Christian family has lost a precious child from addiction, foul play, gang violence, or other tragedy while doing a great job in their moral role. Why would the enemy want to attack a family of whom it already has possession?

To the one who is evil, the prime prize might be the corruption of the innocent. Sometimes it is the blind denial and refusal to open one's eyes and speak up that allows the door to remain open to the enemy. All Christians must keep watch and take a stand whenever detecting a root of wrong-doing, as the enemy prowls around seeking those whom he may devour (1 Peter 5:8). We must always pray for discernment, and through that discernment, the boundaries must be set - the door to evil opportunity must be closed.

Myth 4 – The Miracle Myth

I have to make them apologize, regret what they did, or change.

I call this the *Miracle Myth* because the offender may never choose to apologize, experience remorse, or change. If you believe in this myth, it may forever hold you hostage to the whims of their insensitivity. God is in the business of miracles, not you nor me, and it is not our job to change another person. While this myth keeps you held prisoner emotionally, physically, and spiritually, it will also keep you under strain. There are people who will not ever recognize what they have done and will never apologize nor feel remorse, nor change. While they go around free, you are burdened with stress hormones making you sick.

Have you ever tried carrying a weight that was too much for your physical structure or perhaps been thrown into a job for which you had no training? You likely remember how much strain and pressure you were under. In negative situations, you can focus on the part that you can do, such as speak up, peacefully protest, write your congressperson, pray, and or/leave the situation. Beyond that – leave the rest to God. Holding onto anger with the hope that the other person will finally gain an understanding of their behavior and action is taking on a job that is God's. It is between God and that person or between God and that organization.

Do you remember how you felt when you finally let go of that physical weight or that job that was not meant for you? Peace and order were restored. It is good news that you and I do not have to wait for the offender to wake up and gain wisdom before we can move forward and become free to live our own lives.

Outbreak Upon Outbreak

Late in May 2020, the quarantine in the U.S. from the world pandemic was still in effect to some degree. After most U.S. citizens had been cooped up in their homes for at least two months to comply with the Centers for Disease Control and Prevention (CDC)[xxxiii] guidelines and protect against further spread of this virus, a video in Minneapolis, MN went viral showing the death of a black man named George Floyd while under police custody. What was supposed to be a peaceful arrest went devastatingly wrong and was followed by an investigation. From that point, hysteria erupted with a polarization of views. One group of people began pushing for wide-spread removal and defunding of police officers in general, and the other pushed for increased training and accountability for specific *bad apples* among those in the police force. Initially, peaceful protests began but became infiltrated by extreme radical groups who began tearing down monuments and statues, burning police cars, and destroying business establishments. This led to the deaths of many innocent people caught in the crossfire of this political and emotional hurricane. Now on top of COVID-19, the U.S. had an additional pandemic of hate and violence.

>**A simple math equation taught by my beloved father:**
>
>**"Two wrongs don't make a right."**
>
>**Louis Walter Weathersbee**

Were the rioters trying to get their audience to convert over to their viewpoint or political perspective? A basic marketing-sales class would have taught them that this was not the way to win others over to their views. Instead of this working in their favor, the violence and hate only made things worse, escalating into more and more tragedy.

Myth 5 – The Omniscience Myth

They should know better or understand how I feel.

In 2020, the new and rampant hate pandemic caused a great deal of disruption across some major cities in the U.S. In response to current events, riots erupted against perceived systemic racism, which metastasized into a politicized uproar. Neither side had an accurate picture of what the other group was thinking in their hearts. Rampant misinterpretations were spreading like a psychological infection, causing anger to spin out of control. The radical rioters appeared to be claiming that the police and government systems had pervasive racism. Yet, some individuals positioning themselves as crusaders for racial equality inflicted death and harm on small business owners and innocent citizens, many of whom were also black. The extreme radical individuals or groups caused an enormous amount of death and destruction on those who were financially struggling from the recent pandemic and quarantine. The infiltrating rioters seemed deluded in their assumptions and entitlement that the world should know how they feel and support their destructive behavior, however, they were making the situation exponentially worse. Peaceful protesters and those just trying to live a calm, peaceful life, found it hard to understand the logic behind those trying to burn down cities and attack minorities, including the elderly and financially feeble, in the name of racial freedom.

We assume that the offender should know better. They should know how we feel and the gravity of what they did to us – right? No, not actually. On the surface, much human behavior can seem to be without reason or rhyme. We cannot read their minds, nor can we have a clear picture of their soul. We can estimate probabilities of what has likely influenced them to behave that way. These are only educated guesses or intuitive hunches on our part. They may even have less insight into us if their minds are focused on their own agenda. If you expect them to have such discernment, you may be expecting more from them than what they are willing or able to do. Only God has unlimited knowledge into their minds and hearts.

Human beings have extraordinary complexities that permeate their mind, soul, and physiological body. Behavior is an orchestration of chemicals, hormones, neuronal connections, mediating the individual's perceptions, emotions, and choices, which are influenced by their own interpretations of past and present experiences. Complicated? Yes. There are very plausible reasons why they may even have less insight than most people, as we shall see in subsequent chapters. For now, there is only *one* God, it is not our job to be God, and it is clear that they are not being guided by God as well.

Possibly the most insightful book is one that a teacher gave my son as a graduation gift for his transition from kindergarten to the first grade. It is titled *Seven Blind Mice* by Ed Young (1992).[xxxiv] This simple 36-page book seems to capture the basis of all human conflict. Essentially, all seven individual mice found something strange near their pond, that they did not understand. They each separately went toward the object one at a time and reported back to the group what they perceived it to be. The first mouse went out to look and determined that it was a pillar, but the other mice did not believe it or agree. The second mouse went out to look at it separately and came back, reporting that it was a snake. The remaining mice went on their separate adventures each subsequent day, all returning with totally different conclusions about what this big thing must be. One decided that it was a spear, while another was certain that it was a cliff. Another asserted that it was a fan, yet the sixth mouse clearly felt that it was a rope. They all adamantly disagreed and began to argue. How could there be so many different perceptions with such certainty? All of their individual findings seemed to be correct.

Don't we all do this as humans? It is inevitable that others in your life will have a completely different view of the same situation and refuse to see your side, much less have an understanding, and choose to change over to your way of thinking. As it turned out, each mouse was correct in a sense. They were each only looking at a part of this strange thing that they were trying to understand. When the seventh mouse decided to take a look, this mouse ran all over it, from top to bottom and from side to side. It turns out that they were all correct but only had pieces of the whole picture. The first mouse interpreted a pillar from seeing the leg and foot. The next mouse determined a snake from the trunk, another determined a spear from a sharp area such as a tusk, another saw a great cliff from another angle, while another saw a fan from the large ear, and finally, the last mouse perceived it as a rope from seeing the tail. When the seventh mouse investigated more thoroughly, considering all of the observed parts put together, only then could agreement be reached. It was an elephant. I have often thought, what a wonder it would be to provide each person in Congress a copy of this book.

How often is it that full-grown adults refuse to see an issue beyond the limits of their own perception and experience? It would resolve many conflicts and allow harmonious decisions to be made without wasted time, energy, and expense. There are times when we can encourage others to consider alternate views, consider others' feelings, and come to a compromise; however, it is not always the case. What a difference could be made if simple yet astute books such as this one, could be considered as mandatory curriculum in our schools. If people at all levels would be willing to suspend for a moment their one-sided view to consider all aspects of an issue, there might be fewer divorces, fewer civil legal fights, and more unity. We would find that when all of the pieces are put together into the big picture, we fundamentally agree with each other on many matters.

In this book, I am hopeful that you will come to understand possible underlying reasons for some otherwise unexplainable behavior in others by expanding your perception beyond your own. The tools provided in this book may also help you rise above situations when the other person is not willing to play fairly. Knowledge of the perpetrator's lack of insight is not giving them an excuse for their behavior; it only provides an additional vehicle to help you heal and let go.

Myth 6 – The Self-Deception Myth

I can't help (control, change, prevent) my feelings

I have labeled this myth as such because it is a bald-faced lie that we sometimes tell ourselves. Webster's Dictionary would describe the concept of *can't* as "helpless, powerless, limited, restricted, handcuffed, paralyzed, weak, incapable, incompetent, inept, feeble, and frail." Do you *really* want to label yourself this way? Do you *really* want to tell such lies to yourself that hand over all of your power to the offender?

The first thing to become aware of is your thoughts. Behavioral science, through **Beck, Ellis, Meichenbaum, as early as 1955,**[xxxv] developed cognitive therapy, and later Christian writers such as Caroline Leaf [xxxvi] and others teach on the importance of how our thoughts influence our emotions. Science has shown support for what God has said all along (2 Corinthians 10:5 NKJV). Take hold of your thoughts; take responsibility for them to make them productive rather than destructive.

You can change your emotions by changing your thoughts. Does this seem easier said than done? Keep reading. You have more power than you think you do. The exercises in this book can show you how to get there.

Is Medication a Cop-out or a Sin?

It is important to mention that brain chemistry and hormones have a powerful role as well as hereditary components. Mood disturbance, such as depression, bipolar disorder, and others, are influenced to a considerable degree by brain chemistry and heredity. Furthermore, stress can activate these formerly dormant vulnerabilities. So, while some people can readily take hold of their thoughts and make them captive, others may need the help of medications. This is not a weakness. It is part of being human.

In my work, it is clear that for some people, it is next to impossible to change thoughts and emotions. Most of the time for most people, it takes dedicated effort, time, and repeated practice. For a great number of people, additional tools are needed. If you find it almost impossible to even conjure up one single positive thought or helpful belief, you may need to seek the help of a medical professional. This is not weakness nor disobedience. This is making use of available tools. In fact, this may facilitate your efforts for obedience.

When the Bible says to take all of your thoughts into captivity, the scripture is not specific about how to do so, whether automatically or with the help of useful aids. If you struggle with this and need additional assistance, I believe that you are obedient in applying whatever appropriate resources that are necessary to accomplish this. In many cases, it can be medications when appropriately used.

There is a myriad of examples of God's people using tools to carry out obedience to Him. Noah obeyed God in building the ark with the exact dimensions that God commanded (Genesis 6). Do you think that Noah did this mighty feat with only his bare hands? Do you believe that Noah cut the wood to match those specified dimensions by using his teeth? If you are nearsighted and you want to take food to someone who is shut-in or ill, would God be offended if you drove the meal over to them while wearing your prescription glasses to ensure the safety of others? Medications, when needed and appropriately prescribed, are designed as tools to help balance the chemicals in the brain to balance the mood, anchor the thoughts in reality, and equip us to fully step into obedience to God and His purpose for us here on the earth. A reason for taking medication if needed is that we can feel better, but it is also for the sake of others around us who we can bless because we are no longer hindered by genetic or chemistry-driven mood disorder.

Emotions and cognition are mediated by brain chemistry. There are times when one or more of our physical systems needs medical attention and balance, and brain chemistry can be no exception. Many people struggle with these challenges; you can select a medical doctor of your choice and have an assessment conducted if your moods seem way out of control. This is nothing to be ashamed of and is part of the human condition. Where one person may be on a mood stabilizer, another may be on a blood pressure medication; where one person may be on an antidepressant, another may be on medication to lower cholesterol or adjust their thyroid level. Christian comedian Chonda Pierce pointed out that if prescriptions were a sin, that would mean that near-sighted people would have to, therefore, drive without their eyeglasses, which could be a disaster. If you want to take hold of your thoughts and find it next to impossible to do so, deciding to seek a competent professional who can help you with medication can be seen as taking further steps in obedience to God.

This book will coach you to become aware of the thoughts that you generate and will help you replace them with more fruitful and realistic thinking. We are commanded to take charge of the thoughts on which we choose to dwell (2 Corinthians 10:5 NKJV). As you will see in a later chapter, taking charge of your thoughts can subsequently change the emotions that you feel.

The following are some scriptures that support the idea that we *do* have control over our thoughts. Sometimes taking charge of our thoughts involves the use of whatever appropriate tools are needed. With or without medication, a practical tool involves the repetition of new and healthy thoughts to retrain your brain. If you have a responsibility, you have *response-ability*.

Proverbs 12:7 (KJV)

"As a man thinketh in his heart so is he."

Philippians 4:8 (ESV)

"Finally, brothers, whatever is true, whatever is honorable, whatever is just, whatever is pure, whatever is lovely, whatever is commendable, if there is any excellence, if there is anything worthy of praise, think about these things."

2 Corinthians 10:5 (NIV)

"We demolish arguments and every pretension

that sets itself up against the knowledge of God,

and we take captive every thought

to make it obedient to Christ."

Myth 7 – The Omnipotence Myth

If I hold on to (anger, pain, resentment),

it will fix them, change them, or protect me.

Again (and thankfully), you and I are not God. What a relief that is, because we cannot do any of these things by holding onto our resentment. The person may be oblivious to our pain or, worse, not even care about how we feel. Holding on to resentment, you sacrifice your health and well-being while the perpetrator goes on in ignorant bliss – or at least ignorance. Resentment is a state of tension similar to *bracing*. If always on guard, hyper-alerted, and prepared for the battle it sacrifices your health. As discussed earlier, when you suppress anger and emotional pain, you set your body into a state of chronic fight or flight. When prolonged, the wear and tear will steal your ability to function. We are not designed to remain in such a state, and it does not do one thing to change them nor protect us. Instead, it is the opposite of self-protection. It weakens your health, attacks your immune system, and leads to an array of issues, including anxiety, depression (or anger turned inward), poor concentration, and sleeplessness, as described above. How are you going to protect yourself or change them while so exhausted and in a weakened state? This myth does not work because we are not designed to fight God's battles. Only He can change that person and will do so only if they are willing.

That's right! Even God will not change them if they do not want to change – so why should we try to force change on them? Last I checked, I know that I do not have seniority over God. Therefore, there must be a way for us to heal regardless of the offender's choices so that we can be protected physically, emotionally, and especially spiritually. Harboring resentment does the *opposite* of protecting you. It blocks your recompense and robs you of your life and happiness.

Myths 8 – The Martyrdom Myth

I don't need to forgive myself

Dayle's Story

When Dayle came into the world, she sensed the rejection from the very beginning and did not know why. She was supposed to be born a boy, at least in her mother's mind. When she was born, her mom resented the fact that she was a girl and ignored her much of the time. Therefore, Dayle believed that everything about her was wrong – that somehow, she was a mistake. This resentment became more vivid as she grew older, and her mother would sometimes say hurtful things to her. It did not matter that everyone else in her world cherished her. Her grandparents, her teachers, her peers all adored her. They loved her dearly as if she was their own. Nevertheless, all of this outpouring of love from others could not fill that void where she wanted that unconditional love and acceptance to come from her biological mother. She perceived herself as never being good enough, and this perception translated pervasively into her self-concept, her relationships with others in adulthood, and her perception of God. She also transferred all of that rejection onto herself, distrusted her friends, and truly believed that she was a disappointment to God. For years, she lived her life in such a way to fulfill those negative expectations by making bad choices, which guaranteed to disappoint everyone. She had a hard time taking care of herself, yet she put everyone else on a pedestal, yearning to receive that perpetually elusive acceptance that she could not find from her mother.

In your quest to be thoughtful of others, do you leave yourself completely out in the cold? Do you attempt to forgive everyone else but neglect to forgive yourself? This does no one any good. If you do not choose to extend love, nurturance, unconditional acceptance, and forgiveness to yourself, you will be in a perpetual state of bracing and continual tension. In self-resentment, the tension arises from you having an area of your mind and heart positioned against yourself. This area of self-rejection puts you in a state of internal perpetual attack and defense. When you continue holding something against yourself in unforgiveness, it keeps your mind, spirit, and body in a continual state of fight or flight stress, with your energy tied up in fruitlessness.

The Bible says that when we repent, God removes our transgressions as far as the east is from the west (Psalm 103:12 NKJV). If God is that quick to forgive us of our own mistakes, who are we to be more strict or severe of a disciplinarian than God? If we hold onto anger toward our self, thinking that we are pious, humble, or super spiritual by doing so, we are actually being arrogant. Jesus paid the highest price ever given in the history of existence to free you and me from condemnation - that includes self-condemnation. After such an extreme sacrifice, how could we reject His gift for us? I believe that God must feel hurt as we would feel, if someone we loved were to throw away *our* sincere sacrifice that we made for them. Now, do you feel guilty about possibly not forgiving yourself? Well, before you go down that road, this is false guilt and is unproductive guilt as well.

You are a system, and your whole system – mind, body, and spirit – needs to be in a state of harmony. Think of it this way: you may have watched a movie or had the first-hand experience of a corporation discovering a mole within their organization an (espionage agent or secret intruder) planted there to appear as if they are a part of the company, but are sent to destroy it. Internalized resentment against oneself works the same way as something planted inside that is not meant to be there and is destructive.

How often do we suppress hidden anger at ourselves? Sometimes it is in the form of excessive self-sacrifice or humility and self-shaming thoughts. These features sometimes present themselves as noble and pious attitudes; however, this is not righteousness. It is martyrdom and a waste of your time and God's time for your purpose here on this earth. Worth repeating are the words of a wise Christian therapist,[xxxvii] who stated that the only appropriate guilt that a Christian should feel is for a few minutes – long enough to repent, apologize, and make amends without doing additional harm. I am clear that everything else becomes the enemy's domain and is a waste your energy, time, destiny, and life.

Internalized unforgiveness of yourself or others allows a foot in the door of your heart for the enemy to infiltrate and wreak havoc. It can become an avenue to destroy you emotionally, physically, or spiritually just as a corporate mole can take down an entire enterprise. What good does this prolonged self-punishment serve? The energy you choose to tie up in fight or flight from internal attack and defense is an energy that is continually wasted on false guilt that can steal your present and future.

Rather than choosing to spend your precious energy on beating yourself up because of something you cannot change from the past, will you make a decision today to devote your energies toward your purpose and destiny instead? You can make a decisive choice today to stop abusing yourself in this manner. The exercises later in this book may provide the vehicle to help you further.

Myth 9 – The Bliss Myth

Life shouldn't have these problems.

None of us manage to get through life without some form of insult or injury. Whether in the hospital delivery room or elsewhere, the actual birth process is traumatic for both mother and child.

Consider our first nine months in the womb. If conditions were as designed, you were enveloped in the safety of warmth, protection, and continuous support. We come into the world with foundations for coping – one of which is rest, and another is preparation. If conditions are as expected in the womb, nourishment, oxygen, warmth, and touch all orchestrate together in a beautiful symphony, with the rhythmic heartbeat and gentle sounds of breathing continually present to provide an oasis of peace.

Before entering the world, infants receive constant safety, biological support in terms of nourishment, and emotional support by being positioned at the closest place to their mother's heart. At the very beginning, whether in the womb or the palm of God's hand before the womb, you were wrapped in safety, love, and the provision of all that you need. In God's hand, before the womb, you dwelled at the most intimate place – God's heart. I believe that His heart remains attached to you throughout your entire life, even if you do not feel His presence; you are never actually alone. This initial buffer of safety is necessary before we face the unpredictabilities of life. Although not all pregnancies go smoothly, the initial arrangement of our beginnings is designed for the purpose of giving us a foundation of strength and resiliency.

After approximately nine months, with little advanced warning, something changes. We feel the pressure. Mom feels pressure too. Suddenly we are dashed with a rude awakening, shaking us from this period of bliss by a relentless push that somehow is trying to force us to go through a tunnel that is ridiculously too small for anyone to pass through. *What is happening? Why won't it STOP?* This pushing gradually becomes more frequent and more forceful. *I was so content here! Why can't I stay right here with everything perfect just as it always was? Why is this happening?*

And NOW – OH-NO! What are those horrible lights interrupting my peaceful bliss? Ewww! It's cold! Who is that voice? You're not my Mom! Where's my Mom – and that safe place where I have been all my life (nine months)? I want to go back!

Is it any wonder that God wraps us in a cocoon for several months before we even enter this life? Most likely, our very first introduction to this world through biological birth was traumatic. Then there is childhood. Every childhood is imperfect. Some children have fairly happy homes while growing up, while others suffer abandonment, abuse, or worse. Throughout our lives, we encounter people and situations that can feel hurtful.

William's Story

William was in his second marriage, and this one was a success. She was the love of his life. His new wife was beautiful, smart, and very kind to him. Together they raised his only daughter, who was the apple of his eye. While his business flourished, William and his wife, Shirley, were able to travel abroad. They tasted culture, enjoyed entertainment, and rubbed elbows with important people. It was like a dream. This lasted for several years.

Meanwhile, his daughter grew up, went to college, and eventually married. She and her husband started a family and lived in a small, modest suburb near the city. William was concerned that this town was not going to provide the best schools for his two new grandchildren, so he considered ways to help them. He seemed to get along okay with the son-in-law.

In time, Shirley began to show signs of Alzheimer's disease. It was undetected at first, and then unmistakable indicators started to emerge. First, there was the forgetfulness, then lapses of judgment. Finally, one day as they were getting ready to go out on the town, Shirley could not dress herself appropriately. William realized that their time of carefree bliss was coming to an end. He had sought the best medical treatment for her, but the outcome was inevitable. He was slowly watching the person he knew being taken from him little by little into an abyss from which he could not stop nor protect her.

As Shirley's condition reached a point of needing continual nursing care; William sought ways to remain effective wherever he could, in the midst of a situation that he could not control. At this time, his daughter and her husband's children were approaching school ages. They did not have much income, and William was concerned that the school system where they lived might be academically lacking.

William decided to sell the house that had been his and Shirley's homestead, since it was now becoming empty and *lonely for him anyway. He then purchased a home for his daughter, son-in-law, and their children, located in an upstanding suburb with an excellent school district. William also put this new home in his daughter's name. The mutually agreed-upon plan was for William to live in this home with them for the remainder of his years while he helped them with the children. This would allow both parents to be able to work without babysitter worries.*

Shortly after they all moved into this nice home, his beautiful and dear wife passed away, leaving him a widower. William never remarried again. Instead, he poured all of his energies for the next 25 years into the needs of his daughter and her family. He became Mr. Mom, doing a lot of the cooking, cleaning, ordering of maintenance repairs, and taking care of the children. He was available for the grandchildren 24/7. On several occasions, he advocated for his grandchildren at school when the parents could not. When something went wrong, he was right there at the school in a heartbeat. If either of them needed money, he did not hold back from his savings account.

In 2008 the stock market crashed, and William, in a panic, pulled out the last of his funds to avoid losing what little was left. Now, William did not have the financial resources as before. He was down to a meager monthly social security income that was barely enough on which to live. Thankfully, he had bought that home for all of them so he could rest assured to have a roof over his head in the future.

Time moved forward. He was still there for the family in every way possible outside of finances. He had already supplied that home with beautiful expensive furniture and resources. He was able to see his grandchildren graduate with an excellent education that propelled them toward promising careers. Both of them got accepted into medical school. William's plan to provide a home environment with an academic setting that set them up for success in life had been accomplished. This had been a long-term fulfillment of his commitment, and now William was in his 80's.

Unexpectedly, William's daughter had a medical episode that changed the dynamic of the father-daughter relationship. The relationship between William and his son-in-law changed as well. Matters escalated, and contention grew. As the relationships between them deteriorated, they reportedly began leaving him alone on holidays while visiting other relatives. When they passed each other in a grocery store, his daughter and son-in-law were described as just walking right by William without speaking to him. William did not take disrespect lightly and would sometimes stubbornly stand his ground, but this progressed beyond disrespect, plummeting into heartbreak. Hostility increased to the point that William's sister, while on the phone with him, overheard the daughter threaten to kill him. He confided this threat to a friend, who felt legally compelled to make a report to Adult Protective Services (APS). An investigator visited their home. It seemed that all the APS worker could do was to offer sympathy.

It happened right after the APS visitor had come and gone. One day when William was in his room, a letter came. He opened it and found a formal demand for him to vacate the residence within three days. The son-in-law had hired an attorney with the intent to formally evict William from their home. This letter, written on a lawyer's letterhead, did not include anything else. There were no offers to assist him with moving expenses, no plans for helping him find a suitable place to live, and no thank-you's for his 25 years of serving the family – just an order to be gone within three days.

What was on the third date? Ironically, the third day was William's 87th birthday. They had known him for almost three decades, long enough to know that the target date was also his birthday. At the height of callousness and cold insensitivity, the unwritten words of this letter seemed to say, 'Happy Birthday, and here is our thanks for all that you have done for this family. And, oh, by the way, thanks for buying us this house, and if it's okay since you can't afford a moving truck, we will be happy to keep all of your furniture, too.'

Sometimes things happen that are so unreasonable and incomprehensible that it is hard to wrap your brain around them. If anything perplexing has happened to you, I am here to tell you that you are not alone. As you read further through the next chapters, you may be able to find a way to reconcile the unimaginable ordeals that sometimes come upon us here on this earth.

1 Peter 4:12 (NIV)

"Dear friends, do not be surprised at the fiery ordeal that has come on you to test you, as though something strange were happening to you."

As you will see in the next myth, each of us shapes our perception from our encounters, and, like little professors, we form hypotheses about the world, people, and ourselves. Whether accurate or not, these hypotheses become the framework guiding many of our interpretations and decisions as we read others and determine how to respond. Our perceptions are sometimes misperceptions as we superimpose our own conceptual framework and bias onto every person and situation that we come across throughout our lives.

Myth 10 – The Conclusion-Delusion Myth

I can accurately interpret your intentions.

At the polar opposite of the Omniscience myth (myth 5) is the Conclusion-Delusion myth; where, as opposed to our assumption that they should know how *we* feel (myth 5), we assume that we know what *they* think, feel, and intend. This also applies to the riots that broke out during the pandemic of 2020. The conclusion-delusion ran rampant as polarized groups got seduced into mind-reading games, believing that they clearly knew their opponent's intentions. Some rioting groups were accusing the police departments and other established groups of having systemic racism. Some thought that those rioting had been brainwashed by doctrines from a radical political group. There was also an extreme split in the nation between political parties, each appearing to mind-read the other.

Perceptions in extreme forms generally contain distortion. Not all police officers are racist, and not all of the rioters were brainwashed. Not all Democrats were radical and not all Republicans were extremists. Sometimes radicalism and narcissism can transcend both sides of a polarity. During this time, the tendency for groups to assume that they knew exactly what their opponents thought and felt became a prescription for hysteria.

One solution to the conclusion-delusion is to communicate and clarify. Identify the grains of truth within the hysteria. Sort out what is fact and what is exaggeration. Keep the focus on reality. It is undeniable that there has been a history in our country of racism and the horrible abuse of minorities. While there have been a lot of changes over the decades, there still exist some people who remain racist. The other truth is that among some organizations, the bad apples are still present in our society. If we generalize our assumptions, claiming that the individuals in a group are all the same, we miss out on the full picture of reality.

Our country still bears wounds from the past. Expecting racial minorities to quickly forgive horrendous incidents of history without grieving is highly insensitive. Much more healing is needed. The pain suffered needs to be acknowledged and respected, then resolved with constructive correction, rather than retaliation from any party. In a news presentation from the *700 Club*, senior correspondent Eric Phillips presented a report that included a wise assertion, stating that *un*forgiveness is not the answer. This presentation went on to say that not showing grace is not the answer – but exercising grace and exercising forgiveness without truth is also not the answer.[xxxviii] There are often times that call for taking a strong stand and speaking the truth appropriately. We are to speak the truth in love (Ephesians 4:15) and give the part that you cannot control over to God.

One of the more freeing clarifications of myth 10 is knowing that what people do to you is not about you, but it is because of their own subjective interpretations of the situation. Everyone has their own unique personal experience from the beginning and throughout their life. No two experiences are exactly the same. From these personal experiences, we draw assumptions about ourselves, the world, and others. That person's interpretation of the current situation where you came into the picture was already colored by their earlier life experiences and their own biases.

Even at infancy, we all form early hypotheses and form conclusions about the world and people. Is the world a safe place? Am I worthy of love? Are people trustworthy? Even in utero, there are experiences that are not so sheltered.[xxxix] Perhaps you are floating in this blissful abyss, cradled by the sounds of flowing water and a rhythmic heartbeat. Still, as you are progressing in the womb, it becomes interrupted by a distant scream, or perhaps an abrupt shove, whether accidental or not. You are shaken out of this sense of safety and peace. Perhaps from such an experience, you absorbed a nonverbal impression that the world is not safe and adopted early implicit conclusions such as the following:

It is not OK to feel safe.

I do not deserve to be here.

If things are peaceful, don't trust it to last.

Those early experiences and impressions are not experienced in such verbal terms, yet we tend to download them into our soul and mind nevertheless.

Perhaps, the stressors were subtle. If your parents were stressed about finances or had anxiety about the responsibility that a new birth would bring, this stress may be implicitly experienced instinctively in utero, according to the writers of *The Secret Life of the Unborn Child*.[xl] There may have been some misinterpretations made following birth, where the new infant's introduction to the world is met with sad or worried faces reflecting fear to them.[xli] Although reparable, an unwitting first impression could have been, *I am not welcome, wanted, deserving,* etc., or if ongoing, *I do not deserve love, respect, provisions, fair treatment, etc.*

Babies are born with a certain degree of resilience and a drive to survive, so if your pregnancy was problematic, I believe that God has built resilience into us from the start. In my profession, I encounter many adults who have survived seemingly insurmountable beginnings. Regardless of the start we had, we can retrain our brains to think the way that God wants us to think. *It is biblical* for us to recognize our worth and value.

Psalm 139:14 (NIV)

"I praise you because I am fearfully and wonderfully made;

your works are wonderful; I know that full well."

Even as adults and throughout our lives, we have a tendency to assume that we know the intentions of others. We often conclude that we are being rejected or that the other person has ill will without taking the time to get clarification of the details. This applies to all situations, whether in marriage, work, parenting, and other relationships. As long as communicating is possible or safe, it is worth it to do so.

Some situations become complicated. Either the other person will not talk to you, or they are no longer living. In many cases, the other party chooses to remain very stubborn, regardless of your efforts to ask them to communicate. If the case involves litigation, it can become even more complicated and unnecessarily messy.

Derek and Jacqueline

Derek and Jacqueline eventually divorced because of Derek's excessive drinking and behavior. Jacqueline had kept a blind eye for years. The decree, after a number of modifications, had included an injunction forbidding Derek from drinking and driving with their minor son, Charles. After protests from Derek, the injunction became worded in such a way that cloaked Derek as the party with the behavior, as she felt pressured to protect Derek's image and professional reputation as an airline pilot.

Within one week after the judge had signed the new degree, Derek appeared to have already violated that injunction. Jacqueline knew that she could not just stand by and hold her breath, hoping that no harm would come to their son. Her former willingness to protect Derek's reputation was totally gone. She found the only attorney that she could afford and spent every last penny she had, trying to enforce the protection legally since no amount of negotiation had worked. She told the attorney that her primary goal was to enforce the injunction for their child's safety, asking him to file a motion to enforce. Instead, without any explanation to Jacqueline, this attorney filed a motion to modify the parent-child relationship, a much more intimidating motion for the parent at the receiving end. All Jacqueline had wanted was peace and safety in her child's life and was happy to maintain the agreement for the child to be with both parents 50-50 as long as the child was safe.

When the attorney filed this more robust document, drama erupted. Derek escalated into hysteria and told their son that "Your Mom is trying to take you away from me." Another attorney later explained to Jacqueline that filing a motion to modify allows a judge to have more leeway to enforce the injunction. The motion to modify the parent-child relationship was the exact same document that Derek had filed against Jacqueline just months before. The person it impacted the most, however, was Charles, their son. Jacqueline knew that she needed to stand against Derek's alcohol-related behavior because of its potential impact on their son.

All of the efforts of communication and even mediation had not gotten Derek to stop drinking and driving with their son. Jacqueline believed that this was the only way that she could make sure her son was safe when he was with his dad. She sought prayer before going forward and believed that she should stand firm no matter how scared she had become of Derek's fury. She had no idea of the gigantic tidal wave about to erupt.

Moving from Mythology to Reality

Beginnings

Going back to the first months of our existence, even if your in-utero experience was the perfect place of bliss for the entire nine months, it did not last. Suddenly, out of nowhere, a violent rift began. Contractions started, and within hours, you were pushed and squeezed, thrust, and maybe even pulled with horrible cold metal intrusive things called forceps. Or perhaps for you, maybe it was a cesarean section where all was bliss in the warm cozy, familiar shelter that became suddenly interrupted with bright lights. What an insult! And if *that's* not enough, next comes invasive pokes and probes in the nostrils and mouth with a mucous extractor, and other pricks and probes, ironically with medical 'wellness' tests.

My point is that *none* of us avoid insult in this life even with the most perfect of circumstances. The very first experiences of life introduce us to insult. Life from the very beginning is not perfect, no matter how much anyone tries to buffer and protect us.

Life experiences by each person are unique. Even siblings from the same family system can have a different personal childhood experience to report from the same parents. The first sibling may arrive when the parents are newlyweds and enamored by the excitement of parenthood, while the second and third siblings come into the world with the mother and father exhausted, overworked, or worried about the finances. Conversely, the firstborn may encounter a scared new parent, doubting their abilities in this new role, or encounter a parent with postpartum depression. This child may instinctively interpret these cues from the parent as a message that something is not okay with themselves, rather than the issue being with the parent or situation. The toddler and preschooler may have the experience of a parent trapped in addiction, thus experiencing a myriad of inconsistent interactions, leading to confusion and misinterpretation. The likely result is a negative self-concept and possibly a self-defeating perspective in their life. One child may come into the world with an implied *job*, an unfair proposition from the start. Perhaps this "job" was supposed to save a shaky marriage just by being born. If not therapeutically revised, this child may feel like a failure in adult life and not know why, because from the beginning the impossible was thrust upon them that they were not able to fulfill.

Perhaps another child was overindulged by a parent with unfounded guilt. This child may receive most everything wanted without having to work or show effort. This individual may later encounter a rude awakening when they learn that life is not that way, and the world is not going to be his or her oyster.

Sometimes the beginnings are great. The child is blessed with reasonably loving parents who attend to their needs and operate with honesty and integrity. This child may grow to believe that the world is a safe place. If this child, however, is not taught about some of the realities of the outside world, s/he may become vulnerable to wolves in sheep's clothing, believing that *everyone* is trustworthy.

Background of Derek and Jacqueline

Jacqueline grew up in a family that, like any family, was not perfect but at least was filled with love, and the parents did their best to teach honesty and good morals. Jacqueline felt loved and knew that she could trust her parents. Her upbringing was strict, and she was taught a great deal about humility and putting others first. Although Jacqueline met Derek's parents when their dating became serious, Derek would never talk about his childhood. She didn't push. When Derek and Jacqueline got together, they unconsciously transferred their respective background perceptions onto each other. Jacqueline put him on a pedestal and trusted him unconditionally, as she had done with her parents.

How Our Beginnings Shape Our World View

From these upbringings, each individual forms their own unique, individual conceptual framework of life, self, others, and the world around them. These individuals interact with each other blindly (at least at first), assuming that their significant other, spouse, and close friends share their same idea of the world. As humans, we have an interesting way of gravitating toward the familiar; hence, we may marry someone who consciously or unconsciously reminds us of our mother or father. You can apply your own situation with the descriptives of your parents or caretakers. Were they loving or abusive? Did they give you everything you needed or sometimes ignore your needs? Were you abandoned? Were they attentive, or were they preoccupied or unavailable? Did you receive love, and so on?

Without clear communication, people misread others and conclude that the other person thinks the same way they do and has the same conceptual framework of life. For instance, an event happens that leads to a negative outcome. The individual believes that they correctly interpreted the other person's intention as one of hurtfulness or selfishness. Neither of them communicate to explore the other's actual intent; but instead, they go on silently, presuming, and then concluding that the other is indeed a selfish jerk.

Therefore, the event may be affected by an incorrect conclusion and assumption that the recipient knows precisely why the instigator did what they did. This is a myth that perpetuates false interpretation and leads to destruction before a relationship even gets a chance. Without checking out our impressions and assumptions of others, we can draw conclusions that are erroneously shaded by our previous experiences that had nothing to do with that person presently in our life. From the false mirage that we have constructed of that person, we create barriers. From these barriers, we grow deeper into unnecessary resentment that has been built upon fiction. I have seen couples go years down the road of marriage, fighting a mythical figure that they had constructed in their minds.

When we experience hurt or disappointment and avoid checking out the validity of our subjective assumptions, we may assume that the offender knew better, intended to hurt us, or knew exactly what they were doing to us emotionally. They may not even have a clue because they remain wrapped up in their own biased world view, as well.

Learning to Transcend

In situations where the hurt has not come from a loved one but instead is from a stranger or even criminal behavior, we need to learn to transcend our subjective perceptions of what we think that they think and what we think that their life experiences have been. Chances are their experiences were so negative, so empty, or so devastatingly devoid of genuine love that it is almost as if their world was from another planet altogether.

In this book, you will explore ways in which to experience other people with laser vision – with spiritual eyes – even the eyes of God. The person who causes another's pain may have a roaring tsunami of emotional injury within their own soul.[xlii] For them, gross misperception and illogical confusion may be driving their maladaptive behavior. This does not excuse them, but it serves as a tool for insight that can free you into rising above, moving beyond, and surpassing what happened. No matter how wounded we find ourselves, we all have a responsibility and an opportunity to choose and learn how to heal.

The following picture and table summarize the information described above. The table illustrates the dynamic of negative misperceptions being produced and perpetuated. The table also identifies opposing truths and several scriptures that further clarify and debunk each of the ten mythical beliefs described above.

Negative experiences with a caretaker can warp our perceptions of ourselves, God, and others thereby tainting how we interpret interactions and how we choose to respond. It can even cause a misperception of how God really sees us. What we interpret and choose to digest into our soul can color all of our subsequent relationships and choices unless we make a conscious choice to change.

Figure A shows how this dynamic can happen. Here, the Creator is pouring love into everyone of us, yet sometimes humans either do not detect it or misinterpret the message. Sometimes the caretakers who raised us, or other people we encounter, may have had their perception distorted along the way. In turn, they transfer incorrect messages about value and worth. Into those around them. These negative messages are illustrated as spears or daggers in the picture below. The person who has received negativity from childhood, or at other times, may develop a negative mindset and grow up being unable to detect genuine love and caring from other people or from God. As a result, their reactions to others may be tainted through a lens of negativity. Through this negative expectation or lens, they may misread a gesture of caring from others and respond to it defensively, as if it were an attack or untrustworthy. The other person depicted here, who received genuine love while growing up, is tuned in to and receptive to messages of value, love, and caring from the Creator and from others. These messages of love are depicted as hearts in the picture below. In an encounter with a person who has been severely hurt, and thus taught to have a negative lens through which to view the world, confusion can occur. They find it difficult to trust a genuine act of love, and expecting negativity, they may react with hostility. The person attempting to extend love may feel perplexed and not understand the reason for their harsh response.

Through the following pages, you may become more aware of perceptions about yourself, others, and the Creator. It is hoped that you will heal both spiritually and emotionally.

Figure A: What Was Poured Into You? How Do You Want to Filter the Love Offered to You Now?

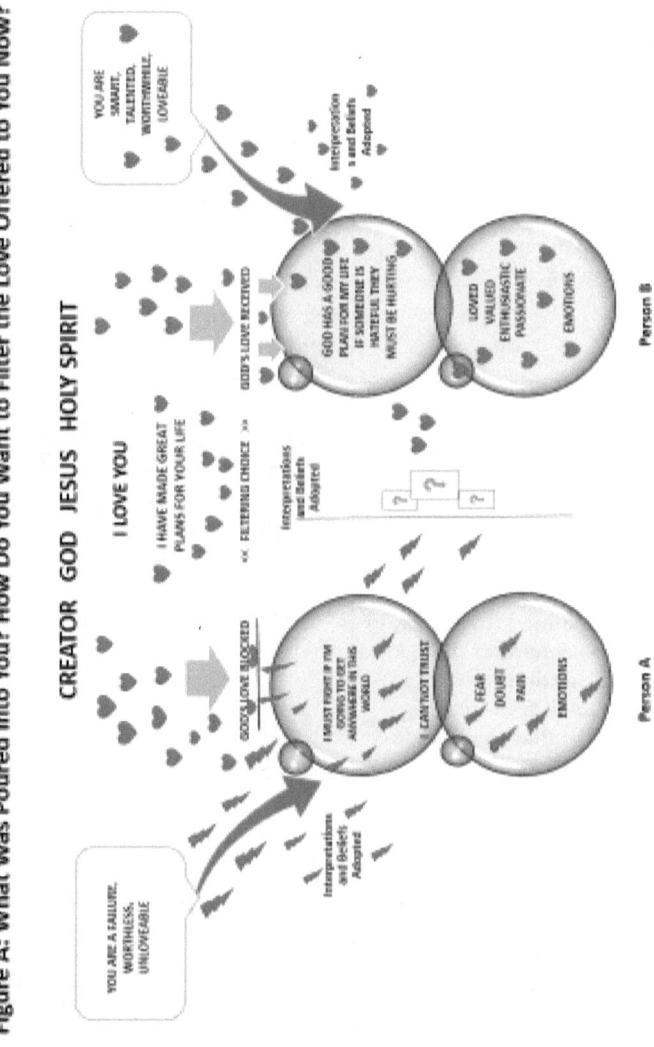

Table 1
Ten Myths of Forgiveness

Myth vs. Truth	Scriptural Support	Reference
1 The Authority Myth	Will I be letting them off the hook?	
Truth: **You are only letting yourself off the hook – not them.** **There are natural consequences that have been already set up.**	Do not be deceived: God cannot be mocked. A man reaps what he sows.	Galatians 6:7 (NIV)
	Do not take revenge, my dear friends, but leave room for God's wrath, for it is written: 'It is mine to avenge; I will repay,' says the Lord.	Romans 12:19 (NIV)
Myth vs. Truth	Scriptural Support	Reference
2 The Amnesia Myth	Will I have to forget what they have done?	
Truth: **There are reasons to remember some infractions, in order to remember the person's limitations and to protect yourself from placing yourself in that same situation in the future.** **Objective knowledge and wisdom are not the same as resentment.**	Behold, I am sending you out as sheep in the midst of wolves, so be wise as serpents and innocent as doves.	Matthew 10:16 (ESV)

*Dr. Joan Weathersbee Ellason, PhD, LPC, Oasis Workshops.

Table 1
Ten Myths of Forgiveness
(Continued)

Myth vs. Truth	Scriptural Support	Reference
3 The Kiss and Makeup Myth	Will I have to maintain the exact same relationship with them?	
Truth: After an infraction, the boundaries and dynamics of the relationship often need to change. *It IS* scriptural to set boundaries with individuals who have shown to be detrimental.	Do not be deceived: "Bad company ruins good morals."	1 Corinthians 15:33 (ESV)
	Whoever walks with the wise becomes wise, but the companion of fools will suffer harm.	Proverbs 13:20 (ESV)
	But mark this: There will be terrible times in the last days. People will be lovers of themselves, lovers of money, boastful, proud, abusive, disobedient to their parents, ungrateful, unholy, without love, unforgiving, slanderous, without self-control, brutal, not lovers of the good, treacherous, rash, conceited, lovers of pleasure rather than lovers of God—having a form of godliness but denying its power. Have nothing to do with such people.	2 Timothy 3:1-5 (NIV)

*Dr. Joan Weathersbee Ellason, PhD, LPC, Oasis Workshops.

Table 1
Ten Myths of Forgiveness (Continued)

Myth vs. Truth	Scriptural Support	Reference
4 The Miracle Myth	I have to make them apologize, regret what they did, change.	
Truth: You can forgive even if the person does not have the appropriate attitude or response.	Judge not, that ye be not judged.	Matthew 7:1 (ESV)
	But mark this: There will be terrible times in the last days. People will be lovers of themselves, lovers of money, … abusive, ….brutal, …treacherous … …while evildoers and impostors will go from bad to worse, deceiving and being deceived. But as for you, continue in what you have learned and have become convinced of, because you know those from whom you learned it, and how from infancy you have known the Holy Scriptures, which are able to make you wise for salvation through faith in Christ Jesus.	2 Timothy 3:1-4, 13-15 (NIV)
Myth vs. Truth	Scriptural Support	Reference
5 The Omniscience Myth	They should know better, act better, understand how I feel.	
Truth: You can forgive regardless of the other person's level of maturity.	Brothers and sisters, I could not address you as people who live by the Spirit but as people who are still worldly—mere infants in Christ. I gave you milk, not solid food, for you were not yet ready for it. Indeed, you are still not ready.	**1 Corinthians 3:1-2 (NIV)**

*Dr. Joan Weathersbee Ellason, PhD, LPC, Oasis Workshops.

Table 1
Ten Myths of Forgiveness
(Continued)

Myth vs. Truth		Scriptural Support	Reference
6 – The Self-Deception Myth	I can't help (control, change, prevent) my feelings.		
Truth: The word 'heart' includes mind in the Bible.		For as he thinketh in his heart, so is he.	Proverbs 23:7 (KJV)
Truth: We are commanded to choose our thoughts and, thus, feelings of the heart; therefore, it must be possible.		Finally, brothers and sisters, whatever is true, whatever is noble, whatever is right, whatever is pure, whatever is lovely, whatever is admirable—if anything is excellent or praiseworthy—think about such things.	Philippians 4:8 (NIV)
Truth: If we have difficulty changing our thoughts, emotions, and heart we can ask for help.		Let the words of my mouth, and the meditation of my heart, be acceptable in thy sight, O LORD, my strength, and my redeemer.	Psalm 19:14 King James Version (KJV)

*Dr. Joan Weathersbee Ellason, PhD, LPC, Oasis Workshops.

Table 1
Ten Myths of Forgiveness
(Continued)

Myth vs. Truth		Scriptural Support	Reference
7 – The Omnipotence Myth	If I hold on to (anger, pain, resentment), It will fix them, change them, protect me.		
Truth: You are not in charge. Therefore, you are not shackled with the job of running the world. This is a huge relief because it turns out that God is much better at getting people to change, and He patiently waits for them to become ready and willing.		Now to him who is able to do immeasurably more than all we ask or imagine, according to his power that is at work within us, to him be glory in the church and in Christ Jesus throughout all generations, forever and ever amen.	Ephesians 3:20-21 (NIV)
Truth: There is permission we can extend to others, accepting the reality of where they currently exist in their own personal journey, growth, and development with God (without condoning their behavior). **Truth:** This frees up our energy and spirit to focus on the wonderful plan and destiny that God has for our lives.		The Weak and the Strong Accept the one whose faith is weak, without quarreling over disputable matters. One person's faith allows them to eat anything, but another, whose faith is weak, eats only vegetables. The one who eats everything must not treat with contempt the one who does not, and the one who does not eat everything must not judge the one who does, for God has accepted them. Who are you to judge someone else's servant? To their own master, servants stand or fall. And they will stand, for the Lord is able to make them stand.	**Romans 14:1-4 (NIV)**

*Dr. Joan Weathersbee Ellason, PhD, LPC, Oasis Workshops.

Table 1
Ten Myths of Forgiveness (Continued)

Myth vs. Truth		Scriptural Support	Reference
8 – The Martyrdom Myth	I don't need to forgive myself.		
Truth: Unforgiveness toward ourselves makes us weak, drains our energy, and distracts us away from our purpose in life.		For All have sinned and fall short of the Glory of God.	Romans 3:23 (NIV)
		He does not treat us as our sins deserve or repay us according to our iniquities.	Psalm 103:10 (NIV)
		There is therefore now no condemnation to them which are in Christ Jesus, who walk not after the flesh, but after the Spirit.	Romans 8:1 (KJV)
Myth vs. Truth		Scriptural Support	Reference
9 – The Bliss Myth	Life shouldn't have these problems.		
Truth: Sometimes terrible things happen that do not make any sense, yet we can get through these situations.		Dear friends, do not be surprised at the fiery ordeal that has come on you to test you as though something strange were happening to you.	1Peter 4:12 (NIV)
Truth: Light has more power than darkness just as one single candle illuminated in a completely dark room will vanquish the darkness		We are pressed on every side, but not crushed, perplexed, but not in despair.	2 Corinthians 4:8 (NIV)
Truth: God is more powerful than Evil.		I have told you these things, so that in me you may have peace. In this world you will have trouble. But take heart! I have overcome the world.	John 16:33 (NIV)

*Dr. Joan Weathersbee Ellason, PhD, LPC, Oasis Workshops.

Table 1
Ten Myths of Forgiveness
(Continued)

Myth vs. Truth		Scriptural Support	Reference
10 – The Conclusion-Delusion Myth	I can accurately interpret your intentions.		
Truth: We do not know everything and cannot read other people's minds.		For my thoughts are not your thoughts, neither are your ways my ways, declares the Lord. As the heavens are higher than the earth, so are my ways higher than your ways and my thoughts higher than your thoughts.	Isaiah 55:8-9 (NIV)
Truth: One day we will know and see more than we do now.		For now we know in part and we prophesy in part, but when the completeness comes, what is in part disappears.	Corinthians 13:9-10 (NIV)

*Dr. Joan Weathersbee Ellason, PhD, LPC, Oasis Workshops.

What to Do with These Concepts

As you continue reading, you will see that interactions are complex. What others do to you is about their perceptions, interpretations, and decisions. It is healthy to examine whether or not you and I have any responsibility in instigating or perpetuating a negative situation. We are to walk about showing kindness, compassion, and appropriate love. It is wise to always consider whether you or I may have played any part in a situation and make wise adjustments in our actions accordingly. You can adopt a balanced perspective of responsibility. We are not to take the full blame for circumstances, nor completely blame others in the dynamic.

Chapter 3

Necessary Tools and How to Use Them

This chapter provides the platform on which to do the work of forgiveness. It is essential that you understand each one of these concepts before embarking upon the three-tier approach and levels of forgiveness. So, please take the time to read the following concepts, and if you need additional support, reach out to a competent pastor, teacher, or counselor of your choice.

Preparatory Prayer

The first strategy to engage in is prayer. Prayer is a powerful resource that reaches into the spiritual and takes on tangible dimensions. Some of us have not considered prayer or others of us have heard it all of our lives and taken it for granted. When we pray and exercise our faith, we literally set in motion supernatural change and partner with God to move situations that we cannot impact on our own. We do the part that we can, and God does the part that we cannot do. Prayer is a way that we can transcend the natural and reach into the supernatural with God's provision.

Several personal accounts indicate that prayers are literally felt in heaven. In the book *Proof of Heaven*,[xliii] an atheist who had been resuscitated from death wrote about his experiences. In this account, he reported that while crossing over from life into the spiritual realm, he felt the realness and impact of prayers in such an intense way that when he returned to life, he became a believer that God exists and that prayers are powerful. In another account, an individual wrote, in the book *90 Minutes in Heaven: A True Story of Death & Life*,[xliv] that he was able to hear the praises of the saints while in Heaven. There have also been scientific studies on prayer that have been encouraging.[xlv]

A profound example of preparatory prayer in advance of an expected traumatic experience is found in the beautiful prayer that Jesus prayed before his imminent crucifixion. After engaging in preparatory prayer, throughout His entire crucifixion,[xlvi] Jesus was able to endure the whole thing without allowing Himself to feel even a twinge of emotional anger or insult. Through this preparation (Matthew 26-27), Jesus was able to rise above the excruciating challenge that was ahead. This is an important example for us, as I do not believe that a person can rise above difficult situations without preparatory prayer.

Preparatory prayer was an ongoing exercise throughout His life as well as the night before His crucifixion. Rising above the situation into a higher order of perspective (H.O.P.E., more in Chapter 7) was His place of existence and His way of life. During the midst of the crucifixion, what strength must it have taken to be able to pray, "Father forgive them for they know not what they do" (Luke 23:34 KJV). I believe the application of preparatory prayer moving throughout our lives can help us deal with *all* of its challenges.

When All Your Supports Seem to Vanish

The prayer in Matthew 26: 36-46 and Mark 14:41, John 18:4 (KJV) is known as one of the most intense prayers of Jesus, understandably since it was right before going to the cross. He had asked for His disciples to pray with him for even just one hour, but they continued to sleep. This was a time when Jesus asked for the support of his disciples, but they seemed to have no clue about the gravity of what was about to happen and the emotions that our Lord was going through. At the one time in his life, when he needed not to feel alone, Jesus experienced abandonment by his closest friends.

Ever had a time when no one seemed to understand when you needed help? They had other things to do, and even though you asked for their help, they just weren't there for you? Jesus went through the entire crucifixion without being able to rely on one single human being. If you wonder why those you counted on were not there for you, it may help to know that Jesus experienced complete abandonment during these most critical moments by those closest to him. None of them was empathetic to what Christ was going through. They scattered, they ran in fear, and one of them even denied knowing him.

In verse 46 of Matthew 26, it appears that after spending a long time in preparatory prayer, Christ's strength was bolstered and He became infused with courage, peace, and power. At the end of this beautiful prayer, He appears fully ready to face the challenge head-on, as he is quoted saying, "Rise! Let us go! Here comes my betrayer!" (Matthew 26:46 NIV).

Many teachers tell us to ask God to help us with the task of forgiveness. Although this book includes several clinical tools and concepts that go beyond general teachings on forgiveness, I concur with this instruction. Spending a lot of time in prayer is the first line of defense to help us face enormous challenges, many of which we do not see coming over the horizon.

In His prayer in the Garden of Gethsemane (Matthew 26: 36-46, Mark 14:41, John 18:4), Jesus already knew that a horrendous injustice was going to take place. He prayed so earnestly that His sweat was like drops of blood (Luke 22:44 NIV). We seldom get advanced warnings about a specific calamity heading our way; however, we *do* get to know that unfair things do happen to the just as well as the unjust. With that in mind, it is a good idea to start every day with a prayer in advance for protection, guidance, and the strength to get through whatever the day may bring.

Awareness of Thoughts and Feelings

Why is it important for us to be in touch with our thoughts and feelings? We all have them. Sometimes they can be very strong, and other times they can be hidden. It is important to know what you are thinking and feeling on a regular basis, but not for the reasons that you may imagine. Feelings contain information about what is going on inside of our hearts and minds so that we can choose appropriate actions. Being unaware of what is going on inside of yourself is similar to trying to administer medication without knowing what is going on inside of your body. How can you know what medication you need if you don't know what hurts? It is like driving without knowing the location of the steering wheel or whether your car battery is fully charged. If you know what is inside your heart, you can more effectively take care of a situation, a loved one, and yourself.

Knowing your feelings and thoughts is not the same thing as allowing them to dictate your actions. Your emotions are not to be the authority over your choices because feelings can be fickle. They sometimes escape logic and, more importantly, can occlude the guidance of the Holy Spirit. The point of this passage is to be aware of them but not necessarily governed by them.

So, then why would I tell you to become aware of your feelings? God gave us emotion for a reason. Jesus experienced emotion; for example, He wept (John 11:35 NKJV), expressed disappointment (Matthew 8:26 NKJV), and even displayed anger (Matthew 21:12-13, Mark 11:15-18 NKJV). Each circumstance is subject to discernment. When, where, and how to use our emotions requires insight, maturity, and wisdom. We are to use them responsibly. Emotional awareness can facilitate judicious choices of action, but we cannot take judicious action without first being aware of what is going on inside of us and our surroundings. Further in this book we will discuss a multidimensional approach to awareness.

This awareness is accomplished with balance so that you do not become continually self-absorbed. It is not healthy to be constantly only thinking of your own feelings and thoughts. We need to be in touch with what is going on inside our own heart along with the needs of the other person. Tune in to your emotions when you need to and then also focus on the needs of others around you. Whenever possible, ask for information about the situation and about the other person's feelings. Awareness of the other person's emotions can give you clarity, helping you to avoid projecting your own bias onto the situation and help you more accurately determine the response needed.

Therefore, it is of great importance that you cultivate awareness as a regular way of life. We are always thinking and feeling something. Sometimes we avoid tuning in to our thoughts and feelings due to business, distraction, or suppression. We may directly try to ignore this awareness through sleep, inappropriate self-medication (alcohol, drug addiction, workaholism), or some other form of avoidance. Our thoughts and feelings are part of the resources that God has given us to use as barometers of information about needs, intuitions, and other insights into the situation in order to help us resolve issues effectively.

You can train yourself to become aware of your moment-to-moment thoughts and feelings. For example, when your alarm clock goes off in the morning, and you roll over to hit the snooze button, what are you thinking at that moment? What are you feeling? Possibly, dread about having to face that work presentation, boss, school assignment, or job search today? Maybe you have thoughts and feelings of gratitude because you *do* have a job even though the boss is a bit scary. Possibly there is excitement and celebration because this is your day off, and you *can* hit that snooze button.

There is always a thought or a belief preceding any emotion or feeling. Rational Emotive Theory (RET)[xlvii] asserts that our emotions are not caused by the event. Our emotions are actually caused by what we choose to think, perceive, and interpret about the event.

How can this be? If someone yells at me or publicly rages at me, am I not to automatically feel humiliated? Wouldn't a person logically become hurt, embarrassed, ashamed, or even mortified? Yet the Bible tells us to take our thoughts into captivity and make sure that they are healthy thoughts. In 2 Corinthians 10:5 (NIV) it states, "We demolish arguments and every pretension that sets itself up against the knowledge of God, and we take captive every thought to make it obedient to Christ." This part, "we take captive every thought to make it obedient to Christ," indicates that we are responsible for what we think. God does not give us responsibility without also giving us the *ability*. If this sounds difficult, read further. This book demonstrates the tools we need to manage our emotions.

God does not give a rule without a tool.

Beginning now, tune in to your thoughts and feelings daily. You may want to start by tuning in to what is easier to notice first. Perhaps you first notice the emotion, then trace it back to the thought that was connected to that feeling. Jot down your thoughts and feelings, or just take five minutes to reflect. Whenever you can, stop at that very moment when something happens to take note of your emotions and thoughts. You may notice that you feel anxious but don't know why. Trace that feeling back to when you first started experiencing it. Then explore what was happening and your thoughts about that event. For instance, did the boss unexpectedly tell you to come to their office later that day? Perhaps, you nodded in agreement and then proceed to pour yourself into the task at hand, not giving further attention to it, but became increasingly tense as the morning went on. Anxiety and worry are forms of fear – what are those thoughts attached to that fear? If you trace fear back and tune in to yourself and the situation, you may discover that you were telling yourself thoughts that created that fear (worry, anxiety, etc.). Examples may be: *On no, what did I do wrong?* Or, *did s/he know that I was late that time last week?*

Remember that throughout our life, we form perceptions and then draw conclusions about ourselves, others, and the world around us, whether accurate or not. Did you somehow find yourself stumbling upon a job or a boss that resembled your childhood family system or your parents? Was your upbringing filled with love and support or hurt and disappointment? These experiences can taint our current day-to-day- perceptions and color our choices in bosses, jobs, friends, and partners.

You may notice that it is easier to detect your thoughts than it is to be in touch with your feelings. That is okay. Trace the thoughts to the event and explore your associated emotions. You may notice neither thoughts nor feelings. It takes practice. If you have an outburst, trace that back to the silent thoughts, emotional origins, and the event(s) that may have felt unpleasant to you. Many of us have learned to suppress this information as a coping mechanism, so be patient with yourself. Start with just five minutes a day or designate a time once per week. As you begin to get in touch with your thoughts and emotions little by little, it will eventually become automatic, requiring little effort.

The next question becomes: now that you are in touch with your thoughts and emotions, what do you do with them. The following sections are designed to help you understand what is going on with you and what you can do about it.

Processing Your Pain

When we believe that we forgave someone but have merely suppressed it, and it comes roaring back, it often means that we have not given sufficient attention to the pain. In Ephesians 4:26 (NKJV) it states, "Be angry and do not sin." We often need to be reminded that it is not a sin to be angry for a period of time. This passage goes on further to tell us not to let the sun go down on our wrath, which gives the devil a foothold. In our efforts to immediately forgive without processing our pain and without using any cognitive tools, we may actually be giving a foothold to the enemy by suppressing it. Stuffing our anger sends it underground, where resentment and bitterness can fester. When anger goes underground, it can derail our emotional and spiritual walk. It can make us sick.

What is the Purpose of Anger in the First Place?

What is *anger*? The best clinical definition of anger that I have heard came from a wise colleague, Dr. Maryanne Watson, Ph.D., ABPP (Personal Communication 1/18/2018). She states, "Anger is a message that a relationship needs to be repaired." Simply put, *anger is energy designed to repair.* The original purpose of anger is to give us the courage to override our fear and allow us to take a brave protective stand when necessary. It supplies us with energy that can be directed toward speaking up against an injustice. This is the healthy purpose of appropriate anger.

Now, if anger (energy designed to repair) for an injustice is still stored in your body or soul, it becomes unfinished business that robs you of your quality of life and destiny. If we do not appropriately make use of our anger or dispose of this energy by processing our pain through tears, talking, praying, or appropriate physical exertion, it can become internalized where it becomes *implosive*. This can lead to an array of emotional and physical problems. Our energy then becomes side-tracked into perpetual repair of the resulting mental or physical symptoms instead of being directed toward resolving the original pain. This is how it steals our energy and, therefore, our destiny. We also remain stuck in the past instead of living in the present and future.

So, What Can a Person Do with Anger?

Worth repeatedly mentioning through this book is the scripture, in Ephesians 4:26, "Be angry, and do not sin: do not let the sun go down on your wrath" (NKJV). This runs counter to what I grew up thinking about anger. I grew up believing that it was a sin. When we believe that we are not supposed to have anger at all and that it is wrong, we likely stuff it in our effort to get rid of it. This is because some people do not know what to do with anger. Many of us did not learn constructive methods of dealing with this emotion.

So, since anger is energy designed to repair (i.e., repair an issue, problem, etc.), there are actually several things that you can do with this emotion. First, you might want to start by noticing that you feel anger. It could be mild, such as annoyance, irritation, or frustration. Tune in to it just to become aware of it, first of all. You cannot deal with anything if you are not first aware of it. Second, if the anger is strong, such as rage, you may need to manage it with a buffer, such as taking a walk, taking slow and deep breaths, or calling a time out for a brief respite to move your attention off of the topic until you are rested and better equipped to manage the emotion. When you are ready to proceed in dealing with the anger, examine what your emotions are beneath the anger. Anger is an emotion with a core need and feeling beneath it. Are you also hurt, sad, scared, or disappointed? Be honest with yourself. Jesus felt all of these emotions at one time or another (John 11:35, Matthew 21:12,

Matthew 26:39 NJKV). Now ask yourself, in these core emotions, what are you needing? With this awareness, consider choices of what to *constructively* do with that anger energy to produce a good solution. This may be to talk to the person who hurt you or talk to a confidant. You may need to take time to cry or vent the emotions through a vigorous, constructive activity. You may want to use that energy to take appropriate action for a social cause or pour your energy into a formal course of training to learn how to correct the injustice. If you are unusually angry, subjective inventory may lead you to get proper rest for balance in your life. If you find that you have excessive, prolonged anger, you may need to make an appointment with a counselor or medical professional to explore hormonal, biochemical, or psychological roots of prolonged anger. Beneath anger can often find a root of pain.

Anger is an emotion with a core need and feeling beneath it.

The pace at which you need to process this pain and anger (i.e., cry, talk to a trusted individual, journal, etc.) depends on the severity of the infraction and the depth of your wound. There is no cookie-cutter formula, and the time you need is just that – the time that *you* need. Be patient with yourself as you grieve. More on grieving is covered in the next chapter.

Derek and Jacqueline

Jacqueline had learned ways to process anger through her clinical training. She had seen clients directed to write a letter that they were not going to mail so that it could contain very candid and raw expressions of the person's anger. This letter is then read to the perpetrator without them actually being present but through the individual's imagination. Then the letter is torn up and thrown away to get rid of the emotional pain.

The events that ensued in Derek and Jacqueline's story were beyond her control to a great extent, and she learned to utilize some of these methods in her own life for reasons that you will see as we go further.

Rest and Balance

Daily rest is necessary, especially for coping with difficult events. Did you ever wonder why, from the very beginning of our existence, that a nine-month period of rest is set up (in the womb) before our feet even hit planet earth? Our creator, God, designed for us to have approximately three-quarters of a year before we even began this journey. During rest, you grow and develop. When you balance your life with periodic rest, you recharge your brain and replenish your soul and spirit. Respite fosters good mental and spiritual health.

If you seldom rest, do you expect yourself to be a super achiever or a superhero? If so, I have an analogy just for you. On the seventh day, God rested (Genesis 2: 2-3 NKJV). It is not only permitted for us to rest, or modeled as a good example, it is an *absolute imperative.* If on the seventh day, even God rested, who are we to be tougher than God? Rest is a necessity for any work that you undertake – especially emotional work on pain. Rest can also be useful as an act of sitting back to take a moment and acknowledge all of your hard work thus far. We are commanded to rest, as it is noted here in Hebrews 4:10-11 (NIV): "for anyone who enters God's rest also rests from their works, just as God did from his. Let us, therefore, make every effort to enter that rest, so that no one will perish by following their example of disobedience." Therefore, we must balance our busy lives with *rest* (respite, sitting time, quiet time, naps, quality and quantity of sleep, work-breaks, vacation days, and an attitude of rest) to remain prepared for the waves of surprises and challenges that life brings and to recover from past stressors.

Genesis 2:2-3 (NIV)

By the seventh day God had finished the work he had been doing so, on the seventh day he rested from all his work.

Then God blessed the seventh day and made it holy, because on it he rested from all the work of creating that he had done.

Another important awareness is the powerfulness of rest. Graham Cooke presents the concept that rest is spiritual warfare. In his work, rest is a weapon.[xlviii] Think about it. How effective are you when you are tired or emotionally drained? In 1 Kings chapters 18 and 19, even though Elijah had just defeated 450 false prophets, right after that when Jezebel subsequently threatened him, he had a complete meltdown. He became afraid, depressed, and even suicidal. Why would such a strong man become reduced to such a state by one single threat? According to a sermon by Dr. Paul Meier,[xlix] you can work so hard that you wash out your serotonin (a chemical that helps prevent depression). Clinically, it appears that such ferocious effort by Elijah had led to his becoming vulnerable to one single threat. What was the medicine that God prescribed for his distraught condition? Elijah was led into God's rest. He slept and was woken by angels who brought him food. After he ate, he slept again. Sometimes just bringing in the balance of rest amidst our work-life is the simple preventative medicine that we need to renew our strength.

Spiritual Insight

One of the most powerful tools that helped me learn to forgive immediately, without stuffing my anger, is the idea that the perpetrator is *not* necessarily the perpetrator. When you learn more about the spiritual dimension that exists, you will see that there is much more than what meets the eye.

In Ephesians 6:12 (NKJV) it states, "For we do not wrestle against flesh and blood, but against principalities against powers, against the rulers of the darkness of this age, against spiritual hosts of wickedness in the heavenly places." The person appearing to try to offend you may be responding to influences that you and I do not see. Think of a marionette. This stringed puppet, originating from the middle ages, has a panel of strings attached to all of its moving parts. Its movements are manipulated by an operator who remains hidden out of sight.

This is a picture of what I think of with human conflict. The only difference is that we *do* have a choice about our perceptions and actions, although some people do not realize that we do. The spiritual realm is not exactly like the strings of the marionette. Still, its influence can be real, subtly presenting negative and destructive thoughts to a vulnerable soul who is willing to heed and follow.

Does a spiritual realm really exist when we cannot see it? Ask yourself if you believe in electricity or oxygen that you benefit from daily. Wi-Fi connections have become a necessity for most productive work. Do you visually see those signals as they move through the airwaves? Do you really believe that these communication signals travel 22,000 miles above the earth to reach a satellite before reaching your recipient's computer or cell phone? Do you see the radio waves or information coming into your television or iPad? A century ago, these ideas might have all been considered psychotic, yet science has supported their existence.

In order for our devices to be influenced by those unseen signals, they have to have an activated receptor. Scripture speaks of spiritual influences, and teaches us that we are to be led by the Holy Spirit and not influenced by other unhealthy input. Toward which spiritual influence do you want to be actively open or receptive? Do you have a highly sensitive receptor that too easily tunes into unhelpful influences like negative thoughts, distorted self-perceptions, or misinterpretations as described in Ephesians 6:12? Or would you like to tune into what God has to say about you and the situation?

The person trying to hurt you may be unknowingly acquiescing themselves to a negative and distorted thought or idea. This may be the real culprit of the situation. The event at the surface level is only one dimension that we see with our eyes and hear with our ears. The person may be reactive, rude, or abusive, but something may be going on with them at another level. The spiritual intent at a deeper level is the unseen dimension. We do not see their perceptions, thoughts, beliefs, or possible negative spiritual influences that may have plagued them for years. Even another co-occurring dimension can be one that has nothing to do with them at all. It could be a distraction to discourage you or throw you off your path. Remember that God loves you, and God wants you to achieve your purpose.

One of the ways the enemy tries to derail the body of Christ is through creating offense. Think of how many church groups, marriages, jobs, and relationships have been destroyed because someone perceived another's actions as an intentional offense. The keyword here is an *intentional* offense. Often in relationships, *both* parties perceive an offense that was not what the other person intended. They can only discover this revelation when they clearly communicate with each other.

Sometimes the offense, however, is intended. Consider a scenario where the offense drama operates at more than one level within the same person. For example, the following describes a person who is trying to exploit or hurt you. None of these explanations serve as an excuse for the individual's poorly chosen behavior; rather, there are possible underlying roots beneath the surface.

1. They may have come from an ugly past, such as a childhood devoid of love and a life full of neglect.

2. They may be going through life with a negative conceptual framework of self, others (you), the world (current situation), and view of life. They may have inaccurately projected those negative perceptions right into the current situation and onto you.

3. The dark spiritual influence (the Enemy, however you may refer to Satan) now tries to take advantage of their negative expectation (of self, others, or life), inserting or whispering distorted interpretations that already fit that person's negative life view.

4. If the person chooses to buy into the lie of misperception or misinterpretation, seeing you as a threat, loser, or adversary, they may create a fanaticized and false narrative about you and the situation that fits the lies.

5. They then make a behavioral choice based on their chosen misperception.

6. They respond according to the perceived actions needed to fit their own subjective world view and consequently their incorrect view of you and the situation (i.e., run, fight, lie, hide, etc.).

A combination of emotional and spiritual influence is at play here. Did you notice how the issue can have very little or nothing to do with you? In the example above it was all about their misinterpretations going on in their mind. We can learn to avoid falling prey to the invitation of offense by learning to perceive situations through wisdom and the eyes of God.

Always remember that what other people do to you is more about them than it is about you. Those who horrendously exploit and abuse others are often abysmally misled and have an inner wounded soul. The person who hurt you, even intentionally, does not get to have the power to define your worth and value, nor the license to steal one single ounce of your purpose and destiny.

Get Support

Seek out someone trustworthy for support as you work through the exercises in this book. You may have helpful friends, or you may not know anyone at all. You may have friends in whom you do not feel comfortable confiding. Listen to these cautions and seek someone trustworthy. It may be wise to seek out the help of a trained professional.

Identifying the intensity of your emotional pain is a personal decision based on how painful it feels to you subjectively. Subjective physical pain is measured on a scale of zero to ten, with zero indicating the absence of pain, 1 indicating the lowest degree of pain, and 10 representing the highest degree of pain. For instance, if your emotional pain feels higher than five, as measured on the zero-to-ten scale, it is prudent for you to make sure that you do not process these emotional exercises alone. If your pain is more significant than a five on this scale, please only do the exercises in this book in the presence of a trained counselor, psychotherapist, social worker, or psychologist. Another reason for seeking an experienced professional is that sometimes friends cannot be objective, and they may try to give you misguided advice. The presence of a trained professional is *not* to provide you with advice but rather to help you remain safe while you process the pain productively.

When selecting the professional, you have the right to interview them to see if you feel comfortable and confident with them. This does not need to take more than a few minutes over the phone or reviewing their webpage. Have your questions ready, and ask the therapist to give you five minutes. They may often have a web site that gives you a sense of how they work. If you have insurance, you can call the member-toll-free line to obtain a list of licensed therapists in your network. Ask for several names in case a counselor on the list is not accepting new clients.

Begin with Self-Forgiveness

You cannot extend anything to anyone that you have not given first to yourself. This is important because you cannot go into any of this work if you become punitive with yourself. It is extremely counterproductive to kick yourself emotionally or criticize yourself for getting misused or abused. This is an example of unproductive processing. It is not helpful.

Furthermore, being harsh with yourself is destructive. *I cannot recommend strongly enough to refrain from dwelling on self-regret as you work through the exercises in this book.* For one thing, if you were upset because someone mistreated you, why would you spend one moment mistreating yourself by berating yourself? If you tell yourself that you were foolish, ignorant, stupid, etc., for trusting that abuser, you are merely telling yourself lies. It was not your fault. Any form of harshness toward yourself for any reason is unnecessary, and it is a form of self-abuse. Make a vow to be kind and compassionate with yourself as you work through the pain.

On planet earth, people have free will, and people will sometimes do wrong things toward others. This is a fact. Since we cannot control the choices of others, it can't be your fault. The fact that you got hurt does not make you foolish. If anything, it probably means that you are more generous than the perpetrator who hurt you, because you provided generosity to them by extending the gift of trust. Giving trust is offering a precious gift. They may not know how to handle it properly, and if they abuse such a privilege. If so, the blemish is on them – not you.

Boundary setting can be learned since you are not required to continue offering trust if it is exploited. Taking assertiveness training and boundary education classes are also forms of receiving support by learning how to protect yourself. There is a time to set limits on your generosity if it continues to be trampled on, and understanding this takes practice. Forgive yourself, learn new tools for self-protection, and then move forward.

Know Your Value

If you believe the Word of God to be truthful, let's start with what *God* says about you. It may be hard to disagree with what He says in his word. The first section of Scripture I invite you to look at is Ephesians chapters one and two. With parts paraphrased, let's look into this treasure chest of God's heart with His attitude toward you and me. We are *blessed* in the heavenly realms with every spiritual blessing in Christ (Ephesians 1:4) Our experience here on planet earth may occlude this truth as things do not often go the way we want them to. We are *chosen* by God before the creation of the world to be *holy* and *blameless in his sight*. *That is the basis and foundation of our very existence*. We cannot negate the fact that He chose us to be holy and blameless from the very start. We are not bigger than He is to override nor cancel what He has already set forth and established for us. There is nothing you can do to make God stop loving you. Verse five continues: In love, He predestined us for adoption to sonship through Jesus Christ, in accordance with His pleasure and will. He has given us *grace* (verse 6) and *redemption* (verse 7) through Christ's blood. We have *forgiveness* of our sins. This forgiveness is not like that which you may have experienced in your life-time with human relationships, where perhaps you got forgiveness accompanied by a stern look. Perhaps a parent might have made you pay mercilessly first or the bitter friend wouldn't let you live down your mistake. This *grace and mercy* He has *already* lavished on us in accordance with the riches of His grace (verse eight). With all wisdom and understanding, he made known to us the mystery of his will according to his good pleasure, which he purposed in Christ, to be put into effect when the times reach their fulfillment—to bring unity to all things in heaven and on earth under Christ. This is indeed a mystery because God's love for us –the *value* that He placed upon us from the very beginning surpasses all that we have ever experienced from another human being – even from the best parent.

Most of us grow up with a theory of our worth and value that has been formed both directly and indirectly by our childhood interpretations of our experiences and interactions. If we were treated harshly by parents, caretakers, teachers, or other leaders, we might tend to download and digest that perception into our self-concept as if it were true. If your parent treated you harshly or told you bad things about yourself, that parent is not God, and they cannot cancel your value that God put in you from the very beginning. The earlier the relationships and experiences, the more formative the self-concept can be. Poor leadership from a misguided human being is likely the result of problems and issues from their own life that had nothing to do with you. The good news is that regardless of the age at which you received negative input, you can get rid of those perceptions and replace all of them with the truth – *you* are valuable, no matter what anyone says.

These negative messages totally unintentional and not meant for us. A mother with postpartum depression may reflect sadness into the face of her infant. Although this sadness has nothing to do with the child, that infant may interpret and internalize negative self-perceptions. These misinterpretations can include an impression that the parent is not pleased with them; therefore, they must be bad, unworthy, or unwelcome. Every parent on the planet will make a mistake several times throughout the child's life, so don't kick yourself for imperfect parenting. The good news is that God has provided resilience within each child. As we grow up we bear the responsibility to take hold of what is true about ourselves and discard any negative false self-perceptions.

If you grew up feeling unwelcome, you can know that God in His Word clearly says that in Him, we were also *chosen* . . . and *included* in Christ when hearing the message of truth, the gospel of our salvation. When you believed, you were "marked in him with a seal, the promised Holy Spirit, who is a deposit guaranteeing our inheritance until the redemption of those who are God's possession — to the praise of his glory" (Ephesians 1:11-14 NIV).

For a more extensive list of how God sees you and me, Joyce Meyer has provided a list in an internet article.[1]

No matter who told you that you are not loveable, good enough, worthy, or forgivable – God sees you as wanted, valued, and chosen by Him. You are *loved* more passionately, sincerely, and deeply than you were by any parent, spouse, child, or human on earth. You can decide to reject the lies that have been offered to you both directly or indirectly by wounded people, whether intended or not, or if misinterpreted by you. You can replace old negative self-perceptions with the *irrefutable truth* that you are eternally precious and that you are profoundly and infinitely cherished by your Creator.

Right now, will you make the decision to realize, download, and accept

the value that you are

as we go through this process?

Part II

Now, On With the HOW
Overview of A Three-Tier Approach to Forgiveness

This book will outline three different levels in the forgiveness process. There is no *cookie-cutter* solution for forgiveness that fits everyone or every situation in the same way. In my upbringing, I was only taught one method, which was to immediately forgive no matter what and ignore my feelings. Fortunately, there is more to learn with greater benefits to enjoy. In Part II, I will describe the three levels of forgiveness with tools for each. All three levels intertwine and build upon each other.

Tier I

Some events are so horrendous that you would be lying to yourself if you thought that you could just forgive immediately. These situations require a grieving process. How long should that grieving process take? This depends upon the situation, the gravity of the offense, your needs, and growth.

Chapter 4 is designed to teach you healthy methods of grieving. A significant number of situations require that we grieve and heal to move past what happened. I have identified grief as a level of forgiveness because it is often necessary to process many emotions before a person can move past the trauma and pain. This level is Tier I because I consider it to be the ground level of forgiveness. It is difficult to move up into the other levels if you still have unprocessed pain.

Grieving involves feeling the feelings that you have. This would seem counter-intuitive since many of us have been brought up to forgive right away, not letting the sun go down on our wrath. If we stuff our sadness or anger, I believe that we are actually letting the sun go down on the wrath. The chapters that follow will help you to understand the use and correct purpose of anger and sadness, which indeed are biblical, as in scriptures stating, "Be angry and do not sin" (Ephesians 4:26, NKJV) and "Jesus wept" (John 11:35, NIV).

Grief, as the first most primary level of forgiveness, is processed for more significant transgressions. The loss of a loved one, the loss of a life-long dream, and criminal victimization are examples of events that cause significant emotional pain. If someone you love was abused or raped by someone, are you really being honest if you immediately tell the perpetrator, "I forgive you?" Sometimes in our most sincere efforts to be a good Christian, we unintentionally deceive ourselves. I interpret Ephesians 4:26, which tells us not to let the sun go down on our wrath, to mean that we are to deal with our emotions as quickly as possible, rather than stuff them underground.

Forgiving immediately, where we recite a statement such as "I forgive you," is a highly moral, respectable act of obedience, and I believe God honors that and sees the sincerity of your intent. Clinically, if we jump to that point without processing pain, it may be merely suppressed. Chapter 4 can show how to deal with emotional pain on a deeper level so that it does not become stuffed into our body, mind, and heart. When pain is stuffed, as mentioned in Part I, it leads to a reoccurrence of emotions that can resurface at the least reminder or trigger. It is important to examine whether you have allowed yourself to grieve.

The exercises in Chapter 6, involve imagery and emotional processing to help you grieve. Some of the processing techniques originated from Gestalt Theory, founded by Frederick Perls, the father of Gestalt Therapy.[li] The emotional processing exercises provided here include components that expand beyond the traditional methods with imagery designed to bring further relief and soothing. As mentioned repeatedly, this section may require the help of a trained clinician for situations involving intense pain.

Tier II

Tier II in Chapter 5 involves a change in your thoughts and perceptions through training. This concept of cognitive change has been written about prolifically in clinical teachings for years by Ellis,[lii] Beck,[liii] and others, with some using Christian application.[liv] The information here builds upon these established teachings by putting them into practical language and application. Changing your cognitions can make your grief periods become less difficult and possibly shorter, the more you grow in this skill.

We must first know what cognition is in the first place. The Oxford Dictionary defines cognition as "the mental action or process of acquiring knowledge and understanding through thought, experience, and the senses."[lv] I like to use the word cognition because it encompasses the whole totality of your thoughts, perceptions, and interpretations of life's experiences. Cognition also includes what you choose to believe about a situation and the perception or perspective that you decide to adopt. Throughout this book, cognition, thought, and perception will be used interchangeably.

Cognition is a very powerful tool that, when applied appropriately, can significantly ameliorate pain. Chapter 5 will show you how to change your thinking appropriately in order to change your emotional life and your reactions to difficult situations. Sometimes this can reduce the traumatic impact and enhance your personal power in such situations.

This process, which I call the Cognitive Shift, actually takes time and practice. New cognitions that replace former negative perceptions must also be believable and realistic for them to be effective. You can learn to replace old thinking with beliefs that promote your healing. This chapter also provides charts with examples of replacement cognitions that can help you achieve a new perspective.

Tier III

Tier III involves the other two levels of forgiveness (Tiers I and II) intertwined. As you begin to retrain yourself to use constructive cognitions that are conducive to healing and you have grieved much of the pain using exercises in Chapter 6, a new perspective can become a more and more automatic way of existing. Tier III, the have third level of forgiveness involves mental and spiritual development that help you rise above many of the events that happen in life. In Philippians 4:7, God desires for us to have a peace that surpasses all understanding. This is a level I like to describe as *ten-foot-tall and bulletproof*, where the darts of the enemy just bounce right off of you. The exercises in Chapter 6 are designed to help you move into this level of existence.

This may seem heroic, allowing a person to go through life with a level of invincible and continual resilience. Jesus did this perfectly. We, of course, cannot achieve it perfectly because we are human and can always encounter events in life that throw us a curve. We can strive to develop this skill with practice, prayer, and growth.

Tier III is the closest to *authentic* immediate forgiveness for which Christians strive. It is where we have trained ourselves to emotionally see the offender with laser vision, spiritual eyes, and through the eyes of God. This can become the emotional, mental, and spiritual perspective that remains a constant for us as a higher-order place in which to exist most of the time. It is a level of functioning where we see the broad, big picture from a multidimensional perspective. This can be freeing as it moves us from the former limited perspective that kept us hampered by narrow interpretations about ourselves and others. At this level our we can let go of many of our discouraging shackles.

As we grow in this level of forgiveness, we begin to see the situation with a multidimensional perspective, aware of many intervening factors that possibly led up to the event. We can see many potential causes of a wounded soul who tries to hurt us. It becomes more clearly apparent why God asks us to pray for that person.

Tier III requires the help of the Holy Spirit. I have learned about people who reached this level without book learning nor therapy but with God's Holy Spirit alone. This is the most freeing level because it involves a higher-order perspective that you can exist within. This means continually walking with in perspective, allowing God to teach you to perceive things, day by day, through His eyes increasingly more. Since this way of living, thinking, and perceiving leads to an ultimate place of hope and peace, I have used the acronym H.O.P.E. for Higher Order Perspective Existence.

This level is anchored in scripture and will be described in more detail in Chapter 7. We are human and it is understandable that we do not exist at this level all of the time. However, the more we change our perspective and perception to achieve this level, the more time we will spend in emotional freedom, peace, and productivity, and the more time we can march forward, unfettered by wiles and distractions. We will be so focused on our purpose in life that we almost become invincible.

John 16:33 (NKJV)

"These things I have spoken to you, that in Me you may have peace.

In the world you will have tribulation; but be of good cheer,

I have overcome the world."

There are limits to all of us in the human condition, and I will *not* tell you that this book will make you impervious to traumas that happen on the earth. All three Tiers are needed at one time or another. All three levels are intertwined, as some situations may be dealt with at Tier III, and others may require the grieving in Tier I with cognitive re-thinking exercised in Tier II. Things happen on planet Earth, regardless of who you and I are. The tools described in these chapters are designed to show you how to move beyond injustices so that you can focus your energies on fulfilling your life's purpose and destiny.

Chapter 4

Tier I:
How to Grieve
(Tier I Level of Forgiveness)

As we know, there are times when the act of verbalizing cerebral forgiveness, though sincerely intentioned, does not seem to stave off the huge tidal wave of tears that flood like an ocean every time we are reminded of that person, marriage, or dream that was lost. Some events are just, no other way to put it – devastating. What do we do for the parents of a son or daughter caught up in addiction or the teen who was abducted into sex trafficking? What can we say to the mother who has lost her baby boy – now a full-grown man – in a random shooting? What do we say for the parent who became alienated from their child through a blundered divorce process and is missing out on their child's entire life? Injustices go on and on. The process of grieving and working through its stages are necessary. It is hoped that the next pages will show you how to go through the process of grieving in order to help you heal. May you transform from victim to victor, from weary to warrior.

Isiah 41:15 (NKJV)

"Behold, I have made you into a new sharp threshing sledge with sharp teeth; You shall thresh the mountains and beat them small, And make the hills like chaff."

This process can take time. The fact that you are working on your grief indicates that you are in the forgiveness process. The next pages describe tools that may help you grieve constructively.

Acknowledgment of Your Grieving

The first step is to acknowledge that you are going through a grief process. This gives you permission to not have to be perfectly on top of things yet. Be patient with yourself and give yourself the time you need.

We grieve an array of losses that do not necessarily involve the loss of a loved one's life. The grief may include the loss of an opportunity, a treasured possession, loss of finances, or the loss of a situation. In your grief, you have also lost the meaning associated with that person or situation. For instance, you may grieve the loss of the dream you had if the loved one were to have lived or stayed. There is the loss of no longer being able to make plans with that person, such as enjoying retirement together, taking trips, or having other meaningful experiences together. You may not have lost material means, but instead, you may feel as if you have lost your dignity if you were betrayed, failed to perform at an expected level, or were robbed. Other losses, such as identity theft, can involve losing your sense of privacy and financial security. Sexual violation leads to a sense of loss of safety, innocence, and/or personal power. An affair, even if the relationship is repaired, can involve a loss of that sacred sense of trust, which may never be restored to its original level. If someone left you or someone was taken from you through death, you have not only lost them, but you also may grieve the dream of what the future would have been if they had remained by your side.

Give Yourself Time

There is no specific timetable for grief, and each person needs different time lengths to heal. Don't pressure yourself, but instead, be kind and gentle with yourself, just as you would be to a child or a loved one who is grieving. This is a time to become your own best friend.

What to Do with Your Feelings

If you have not already done so, tune into your feelings regularly and give yourself time and space to express the emotions. God gave us emotions for a reason. There is a purpose for their expression through talking, crying, journaling, art, and music, for example. In the old testament, God recognized that a period of time was needed to be set aside for his children to work through their grief process. Jesus has walked on this earth in order to truly know what it is like to be in the human condition, with all of the struggles that we experience. You are not alone in your grieving. Sometimes it is helpful to call a friend or to just sit with God.

Our emotions, when handled appropriately, can bring us relief. There is a difference between being aware of your emotions and processing them constructively versus allowing them to control you. In fact, they are more likely to control you when you try to suppress them or block them out. They will remain inside, waiting to be dealt with one way or another.

Being in touch with and aware of your emotions allows you to know that something is going on inside that needs attention. Emotions are designed to be signals pointing us to a need that we have. A parallel example involves the dashboard of your car. These days our dashboards give us a multitude of information.

Some vehicles have an oil light that illuminates if the vehicle is low on oil. The oil light comes on when your engine needs oil to keep working properly. If you continue to ignore the oil light long enough, your engine will burn up, and your vehicle will stop running. Modern vehicles have a window showing how close you are to objects behind you when backing up. If you ignore these warning signals as you back up, you can damage your vehicle and worse seriously injure someone if they are behind you.

Like the signals in our vehicle to preserve and protect, our emotions were designed by God to provide us a signal when we need something. If we tune into feeling tired, we need rest. If we tune into anger, we need to attend to something that is going wrong. If we have something going on inside of us and continue to ignore the fact that we are hurting, we can eventually breakdown. We can burn out just like our vehicle can if we become too depleted of our necessary resources. Fear can be an intuitive warning signal of wise caution for us to stop or choose a different path.

While feelings have a purpose, they also need to be handled in balance. Most of us understand clearly to avoid exhibiting extreme emotions. Alternatively, some of us do not give proper attention to emotions at all. Would we ever dare to scold our vehicle for having its oil light illuminate or ignore the back-up sensors making noise? Our emotions are usually there to let us know that we are hurting and need healing or to caution us before we make a move that could be detrimental. Ignoring or even shaming ourselves for having an emotion is just as unproductive as scolding our vehicle for having its warning light come on.

These God-given emotions can help navigate our choice of action. If you are sad, you may need to cry. If you are scared, you may need to stop, leave, run, cancel a transaction, or set a boundary with someone. If you are angry, it is important to know that there is always an original/primary/root emotion beneath your anger that contains the basis of the needed information.

Learn to trace your anger to the root, which is often hurt, fear, or sadness. The emotion beneath the anger will tell you what you are needing. Remember that anger is energy designed to repair, so consider the constructive methods needed to repair the hurt or injury. You may be needing safety, comfort, encouragement, perspective, or a decision change. Respect the information that your emotional signals can give you.

Scriptural Balance with Anger

It is also important to discuss spiritual perspectives of anger. Let's clarify what the scripture says about anger. The Bible says for us to be slow to anger (James 1:19), so when we feel a twinge of anger, we may try not to have anger at all in our effort to be obedient. However, since it is already there, we may then suppress it and deny its existence. When we stuff it in this manner, it is still there inside us, waiting to either be processed and drained or waiting to surface when we don't want it to.

There are a number of unhealthy ways to mismanage anger. One is to suppress it. This is compared to allowing the sun to go down on your wrath. The other two ways of mismanaging anger are to allow it to have an unhealthy level of intensity and to allow it to have an excessive length of time. Stuffing, intensifying, and extending anger enables the enemy to get a foothold in our emotional and spiritual life. James 1:20 states that "Human anger does not produce the righteousness that God desires" (NIV). We are to deal with anger as quickly as possible. The exercises in Chapter 6 show you how to give your anger and pain to God. Since Ephesians 4:26 states, "Be angry and do not sin" (NKJV), we are allowed to have anger, yet deal with it quickly and manage it properly. Therefore, the key is balance and healthy, wise management of that anger (energy designed to repair) so that it can truly accomplish a repair.

We can learn to feel anger while remaining constructive.

Processing emotions can be done in various forms. Talking to a trusted friend, praying, crying, taking a walk, and exercising are some methods. You may also want to journal your emotions. Journaling is a form of moving the emotions through and out of you. Take time to *feel* your feelings for a period of time in small doses. Give yourself time to cry, yell (not at a person), or perhaps have a passionate candid conversation with God.

Five Basic Stages of Grief

A legendary writer on grief is Elisabeth Kübler-Ross, a Swiss-born psychiatrist who, in 1969, conceptualized the well-known five stages of grief.[lvi] I have integrated Dr. Kübler-Ross' five stages of grief into this forgiveness process because it provides an excellent framework and parallel for the steps necessary to recover from difficult experiences. It is a valid consideration that many events require a grieving process before we can fully let go. Some infractions are so impactful, so painful and devastating, that we would not be human if we did not grieve. Processing grief can help you get to the point of being more impervious to triggers and reminders about the painful event. The next section provides a correspondence of forgiveness work with the five stages of grief.

The first stage is *Denial* (sometimes called shock or numbness), followed by *Anger* (ranging from frustration to rage), then *Bargaining* (asking why and trying to make a deal or ponder what one could have done to prevent it), then *Depression* (sadness, emotional pain), and finally *Acceptance* (peace). These five fundamental stages do not necessarily occur in the same order listed and they may be re-experienced in different sequences and levels throughout the grief process. There may also be times that you feel two or more of them all at once. There is no specific order in which to walk through them.

It is important to understand that many of these emotions and stages can manifest in our physical body. For instance, fatigue can be a manifestation of turning anger or sadness inward. Have you ever been hit with shocking or sad news and found that afterward, you had little or no energy? Often prolonged fatigue, excessive sleep, and lethargy are part of the symptom picture associated with stress, as emotions impact the body as well as the heart and mind. You may be manifesting grief in the form of low physical energy. Be patient with yourself, and also consider giving yourself the proper physical care as well as emotional solace.

While we may usually start with numbness or shock and denial, we may feel sadness or anger first, then shock all over again, or all at the same time, before we ever begin to see acceptance on the horizon. Acceptance does not mean that we are happy and thrilled about what happened. We may never be. Acceptance is a stage where the pain is no longer dominating our emotional life the way that it used to. The acceptance stage of grief is more about arriving at a level of peace or having a perspective of hope despite what happened. The next section describes examples of ways to process the pain through each of these stages.

Table 2
The Grieving Process of Forgiveness Work

Denial, Shock, Numbness	**Unhealthy Forms** Thinking 'I'm Not Angry' Thinking 'I Have Forgiven [him/her/myself]' Stuffing Anger Leading to Physical Issues
	Healthy Forms Acknowledging Initial Numbness as a Form of Emotional Buffer and Protection Giving Time for Feelings to Surface Gradually
Anger, Frustration	**Unhealthy Forms** Holding a Grudge through Resentment or Bitterness Raging
	Healthy Forms Processing Anger Appropriately by Talking, Journaling, Expending Energy,
Bargaining, Questioning	**Unhealthy Forms** (Direct or Indirect) Engaging in Destructive Efforts to Fix, Avoid, or Undo the Issue by Obsessing, Worrying, Working too Much, Drinking Excessively, Over Eating, Self-Medicating through Addiction
	Healthy Forms Exploring the Lessons in the Tragedy, Contemplating Methods of Prevention in the Future, Making Decisions for Change

*Dr. Joan Weathersbee Ellason, PhD, LPC, Oasis Workshops.

Table 2
The Grieving Process of Forgiveness Work
(Continued)

Depression, Sadness	**Unhealthy Forms**
	Prolonging Sadness, Severe Low Energy, Carrying Heavy Emotional Weight on Your Shoulders
	Healthy Forms
	Connecting with Feelings of Sadness, Shedding Tears When Needed
Acceptance, Moving Forward	**Unhealthy Forms**
	Cycling Back into Denial
	Suppressing Your Emotions
	Giving Up all Hope
	Resigning to a Gloom and Doom Perspective
	Healthy Forms
	Giving the Situation Over to God
	Letting Go of the Pain & Anger
	Resuming/Pursuing Your Destiny
	Inviting/Allowing/Receiving Blessings
	Finding the Gift or Lessons within the Event
	Allocating Time and Energy to Help Others Through Similar Circumstances

*Dr. Joan Weathersbee Ellason, PhD, LPC, Oasis Workshops.

Processing the Sadness

After the shock, the emotions begin to emerge. One of them is sadness. Many of us were taught in our culture to avoid crying. Why should this be? We *all* need to cry at one time or another. Some of us were taught to *keep a stiff upper lip* or to *be strong*. These mandates are recipes for a physical and emotional train wreck. It is not natural to *not* cry. Many cultures impress this injunction more on males than on females. Jesus, who came to earth as a male and is Lord of the universe, also wept (John 11:35). Therefore, the gender basis for avoiding tears can be debunked.

Give yourself permission to cry. You may prefer to cry in private or avoid situations where it may not be fruitful; however, it is okay to cry. You can choose to cry in front of someone with whom you feel safe to confide, such as a close friend or a counseling professional. You can also come before God and lay it all out there with candid honesty. Did you think that He did not already know how you feel and the negative thoughts that have been swirling around in your mind? Whatever you do, move those feelings out of you appropriately.

We need to pace ourselves at the level and amount of grief that we can tolerate at a given time. Everyone grieves differently, and there is no cookie-cutter formula. The key is balance. Make sure that you are grieving in a healthy manner, and don't hesitate to consult with a professional when needed.

If you find that you are having emotional intensity that interferes with your functioning, see a professional to help you bring your grief back into balance. There are legitimate situations where medication is a necessary tool. Consult with a provider whom you trust.

There are some chemical gender differences in grief. Recent physiological findings show a biological basis for gender differences in exhibiting tears. At the age of approximately 12 years old, males and females under-go hormonal changes that render them basically different in the amount of tears produced. As testosterone increases in males, tear-producing prolactin decreases. This explains why males from adolescence forward do not seem to shed as many tears as females. This does not mean that they *cannot* shed tears; it just means that they tend to shed *fewer* tears as compared to females. This may help relieve you of unnecessary guilt if you are male and pressured to gush with tears, like your female counterparts, but the well is dry. Just because you are not shedding as many tears does not mean that you are feeling less pain.

In most cases, males process grief by first acknowledging that there is pain, sadness, hurt, anger, or all of the above. After the acknowledgment, males tend to seek constructive action, which is an essential step of healing. This manifestation can apply to *both* males and females. If you don't acknowledge, feel, and let your sadness and pain take constructive action, it may fester and turn into complicated bereavement or depression.

Constructive Action

After an appropriate healing period, some people volunteer to help victims going through a similar plight as their former ordeal. Others may become motivated to teach constructive lessons for the purpose of prevention. Taking constructive action can alleviate feelings of helplessness and can provide healing as we transform our pain into efforts that are within our control.

General Self-care

Take good care of your physical, emotional, mental, and spiritual self. Physical care includes healthy nutrition, physical activity that is within range of your medical professional's advice, and plenty of rest. Some emotional self-care includes relaxation exercises that involve slow deep breathing and positive or peaceful visualization. You may also very well need to release your emotions, even if that means screaming into a pillow or going to a private place and making noise by sobbing, wailing, or possibly even singing (yes, some cultures include singing). Following any intense release, you will need to rest and turn to a soothing activity.

Self-soothing

Soothing activity is through both thought and action. This is very important. Your thought life during this time is a form of medicine for your soul. Treat yourself as you would a very special loved one in both action and thought. How would you deal with a very dear friend who is grieving? You would most likely try to comfort them with soothing words. Do this same thing for yourself. This is where you need to be your best friend.

Internal thoughts, though subtle and in the background, are very powerful. Communicate supportive messages to yourself. Examples would include permission to rest more or permission to reduce the pressure to perform at your previous level for a while. Other supportive messages include reminders that what happened was not your fault or messages of how the disappointment can be repaired or resolved. The next chapter on the Cognitive Shift gives several specific examples of reality-based hopeful thoughts to replace discouraging ones.

Pampering activities are in the eye of the beholder. Choose activities that you find to be relaxing and recharging personally. For many people, pampering can be taking a walk, finding a quiet place to read, doing prayer and meditation, turning off all technology for an hour, getting a massage or a facial, taking time at the gym, or spending time with friends. Whatever it is that soothes you the most, set a commitment to include these activities regularly. Schedule it with the same priority level that you would a meeting with your boss and stick to it. Your needs are important, and if you expect to fuel your spiritual and emotional tank with healing and strength, then the soothing activity is imperative.

Creative Empowerment

Once your own original pain no longer consumes your concentration or focus, and you are not easily triggered by it, you may find it to be further healing to provide support for others. It is important to work through the initial intensity of your own pain first.

You may want to create a ceremony that helps you to acknowledge the loss in a healthy manner. Funerals are helpful to the living to help them acknowledge the loss or celebrate the life of a loved one.. If it is a type of loss where there has not been a ceremony to help bring closure – create one. Invite who you wish and honor that person or situation that was lost. It could be a period of your life that once was and is now over. It could be a career dream that perhaps was not realized but has actually been moved out of the way to open your sights up to something better. Grieve the loss of the dream, person, plan, expectation, or identity that you had so that you can close that chapter and become open to the next mission in your future.

In many cases, you may find healing by taking action to study the phenomenon that hurt you. There is truth to the saying that knowledge is power. Often just understanding the dynamics or issues can give you a sense of control and empowerment. When I was 11 years old, my father died unexpectedly of a heart attack. For my seventh-grade research paper, I wrote a very lengthy report about the heart. I did not become a cardiologist, but just facing the issue head-on and studying about it, allowed me some sense of control through knowledge.

The chart below outlines some examples of actions that can be taken in both thought and deed. Some of the deeds involve seeking insight into the perpetrator's mindset beneath their behavior, which can be eye-opening. Knowledge of the perpetrator psychologically and emotionally can sometimes reduce their power in your mind and help you claim back your own power over them.

Grief Support

You do not need to go through this process alone. Healthy support may be a close friend or a professional. You may not have anyone in your life with whom you feel comfortable sharing your deepest hurts. This is not uncommon. That is why, across the nation, there are 24/7 crisis hotlines in most major counties. The people who answer those phones are usually trained and often have a list of supportive resources in your area, such as grief groups, churches, hospitals, and other sources in the community. You can enter the following cue words into an internet search window that include "24/7," "crisis," and "____" (the name of your county or city) to find a nearby crisis line that may be available, in addition to dialing 911 for emergencies.

During your grief, maintain healthy, supportive connections, whether personal or professional. Nurture those relationships when you find them, as they are precious. Supportive people are those who will not blame you nor point out what you could, would, or should have done differently. True supportive resources provide listening without judgment. They may also provide some understanding words to say, or they may have no words to say at all but can show genuine empathy. It takes time and effort to cultivate these types of supports, and when you have them treat those relationships with appreciation and respect. Sometimes they become more of a family to you than some of your own biological family members.

Grieving within Your Own Pace and Process

No one can tell you the correct way to grieve nor how long it should take. It is an individual and personal journey. Some losses may seem never to have an end in sight, such as the loss of a child. Be gentle with yourself. You may find that you experience each of the five stages in waves, with them reducing in intensity each time that you cycle back through them. You may suddenly be struck with an unexpected and surprisingly strong emotion when you thought you should already be over it by now. Don't pressure yourself. Instead, nurture and love yourself and connect with supports who can just be there with you as you go through this.

Sometimes grief is done in advance, as you know what's over the horizon. Other times grief occurs in an ongoing fashion, as new events happen again and again. Often, we discover that we have, yet again, unknowingly stuffed some of the emotions. We all do this to some extent. All grieving is an individual process.

Derek and Jacqueline

Jacqueline had lost her father when she was 11 years old. He was on his way to church alone on a Sunday night and stopped just in time to pull his pickup over and put the gear into park before having a fatal heart attack. At that time, no one in her family knew how to grieve, so everyone stuffed their feelings. This led to suppressed pain in the family that ricocheted into all kinds of difficulties.

Since then, Jacqueline had learned, for the most part, to refrain from suppressing her emotions. After nine years of marriage had passed, it had gradually begun to deteriorate. Everything from the beginning had been so sweet, yet there was a progression of neglect regardless of her communication efforts through the years. This dynamic had eventually eroded into what seemed to be Derek's expectation of intimacy without the engagement of relationship. He frequently went out with his motorcycle friends from bar to bar, leaving her and their son home at night. At this stage in her life, bar touring was not her cup of tea, but she wanted to nurture their relationship through other forms of quality time. Her efforts fell on deaf ears, as he would not even sit on the couch with her to watch a movie, much less take her out to dinner or a date.

One Sunday at lunch, he had finally taken her to a decent restaurant. After the meal, the ticket came, and she noticed it was slightly over $20. When he proceeded to pay, the topic *came up about whether or not she was going to be intimate with him after his buying her lunch. She responded, indicating that she did not want the two events to be contingent upon each other. He then responded by saying that if he had known that she was not going to be intimate with him, then he would not have bothered to take her to lunch at all. Jacqueline felt deeply mortified as if reduced down to the level of some $20 worker who had to produce such favors in order to even have a meal. She did not say anything back to Derek on the spot, but her anger ran underground, and she stuffed it into her body that night.*

Later that night, while Derek was back out on a trip, she was woken by a paralyzing pain in her back between her shoulders. She called for help, and since their young son was the only one there, he ran to the phone and called 911. The ambulance came and ruled out a heart attack. She had tensed her back and stuffed her anger so deeply into her muscles between her shoulder blades, that she had dislocated that area and was having spasms up and down her back. It took months for this to heal. Over the years, Derek's continued acts of devaluation and contempt toward her continued, so she grew further and further away from him emotionally. She turned her energies more and more toward work and school and began to process her grief in moments of privacy.

How could it have deteriorated to this level when it had all been so true and solid? The descending spiral progressed. She sought after her missing sense of value in career and school while he increasingly romanced the bottle. The further she progressed in school, the closer he migrated toward alcohol.

The marriage in the beginning, at least she thought, had been originally founded upon the mutual agreement of partnership in building each other up to fulfill God's purpose. Yet that seemed to be no more. To cope and to avoid further hurt and disappointment, she relegated her definition of marriage down to a situation where you do not expect to receive emotional support or have your needs met. She was committed to sticking with her vows, but it became as empty as a business arrangement. She decided that maybe marriage is just a neutral arrangement where you dutifully walk with that person through their ups and downs of life, expecting nothing in return.

What once was - was no more. The dream had died. Jacqueline was grieving the death of a marriage and what had once been so sweet and loving. She knew she needed to mourn what she saw gradually slipping away. Every day while driving to school, she would sing Whitney Houston's song I believe in You and Me with tears rolling down her face. Her faith in the relationship, that implicit trust, was going into an early grave. The unconditional and complete faith without question and innocence had gone. She committed to staying in the marriage for the stability of their son. After a time, she had grieved out her pain and was now more neutral about Derek. They eventually divorced several years later.

Was Jacqueline wise to have grieved in advance? Maybe. She knew it was inevitable and wanted to get rid of all those unpleasant feelings.

There had been periods where Derek had expressed willingness to moderate his drinking and to work on the relationship. She willingly gave it a try again each time. One weekend during one of those periods of trying again and Derek's expressed commitment to change, she had taken their son with her out of town to an educational event. When her part was fulfilled, she decided to return home earlier than planned. Derek had just talked to her the night before on the phone, saying that he had no plans at all that next night. Their relationship seemed hopeful. When she and their son arrived home that next evening, she realized that she had walked right into a lie. She noticed two trashcans, including the extra-large outdoor trashcan overflowing with empty beer cans. In the bedroom, their laptop was placed on their bed with the webcam set up showing recent visits to triple x websites. Hours passed and he did not come home that whole night.

When he did walk in the door at 6 a.m. the next morning, he looked as white as a sheet with shock. He was supposed to go to work to train a pilot that very morning; however, he expressed a concern that if he went to work, he might return to an empty house with Jacqueline and their son gone. She instead reassured him, "Go to work, and when you return, Charles and I will be here" (to talk, etc.). She had been raised to be slow to anger, so being reactive was not her style, although she often wished that it had been.

When he returned, his attitude had changed, and he told her that if she were not willing to compromise, it would not work. What compromise? That he could continue indulging in internet porn, guzzle all the beer that he wants, and leave her alone at night while he partied? What kind of compromise was that? Compromise may have meant that Derek would have his entire way, while Jacqueline would have no say. She did not argue nor try to stop him as she watched him pack up all of his things and move out.

Jacqueline still had much to learn about addiction. She grew up in a household where there was no drinking in the home. Tobacco was the only addiction she witnessed.

When Derek had packed and moved out, Jacqueline had already done her grieving. After running face to face into such an abrupt lie, she was completely done with trying anything further to save the marriage. She was relieved and even happy about it finally being over. She had her young son sitting beside her and she needed to mute these emotions so as to not confuse him.

The divorce process moved along smoothly at first. She did not want anything from him except to be able to raise their son in an environment that did not model excessive alcohol and to be able to stay in the house to raise their son where he was accustomed. When she filed for divorce, the attorney asked her if she wanted any money from Derek other than child support. Even though she qualified for alimony, she declined to receive any additional financial assistance from Derek.

During their separation and before the final agreements were written, Jacqueline had a rude awakening. On one Wednesday evening, Derek had taken their son out on Derek's motorcycle. Jacqueline had always assumed that Derek would use good judgment if their son Charles were with him; however, when Derek brought him back and came into the house, Derek's speech was slurred. Jacqueline, in astonishment, confronted him. Derek replied with slurred speech, "Id-duzent madder annny-morr." Jacqueline was furious, and though in exasperation, WHAT? It doesn't matter anymore? So, now you are going to just kill our child? Her eyelids flew wide open. Jacqueline went back to her attorney, who gladly added injunctions into the decree draft, stating that Derek was to refrain from drinking and driving with their son. This was not the only occurrence of this problem. At a later time, a babysitter and family friend called Jacqueline while she was at work, telling her that Derek had picked Charles up at the house while wreaking of alcohol. Later that same night, with Charles in his care, Derek left Jacqueline scathing vitriolic voice mail messages with grossly slurred speech, demanding that Charles was going to be at his house whenever Derek wanted him to be. When she spoke up to Derek about the alcohol issue regarding their son's safety, he threatened to turn their son against her because of it. Derek's behavior was out of control, and Jacqueline did not know what to do. She wanted their son to be safe and shielded from the alcohol influences when with his dad. From that point on, she knew she had to focus her energies on her son's safety, because she learned that she could not trust Derek to do so.

Another issue involved finances. Jacqueline asked that the debts be divided equitably. Jacqueline would take all of the mortgage since she was to be in the house, and she would take an additional portion of their credit card debts that matched her salary, while Derek would be responsible for the amount congruent with his salary. In the marriage, she had used all of her inheritance from her mother's death to pay off their other debts, thinking that it would render them debt-free, and they almost were. But, as the dysfunction in the marriage ensued, the new debts grew like a cancer. She discovered that Derek would allow his buddies to contribute cash to him for their bar tabs, and he was putting the whole table's ticket on their credit cards. Jacqueline had not asked for a reimbursement of her inheritance that she had used to cover his and her debts.

When he saw the first draft of the decree that her attorney had written up with his credit card debt responsibilities, the harassing messages ensued. He relentlessly tormented her with threats to make her "lose the house," "lose [their son-Charles]," "lose it all." In these voice mails, he threatened to destroy her financially, which terrified her because she already only made around $24,000 per year compared to his pilot's salary. She already had no idea how she was going to make it financially in the neighborhood in which their child was accustomed. With these threats, she was plagued in the middle of the night being woken with vigorous nerve twitches convulsing up and down her throat. How could he threaten her sense of security that way? She became petrified of Derek's rage and was afraid to do anything that might set him off.

Finally, the decree was about to be signed and she was exhausted. He wore her down with his bullying. He demanded that nothing be written in a public document about his alcohol and driving because he said that it would hurt his career as an airline pilot. She did not want to do anything to hurt him professionally nor in any other way. She had an injunction removed from the decree before it went to the judge, believing that if she compromised with him, respecting his concern that he would respect her concern and stick to his agreement to refrain from drinking and driving with their son.

She had forgiven Derek for what he had done that led to their separation, but she had no idea of the things that were to come. This was only a drop in the bucket of the learning that she was about to embark upon. As the next several years unfolded, she would be faced with things far beyond what she ever imagined and would become angry and worried over and over again.

Process the stages of grief as you become ready and do not push yourself too hard. The following chart may provide some cognitive and behavioral tools for various situations as you make a choice to nurture yourself through your grieving process.

Table 3
Examples of Taking Care of Yourself Through Positive Thought and Action

Traumatic Event	Positive Self-Thought	Possible Outward Actions
Abandonment	I refuse to interpret this as a personal failure. I am going to become my own best friend. I will remind myself of my good qualities that the other person or situation is missing out on. I am a good [friend, spouse, business partner]. God is with me - therefore, I am _never_ alone.	Attend a support group and/or counseling. Find your passion and fill your life with purposeful activities that you now have time to fulfill. Constructively take an inventory of any skills that you can apply to the next friendship or situation to reduce the risk of repeating past mistakes. Volunteer to help others in similar situations.

*Dr. Joan Weathersbee Ellason, PhD, LPC, Oasis Workshops.

Table 3
Examples of Taking Care of Yourself Through Positive Thought and Action
(Continued)

Traumatic Event	Positive Self-Thought	Possible Outward Actions
Robbery/Theft	I refuse to be a victim. What happened to me was not about me – it was about the robber. I can take action to increase my protection. I will remind myself of what the robber couldn't/didn't steal. I will acknowledge and appreciate that: I am still alive. God can replace all of the things I need. I am grateful that this did not happen to those I love and want to protect. Eternity Thinking -No one has the power to ultimately take anything from me.	Attend a support group and/or counseling. Press charges. Enroll in a self-defense course. Install a security system and/or camera system. Volunteer to help those who have experienced a robbery (when you are ready). Receive training or enhance professional skills to help other survivors of crime. Study to increase insight into what leads a person to rob or steal.

*Dr. Joan Weathersbee Ellason, PhD, LPC, Oasis Workshops.

Table 3
Examples of Taking Care of Yourself Through Positive Thought and Action

Traumatic Event	Positive Self-Thought	Possible Outward Actions
Rape	It is not my fault.	Attend a support group and/or counseling.
	I refuse to shame myself for what happened.	Press charges.
	I refuse to allow this to define me.	Volunteer to help others surviving a rape (after your own healing).
	They do not have the power to taint me in any way, shape, or form.	Become trained to professionally help rape survivors.
	I am still a virgin/pure/innocent in God's eyes.	Study/increase education to gain insight into what leads someone to become a rapist.

Traumatic Event	Positive Self-Thought	Possible Outward Actions
Loss of Job, Dream, or Career Opportunity	This was not the only opportunity for me.	Make a list of all of your positive skills and attributes
	I have other talents.	Consider this a practice rehearsal, identify any errors, and create a strategy to perform better in the future
	When one door closes, another one will open.	
	I will make a list of the attributes that make me a strong candidate for future opportunities.	Create a vision board with pictures, words, scriptures, and drawings that represent the positive plans that you want to put into your life to overcome the loss.
	I will take a constructive inventory of any areas that need to grow.	Take charge of the situation by learning more than you knew before so that you can come back even stronger than ever.
	I will review ways that I can improve and create a better outcome for the next opportunity.	

*Dr. Joan Weathersbee Ellason, PhD, LPC, Oasis Workshops.

Table 3
Examples of Taking Care of Yourself Through Positive Thought and Action
(Continued)

Traumatic Event	Positive Self-Thought	Possible Outward Actions
Loss of Loved One	I will give myself time to grieve and receive healthy support.	Attend a support group and/or counseling.
	It was not my fault (nothing I could have or should have done differently). (Ecclesiastes 8:8)	Create a ritual that honors their memory, such as a memorial or shrine in a special location.
	I will hold them close in my heart.	Maintain relationships with healthy supports.
	I believe that I will be able to see them again one day in Heaven.	Reach out to their family members to help them also.
	I will hold onto the positive memories of them.	Increase your education on Grief and ways to deal with it.
	I will help their legacy live on.	Place fresh flowers in their place of memorial.
	I will choose to live a full life to honor them because I know they would want me to do so.	
	Eternity Thinking -No one has the power to ultimately take my loved one from me.	Release balloons into the Heavens to spiritually and symbolically reach up to them and to honor them.

*Dr. Joan Weathersbee Ellason, PhD, LPC, Oasis Workshops.

No matter how good we are at taking care of ourselves or even if we have not caught onto these principles yet, sometimes this help comes from above. It can come through people who are responding in obedience to God's prompting.

The Rest of William's Story

Remember William, who gave up everything for his daughter and family to find himself kicked out of the home he bought for them with virtually only the shirt on his back? When someone saw what was happening to William, the Holy Spirit clutched their heart. This seemed to grab hold and not let go. They did not have a big salary and had to work two jobs to make ends meet, so it was not logical for them to be the person to step in and help. Logic did not matter. They could not stand by and do nothing. The friend found a way to hire an attorney on William's behalf. They also raised funds to supply moving expenses for him and helped him find a modest place to live. William eventually had to move in with a supportive friend until the time came for him to need assisted living. This level of care was a staggering expense, so the friend had to come up with ways to help raise the necessary finances for him. At each point, when the financial feat seemed impossible, solutions emerged. As William aged further and needed a higher level of nursing care, his lack of funds qualified him for placement in a very clean and attentive nursing facility. To this day, William continues to be well cared for, protected, and nurtured by the professionals around him. He is actually cared for more effectively than he might have been with his original plan to stay in the home with his family.

Often when those around us let us down, we can still count on God to come through in unexpected ways. Psalms 27:10-14 states, "Although my father and my mother have abandoned me, Yet the LORD will take me up [adopt me as His child]" (AMP). Also, another awesome promise in the scripture is found in Isaiah 46:3-4 (NIV), where it states, "...you whom I have upheld since your birth, and have carried since you were born. Even to your old age and gray hairs I am he, I am he who will sustain you. I have made you and I will carry you; I will sustain you and I will rescue you." No matter who has abandoned or rejected you or thrown you out of a job, home, social group, or anything – you are <u>not</u> rejected by God. You are not alone.

Chapter 5

Tier II:
The Cognitive Shift
(Tier II Level of Forgiveness)

After you have moved through much of the grief, you can begin to consider the replacement of many of the painful emotions. This chapter will show you how to move your mind from deficit thinking into abundance thinking by learning how to renew your mind with God-ordained uplifting beliefs and perceptions. This chapter involves building a repertoire of constructive thoughts, beliefs, and perspectives that can become a resource from within, in addition to your external supports. At first, this usually feels like an uphill climb, yet eventually, it can begin to become automatic. You truly can reach a point of automatically having hope-based thoughts. Changing your perspective and awareness from defeat and deficit to abundance and victory thinking is scriptural (John 10:10, John 16:33, 1John 5:4, Romans 8:31, Ephesians 6:13, Joshua 1:1-9, Isaiah 61:3, Jeremiah 29:11, Zechariah 9:12).

Change Your Thinking from Deficit Thinking to Abundance Thinking

The new positive thoughts and perceptions also will need to be realistic and anchored in truth. Exchanging negative thoughts for helpful positive ones involves learning to let go of your old negative beliefs, which are often not true anyway, and align them with positive reality. If you find this work to be almost impossible, you may need to give yourself a little more time to grieve, or you may also benefit from appropriate prescriptions recommended by a competent MD. Remember to be patient with yourself. Everyone heals at different rates and needs different resources.

Making a shift from negative to positive thinking is not the same thing as being gullible or naïve. You are still firmly planted in reality. The fact that the person *did* do harm is not negated. You can become trained to reach a higher platform of insight and move beyond the immediate circumstance. You can learn how to grab hold of restoration for your mind, soul, and spirit while maintaining your grasp on reality. A specific example of this change in thinking is, for instance, 'Yes, that person really did hit me,' 'Yes, s/he likely has severe issues that are not about me,' and 'No, I refuse to be their victim.' So, it is true that what the person did is wrong, unfair, and should not have happened to you. It is also true that their action is not about you but is about many other possible things, such as their past, their current interpretation of the situation or an old nemesis that they are reminded of when they look at you, and their own individually chosen repertoire of actions. It is further true that not one ounce of your emotional life has to be controlled by them. Alternatively, you could have contributed to the outcome but are not the cause of *all* of it. You do not have the power to *cause* that person's actions. They choose their actions – not you.

After practicing this new method of thinking and perceiving reality, your new thoughts and beliefs become a powerful arsenal of defense and protection that gives you resilience and brings you into recovery. This process sometimes involves an adjustment.

Why Do We Sometimes Remain in a Negative Mindset?

There are many reasons why we may choose to hang onto a negative mindset. One of the payoffs of negative beliefs and perceptions is the attempt to retain a sense of power. This, however, is false power.

For some, being sad and helpless did help in the past. Perhaps someone came and rescued you from that mean bully. Possibly, it has been an indirect way for you to receive love and protection. Maybe a negative mindset has served as a protection for you, where you made a decision long ago to refuse to trust anyone because of disappointments. The belief that you have to do it all on your own seems independent and noble, but may feel lonely to you.

There are parts of these beliefs that have some truth, but they are not totally true. First, people are human and will sometimes let you down. It is good to be independent and not need a rescuer, yet it is also good to allow some help when appropriate. Taking these beliefs into balance is important. When we overly dwell in the negative, we actually rob ourselves of true power.

To get a taste of this level of forgiveness, I encourage you to first begin the exercises in this and the next chapters with mild examples of frustration and mild tasks of forgiveness. So, shall we? Let's start with some examples.

Let's Begin with Ease

Here is a mild example of shifting from a negative to a positive mindset to deal with a recent frustration that I experienced. Earlier this year, I ordered a newly released movie for my sister. I was proud that my fledgling technological effort succeeded in requesting to have it shipped to her house instead of my regular address. The update indicated that it would arrive that next Sunday night, so I asked her to watch for it in the mail.

When it did not arrive at the expected time by this well-known delivery company, I noticed a mental opportunity to indulge in negative thinking. One possible negative assumption I observed that could have, was that the person who was supposed to do the delivery must be a bumbling idiot or moron. I could also assume that the delivery guy was lazy or just a loser in general. Now, with this cognitive perception, I could sit back, feeling superior, and gloat with pride, but I would only be poisoning myself with toxic chemicals that are associated with negative thinking.

My first interpretation was to picture the delivery person as an incompetent individual. Why, I don't know, since I didn't even know that person. The fact was that I had no idea what happened. Did the communication fail so that the individual did not receive the needed information about the pending delivery? Did the delivery person get sick with the flu? Remember the conclusion-delusion mentioned in Chapter 2? I had been tempted to fall for that myth, but I chose to replace that thought with better perceptions. When we assume that the other person is an idiot, we have a false sense of power, but how powerful are we really when we are operating out of delusional thinking and permeating our body with excessive cortisol?

Another negative cognitive mindset that we can get into is to believe that it is all our fault, and we cannot do anything right. For example, I could have berated myself for failing to order it correctly and begin a litany of self-disparaging thoughts. If you are inclined to go in this direction, the underlying payoff from this way of thinking may be to reinforce a negative self-perception. That may have worked for you in the past but is not helpful to you now. This may have been a way that you managed to keep the peace in your home, while growing up, or appease a condescending individual. The belief that it is all your fault or that you cannot do anything right is a lie – plain and simple. Unless you have superpowers to make others do things that you want them to do, external choices of others cannot be your fault. Remember that each individual chooses their own actions out of free will and that you and I cannot control them because you and I are not God, and thank God for that.

Difficult Situations

Often, our circumstances are much more serious than just a delivery being missed. Often life throws us a curveball. Some events defy all logic and expectation.

Derek and Jacqueline

The divorce was final, yet there was bitterness between Derek and Jacqueline. Jacqueline had not yet forgiven Derek for his harassing messages to her during their separation. Derek had signed over sole custody to her because she informed him that all of his alcohol behaviors would come to light if the case went to court. He also resented Jacqueline because when she filed their last married income tax return, she had not given him half of the refund. Jacqueline had spent days adding up and counting every receipt that she thought could apply in preparation for their taxes. Derek would come around while she was working on the tax return, saying that he would contribute by bringing deductible receipts that could help them, but he ended up not following through. He showed only casual interest and did not put any effort into the tedious work of searching through his own financial records. Jacqueline, however, spent pain-staking hours and days digging through receipts, organizing and tabulating everything that could possibly be listed as a deduction, and filled out the forms to get it filed. When he learned that they actually got a refund, because she answered honestly when he asked, he suddenly had intense interest and energy all over it. Derek suddenly became full of motivation and entitlement, demanding his half. She was struck by Derek's lack of effort to help with the hard work that it took to obtain a refund, in contrast with his effort to cash in on the result. Jacqueline was afraid to hand him over half of it because this was the first time that she recalled them ever having received a refund, and she was not sure if it was done correctly. She knew that if she gave him the money and had to return it because of a filing error, she would not be able to get it back from his hands. She stood her ground and all seemed peaceful for a while after this. Jacqueline began trying to put her anger at Derek aside, yet the events about to unfold showed that Derek's anger toward her was not over.

Time passed. Jacqueline worked at least two jobs in order to make ends meet, and Derek had a standard pattern of time with their son Charles. Derek would not communicate with Jacqueline directly, but when he and his new wife, who I will call Lucy, wanted to introduce a change to the father-son time, they would send that information through the child instead of discussing it with Jacqueline. Soon, Jacqueline began to notice an increasing pattern of disrespect beginning to emerge toward her from their son. Jacqueline did not know it yet, but Derek and Lucy had started a campaign to lure Charles into wanting to live with them full-time. This became evident as events unfolded.

One day there was a certified envelope on the kitchen counter. Young Charles had answered the door to sign for it while Jacqueline was busy. Charles stood there next to it, nervously watching her open it. Seeing that it was from an attorney, she thought that it might be a professional request for her to testify on behalf of someone. When she opened it, she saw an affidavit from an attorney, signed by her son, stating that he wanted Derek to have sole custody.

The document had legal jargon in it that she was sure that a 12-year-old was not old enough to understand. Jacqueline also later learned that it was Lucy who had taken Charles to the attorney's office to sign the affidavit, without either Derek nor Jacqueline present. Moreover, Derek and Lucy knew Charles' schedule – the days he was with Mom, and the days he was with Dad. Why did they allow that letter to be delivered on a day when the child would be alone there with his mother, to deal with whatever reaction that she would have? What were they thinking – or were they thinking? If Jacqueline were the nightmare that Derek had portrayed her to be, wouldn't that have been deliberately putting a 12-year-old in a difficult position to deal with the fallout all by himself? Charles looked at his mother with worried eyes, trying to read her emotions. Jacqueline was not angry with Charles; she knew that he had been manipulated. Jacqueline excused herself from the room to call a friend. She was devastated.

Why did Derek want to take Charles away from Jacqueline? And how could Lucy, who was a mother herself, do something so surreptitious and devious to another mother? This seemed unforgivable. To get through this, Jacqueline had to learn how to change her thoughts, perceptions, and interpretations of this situation. She needed to make that cognitive shift in her mind.

Making the Cognitive Shift

The cognitive thoughts (beliefs, perceptions, and interpretations) that you are invited to consider here in this chapter are more empowering than negative ones. There are plenty of alternate cognitive thoughts to choose from that are reality-based. This is not a weak-minded strategy of floating along on a cloud being out of touch with the gravity of what is happening. These new cognitive alternatives do not remove you from the options often necessary to take care of or protect yourself and your loved ones. The following section outlines some of these alternative cognitions. This section also invites you to transcend the present here and now by learning how to see events at a number of levels and through God's eyes.

The fact that this cognitive retraining process takes time and practice is supported by scientific findings. Learning to practice new thoughts and perceptions through repetition has been shown repeatedly in cognitive research to be successful in changing our habitual thought patterns. Neuroscientists have substantially verified that when you repeat a new perception or way of thinking over and over, you strengthen those particular neuronal connections of that new thought pattern within the brain. The older thought processes become weakened when you cease to think about them and replace them with new healthier thoughts.

God already knew before science learned that we could indeed change our brains. This is why God asks for us to think about healthy thoughts – because (1) He knows we can, and (2) He knows that it is healing to do so. If you resort back to the old negative thoughts, however, they become strengthened as you go back to ruminating on them again. God set up our brains with a capacity to heal, and we get to decide which direction we are going to go, by what we choose to dwell on in our minds – destructive lies or healing facts.

Philippians 4:8 (NIV)

"Finally brothers and sisters whatever is true, whatever is noble, whatever is right, whatever is pure, whatever is lovely, whatever is admirable – if anything is excellent or praiseworthy think about such things."

Permissions for Others

As already mentioned, God grants free will. This is one of the answers to the question of why bad things sometimes happen here on earth. If even GOD is not a control freak, why would we blame ourselves for what the other person did? And why doesn't God make them stop? Frankly, God does not consider it loving to force a person to choose the right behavior. He wants us to choose what is right, and sometimes we don't. If another person does wrong to you, it is not your fault., It cannot be your job to control that person since even God does not forcefully impose control in this manner.

This permission, therefore, is a release. We release that person to be right wherever they are in their own growth process (or lack thereof). They have been given the freedom by God to choose whether or not to grow, progress, regress, stay stuck, stay sick, or get well. Being able to give permission for others to make their own choices can bring you freedom and is a hallmark of good mental health.

When we decide to grant this type of permission to others, it frees us. Luke 6:28 tells us to bless those who curse you and to pray for those who mistreat you. The exercises later in this book may help you to gain a deeper understanding of why God wants us to pray for the people who hurt us. Frankly, it is because they need it - terribly.

As mentioned earlier, this type of permission is not the same thing as condoning that negative behavior. It also does not negate the necessity at times to stand up against evil. Often, while simultaneously in a state of forgiveness, you can still put your hand up to say no, remove the child from that situation, call the police, or shut the door. Therefore, this form of permission does *not* mean permissiveness. The next sections outline more specific types of permissions extended to others as well as to ourselves.

Permissions that we can bestow upon others empower and free us up to continue putting our energy into our own destiny instead of wasting it on the perpetrator. The cognitive task in this type of permission is an acknowledgment that no one is perfect, people are in a process, and that this is planet Earth where things are not perfect. The person who has initiated the offense is not excused from natural consequences. It is just that the burden of imposing those consequences does not necessarily have to fall upon your shoulders, draining your own time and energy.

Remember, in an earlier chapter, it was discussed that if we are giving up our own right for revenge, it does not mean that God suddenly cancels the natural consequence coming to them. Consequences are powerful teachers that help people grow. This permission is for our own benefit, not theirs. Therefore, you are not giving them an endorsement of their wrong behavior. You are just washing your hands of having to be the one to do the job of fixing them.

Indirect attempts to fix them (or the situation) come in forms of incessantly thinking about them, fuming about what happened, seething, obsessing, and worrying, which can often lead to a litany of medical and emotional problems that can steal your happiness. To reiterate: this anger, which is energy designed to *repair* the situation or the person, becomes either displaced outwardly (explosive) or becomes turned inwardly, suppressed (implosive). This can impact not only ourselves but our loved ones as well, while the person of concern goes about clueless and unaffected by our pain.

When you give others permission to stay sick, ignorant, selfish, or in other words, impaired, you do this by replacing your negative thoughts about them with thoughts that free you from having to *fix* them. Your replacement thoughts may be interpretations such as *I refuse to take on the job of fixing them, because they likely have a wounded soul* or *something really awful may have happened to them to lead them to behave this way.* Exercises that follow later in this book can show you more about making this shift and moving into a perspective to let go.

Whether to fix or not to fix is a case by case decision. There may be times when trying to fix another person is motivated by efforts to protect a loved one. This book is not designed to guide you on whether or not to take a stand, nor the strategies to use to achieve a desired outcome. Even if you have put forth your energies to attempt to fix a situation and it was difficult, remember that nothing is wasted and God has a way of taking our effort and turning our situations right-side-up again. The following involves one such story of an effort to fix a situation.

Derek and Jacqueline

Jacqueline told Derek that she wanted to have mediation to discuss the adult matters with an impartial third party. When they first sat down at the mediation meeting, Derek told the attorneys that when Jacqueline had filed their income tax before, she had not given him his half, which was less than a half month's salary), so he wanted to have Charles come and live with him so he could make Jacqueline have to pay him child support in return. Was this about custody or was it really about money?

This was a shock. They mediated and ended up with the same 50% parent-child time arrangement that they had been applying beyond Derek's standard time already, except this time, Jacqueline asked that the injunction be put back into the new modified decree. She had learned that the previous verbal agreement about this had not worked and hoped that this would ensure that Derek would refrain from drinking and driving with their son. She had it written in such a way that the wording did not reveal that Derek was the topic of that injunction in order to protect his reputation.

They mediated all day, and it also became clear that Lucy wanted Jacqueline to not receive any further child support from Derek. Was this what it was all about, after all? They dragged Charles through splitting dynamics with his mother over money? This was ironic because their household had two separate adult incomes plus Lucy was receiving child support from her ex-husband for their two kids, yet Jacqueline was working two jobs to try to cover expenses.

During this extended period of drama, Charles began to become increasingly disrespectful toward his mother every time he returned from his father's house. As this escalated, Jacqueline wanting Charles to remember the type of person that he truly was, told him in the middle of one of his tirades, "You are still a good person even though you are acting this way." Charles responded with tears in his eyes and said, "How can I be when I act this way?" Jacqueline knew that Derek's animosity toward her was being channeled through their son, and it was toxically impacting him at many levels. She kept Charles connected to church, counseling, prayer over him, and other healthy mentoring supports to help provide relief from this pressure. He often apologized to his mother for his behavior, but it was still taking a toll on him because he did not forgive himself, and he did not want to hurt either parent.

A child naturally loves and needs both parents, but when one household's attitude is contempt toward the other parent, the child is put in an impossible lose-lose, double-bind position emotionally. The child needs the love, acceptance, and approval of both parents, so when one of them promotes an anti-mom or anti-dad culture in their household, the young person at any age can feel split in two. Because of the child's need for acceptance from their parents, outward ridicule or open criticism against the other parent creates an implicit atmosphere of peer pressure for the child to also reject that other parent. This is not just the simple peer pressure that can happen at school. This is peer pressure coming from a parent whose approval and attachment are crucial for emotional survival, security, development, and (at a subconscious level) life. At an unconscious survival level, particularly during childhood, we are biologically wired to need attachment and approval from both of our parents. Perceived rejection from either parent strikes at the very core of existence in the child. Since this attachment is deep-rooted into the innermost fiber of our being, parental rejection of that other parent that is outwardly displayed or even tacitly expected can lead the child to feel as if part of themself at their basic core is fundamentally wrong or defective. It was no surprise that Charles emerged from this situation, labeling himself as a problem child and the 'black sheep' of the family.

Jacqueline wondered why they would put Charles through this. Derek's childhood was pretty much a secret. It was learned later that Derek had resentment toward his own mother. Derek had cut himself off from his own mother during adulthood, but Jacqueline learned that there might have been a splitting dynamic already at place when Derek was young. During their marriage, Jacqueline would try to get Derek to call his mother, but to no avail. Derek's mother died, still in bewilderment, not knowing what she must have done so awful to cause him to be estranged from her. His mother would call, crying and begging Derek to call her, but he still would not. He never gave a reason, except that she was "controlling." This was a common term Derek often used to describe anyone with whom he had a falling out or a disagreement. There were other mysteries in that family system that had never been fully explained. The point is that Derek had learned distrust long before Jacqueline came along. Derek had a tendency to put people in one of two categories - all good or all bad. If you were one of the people who he saw as 'good', you only received warmth and charm from him. If you were placed in the 'bad' category, you were rejected and received contempt. In her stand against Derek's behavior, Jacqueline had moved from the all-good category to the all-bad category in Derek's mind, and like his own mother, he seemed to want Charles to cut Jacqueline out as well.

Why would the characters in this story act the way they do? People who hurt others are operating from a wounded soul. In cases where you cannot persuade the other person to change, you can take charge of the aspects of the situation that are within your control and responsibility. Then you hand the rest over to God.

For less severe matters, humor can be used to diffuse an unpleasant situation. I have used it sometimes in private thought. Depending on the situation, it can be used outwardly to diffuse disagreements. The cognitive permission of *I give you permission to be wrong* can be used privately in your thoughts or sometimes outwardly in a bantering manner. In many situations, the use of humor may need to remain in the silence of your own mind with possibly only a covert chuckle. In a relationship where I was permitted to outwardly use this strategy with humor, I would say, "I love you enough to allow you to be wrong," and then give them a little smile.

What about Permissions for Yourself?

Unburden yourself. You do not have to make everyone see things the same way that you do. You can still consider yourself just as valued, successful, and right even if they disagree or do not see you that way. How many people do you know of who disagree with God, and He is still Lord of the universe? Does that make him of any less value or worth? No. Does a person's rejection of His opinion make Him wrong? Absolutely not!

Give yourself a break also. Giving yourself the grace to learn from mistakes and permission to not have handled a situation perfectly is important. It often takes several attempts to master a task, and practice will increase your chances of succeeding in the future. Instead of wasting time on self-criticism, fill up your mind's cognitive space with thoughts of what you did that was right and the next areas to change going forward. This form of self-assessment carries acceptance.

The fictional movie *Twister* (Jan de Bont, director, 1996, Warner Bros., Universal Pictures) involved scientists who were trying to create sensors that could go up inside of a tornado and measure the velocity dynamics and predict its patterns. They created a tool that they called Dorothy. At each twister they encountered, Dorothy was either destroyed or picked up and thrown back down to the ground, sensors and all scattered all over the road –wasted. They identified what was lacking at each mistake and could pinpoint a new strategy that inched them closer toward their goal. One strategy was to anchor Dorothy down to allow the twister to exclusively pick up the sensors. The next error showed them that the sensors needed to be made of aluminum because the original material had been the wrong kind.

Fiction? Yes. Useful metaphor? Most definitely. Don't let yourself stay bogged down in the heaviness of your mistakes. Use these mistakes as building blocks to ultimate success. Don't waste time beating yourself up. Dr. Judith Wilkins PhD, LMFT, LPC asserts that the only guilt that a Christian needs to feel lasts only a few minutes, long enough to apologize and to make amends, while doing no harm.[lvii] Identify your error – without shaming yourself. Keep getting back on track, and do not give up. Addiction counselors that I have worked with have said in consensus that it often takes more than one and often more than several treatment periods for a person to overcome their addiction. Whatever area of growth in which you are striving, choose to give yourself grace and permission to try again, *and again*.

"I have never seen a strong person with an easy past."

Jay Shetty

How Do I Move the Self-forgiveness from My Head to My Heart?

In addition to some of the exercises outlined in the next chapter, here are some basic keys that you may find helpful:

1. <u>Give Yourself Appropriate Permissions.</u> Give yourself permission for imperfection. This is not a license to deliberately do wrong. It merely recognizes the fact that you are human, and Jesus already knew that you would err. Otherwise, He would not have gone to the trouble of dying for you. God knows that you are in a process.

2. <u>Know God. Truly Recognize God as He Really Is – A Loving God</u>. If you perceive God as punitive, harsh, or condemning as some of the people you have known, you do not have a true picture of who God really is. Do you *really* know Him? Do you have an accurate picture of God's personality? Jesus said in John 14:9 that he who has seen Jesus has seen the Father. Read through the New Testament to follow the teachings and actions of Jesus to learn exactly how the Creator really thinks and demonstrates forgiveness.

3. <u>Become Aware of the Thought-Life Inside your Head.</u> Tune in to the thoughts that you tell yourself in your head. Are you judging or punitive with yourself? Are you choosing to scare yourself? Become aware of this and make the needed changes in your perception.

4. <u>Develop an Accurate Relational Connection with God.</u> Begin to see yourself as the child that God is raising and loves unconditionally. Then begin to remind yourself over and over how precious you truly are- *Yes, you are*. Think about a person who you have had so much compassion for, such as one of your own children or relatives, that you forgave them willingly with no regrets. Notice the love and mercy you feel toward them. This is only a tiny fraction of the abundant love that God has for you, even if you are not aware of it. Begin to see yourself as such a child on the inside. The only reason you did something wrong was that you had woundedness yet to be healed or were misguided. Give yourself permission to be in a growth process and know that God is working with you in it.

5. <u>Develop an Accurate Relational Connection with Yourself.</u> Make a decision to have a positive parental relationship with yourself. This is done by deliberately giving yourself reality-based, loving thoughts in the privacy of your mind and through your spoken words out loud. We often internally judge and parent ourselves like someone who may have raised us or influenced us. If you had a punitive parent or teacher, the chances are that you may be giving yourself the same harshness with which you grew up. On the other hand, you may be harsh with yourself to overcompensate for a permissive parent. Either way, begin to see that tender, sweet innocent child that you once were (and still are on the inside) and allow God to help you grow. Stop emotionally abusing yourself and make a decision to treat yourself with love, appropriate limit-setting, and patience.

6. <u>Appropriately Use Self-Management</u>. Just as parenting can be considered abusive or overindulgent, over permissive parenting can be considered neglectful. Give yourself appropriate self-management through constructive limit setting, learning, and wise counsel. When you make a mistake, constructively review the behaviors to change, make amends, and proceed with constructive new choices.

7. <u>Recognize that the Bill is Already Paid in Full.</u> Finally, stop trying to pay for the debt that Jesus has already removed. Ruminating over and over, telling ourselves self-punitive lies inside our minds about being bad, and self-shaming is all a futile waste of time. Your purpose is far too valuable to waste.

So, imagine that you are extremely wealthy, and someone you cared for deeply had been struggling with insurmountable long-term debt for years. It kept them strapped and unable to move forward productively in their life. You have such an overflow of funds that it would only subtract a tiny fraction from your bank account to completely wipe out all of their debt, giving them a fresh new start. Imagine that you pay *all* of the money of the entire debt, bring all of the balances entirely down to zero. Imagine what glee and excitement you feel at being able to do this – to completely set them free so that they can concentrate on their purpose and live their life unencumbered. What joy that is for you to be able to do that for them! Now see them spend all of their energy as they commence to pay all of their hard-earned money to those accounts even though they paid in full. The money that they continue to pour into those accounts does not create a new credit on those accounts, but rather those dollars get wasted and poured out into nothing. How frustrating this may feel to Jesus who gave everything that He had to set us free, if we still carry the guilt around on our backs?

God has an overflow of mercy, grace, and compassion for us. He wants you to accept and receive His forgiveness so that you become an overflowing vessel that He can move through as you rise to your purpose here on this earth. Your overflow can pour good into others. You must allow *self*-forgiveness so that your energy can extend forgiveness to others. This makes self-forgiveness a *non*-selfish act. Self-forgiveness is not for you only; it is also for others and for God to completely flow through you, uninhibited and unlimited.

Re-training Your Thinking

Train yourself to notice what you are thinking at any given moment. What are you telling yourself in your head about that person's actions or the situation? What are you telling yourself about yourself? We are continuously making interpretations about situations and drawing conclusions. We are just often not aware of doing it. Often these conclusions come from our unchecked assumptions, so don't judge yourself too harshly. Just begin to tune in to what you are thinking so that you can examine those thoughts.

If someone is hurtful to you, what do you think in your mind about them, the situation, or yourself? If another person disagrees with your opinion, do you interpret that as a personal rejection of you? Do you think to yourself, *I am stupid,* or *S/he does not like me?* These perceptions are not helpful to you - nor them.

What if the rejection of your opinion or request comes from a high authority? Do we expect that the courts are always right? On the contrary, we see innocent people wrongly convicted throughout the courts because the judge cannot tell when a person is lying on the stand under oath, and the judge is completely blind to evidence if it is unethically withheld. Often all three elements of morality, ethics, and legal matters can clash when they should all coincide. The judge and jury's eyes in both criminal court and civil court are mere human eyes and have limitations. They cannot always be counted on to be your vindicator. Even if an authority figure rules against your case, do not assume that this entity has power over your ultimate destiny. Only God does.

"Any rejection is just redirection."
Jay Shetty[lviii]

My belief is that when you learn to see barriers or closed doors as God's redirection and even sometimes as your protection, your emotions can change readily. This is called a cognitive reframe, which will be discussed further ahead. You shift the frame with which you view the situation. Using a reframe to forgive a rejection, for instance, could involve the idea that being accepted by that person, job, bank, authority, etc., may have encumbered you with a relationship, work environment, or loan that would have steered you away from a better opportunity. The truth is that with some closed doors, you may very well have dodged a bullet.

Begin to notice your interpretations in your mind for each situation that you encounter. What if that person really does not like you? Who made them the authority over your life and value? What if they are more educated than you? Every person has their own set of gifts and talents. You do not have to possess the same ones that they have in order to be valuable.

Explore more options beyond your customary self-perceptions. Just because you feel something (dumb, ugly, bad) does not make it true. Even if another person believes something negative about you, it does not make it so. Just because that person hurt you or was able to get away with exploiting you does not make you into a fool.

The first moments after my child was born, following the nine-month safe protective oasis in the womb (coddled and wrapped in a cocoon of safety, listening to an orchestra of rhythmic heartbeats and the muffled sound of my singing voice), an aggressive obstetric nurse grabbed him abruptly from my chest! I'll never forget the look on his face when she turned him to face her. It was as if he were thinking, *"Who are you? What planet are you from?"* It was an interesting look implying that he seemed to assume that something was wrong with *her* – not with him. I wonder if we initially start with this wisdom before life, environment, and socialization take us in the wrong direction of erring toward self-blame.

My newborn son's immediate response seemed to be the awareness, after the initial shock, that something was wrong with that external person. Beyond those first few seconds of the introduction to the outside world, babies internalize their sense of self-awareness and worth from the reflections that others mirror back to them. However, at that initial moment, it seemed to be a correct assessment that something was wrong with the *other* rather than the *self*. We all need to know that —what other people do *to* you is not about you; it is about them.

What other people do TO you
is <u>NOT</u> about you – it <u>is</u> about THEM.

Regardless of what we learned growing up and any impact we may have had on others around us, we all *can* and *do* have the responsibility to retrain our thinking. The following tables are designed to assist you in that process. The first table has examples of situations followed by a negative perception in the first column, and some suggested positive cognitions in the second column. Choose alternative beliefs that are reality-based for your situation, and feel free to make up a few of your own. As long as they are constructive and positive, they can transform your hurt into healing. Take a look at some examples of changes that you can make to your thought-life and perspective.

Table 4
Situations for Alternative Ways of Thinking

A. You auditioned for a role or interviewed for a career position and were not selected.

Negative Thoughts	Hope-based Thoughts
I am a loser, failure, etc.	I have good skills to offer.
They are a fool, stupid to reject me.	They may be looking for a different type of person and a different fit.
I'll never get selected.	There is a right position for me and I will find it.
Those people are not good enough for me.	This position was not meant for me, and I know that there is something that will be a better match for me.
It is hopeless.	God has a plan for me.
I give up.	I trust God; I will choose to believe in myself and continue looking.

*Dr. Joan Weathersbee Ellason, PhD, LPC, Oasis Workshops.

Table 4
Situations for Alternative Ways of Thinking (Continued)

B. You have been exploited by someone you trusted.

Negative Thoughts	Hope-based Thoughts
How could I have been so stupid ?!	This is not my fault. I did not ask that person to rob me.
What a fool I was to trust them!	When I gave them the trust/benefit of the doubt, I offered them a precious opportunity that they have mishandled terribly.
They have taken everything from me.	They were not able to take my life, my health, my loved ones, my dignity, nor my destiny.
Those people who robbed me are evil and deserve to have a horrible calamity come upon them.	Something must have happened to them to make them do this, although it is no excuse. What a sad existence they must have.
I will hunt them down and make them pay.	Revenge is not my job – God does a much better job at it. They do not get to steal even one more ounce of my time or energy.
It took a lifetime to acquire all of those things. I can never be the same again.	God has got this. God will restore all that I need and even double what was taken from me in one way or another.

*Dr. Joan Weathersbee Ellason, PhD, LPC, Oasis Workshops.

Table 4
Situations for Alternative Ways of Thinking (Continued)

C. Your partner, spouse, fiancé cheated on you.

Negative Thoughts	Hope-based Thoughts
I am so ashamed and embarrassed.	I refuse to shame myself. Anyone who also shames me is not my friend.
This happened because I must not be enough -I am not [smart, pretty, handsome, appealing, good] enough.	I did not cause them to choose to cheat on me. I don't have to be perfect in order to be loved or for someone to be loyal to me.
It is all my fault.	Good and faithful partners are sometimes cheated on, without it being their fault. There are some individuals who choose cheating as their token coping mechanism or escape hatch, and I did not cause them to make that choice.
I must have deserved it.	No one deserves to get cheated on. I refuse to blame myself.

*Dr. Joan Weathersbee Ellason, PhD, LPC, Oasis Workshops.

Table 4
Situations for Alternative Ways of Thinking (Continued)

C. Your partner, spouse, fiancé cheated on you.

I cannot live without that person.	I will learn to live without having to depend on a person who I cannot trust. My partner has lost me - Not the other way around and their loss is greater than mine.
I will get revenge on the person who invaded our relationship.	Maybe the intruder took my partner, but I will not allow them to take my time, energy, or power – I do not need to waste my precious time or energy on them. God is my vindicator.
This has devastated my whole life.	I will not allow this to define me or my life.
I am a failure.	I did not cheat on them (and/or) I was a good partner in __(list)__ ways - therefore, I succeeded where my part is concerned. I will take time to acknowledge all of the right things that I did do. I will also examine any growth needed to avoid having the same situation repeat itself in my future. I will wrap my arms around me, be loving toward myself, and take time to heal.

*Dr. Joan Weathersbee Ellason, PhD, LPC, Oasis Workshops.

Notice as you review some of the negative options above how you may have felt physically if you were ever in those places of thought. Negative thoughts are toxic by nature. Notice how the positive, hope-based alternative thoughts in the right column can also be understood as grounded in reality, truthful, and are also life-giving. When you imagine applying some of these positive choices, notice how you feel in your mind, body, spirit, and soul. When you select a positive belief that fits with reality, notice that it actually feels better not only emotionally but also physically. This is why God wants us to dwell on hope-based thinking. God wants us to be healthy.

These are just a few situations, that may require grieving and time for recovery before making a shift to the alternate, hopeful perception. A cognitive shift from the negative to the positive is not an instantaneous, shallow event. It often takes time and practice intermingled with a bit more grieving. This does not ignore the fact that horrendous events occur, such as rape, physical and sexual abuse, loss of a loved one, or loss of a child that clearly merit a considerable grieving process. Review Chapter 5 and other resources (see suggested Reading List at the end of this book) whenever you find that you need to do so.

Cognitive Reframes

After we grieve, we can apply a cognitive reframe. This is a tool involving a change in the frame or lens through which you view the situation. When we retrain our thoughts to this level, we give ourselves a wealth of perspectives that can reshape our perception and ameliorate our pain. The development of this cognitive skill can also help buffer us through a number of emotional or interpersonal storms.

Derek and Jacqueline

Through the next few years, every effort that Jacqueline made to stand up against the alcohol issue was met by Derek increasing his efforts to vilify Jacqueline in their son's eyes. Every time their son would come back home from his father's house, he would rage against Jacqueline, yelling at her, telling her to get out of his room, and disregarding all of her rules. She was a one-woman team; she had no living parents, no grandparents, no nearby siblings, and no new partner nor spouse in the picture. She was left to deal with this single-handedly. Other than confiding in some friends who she could call, there was no one to step in as co-parent to help fortify the moral standards she was trying to instill in him. Since she was on the front lines by herself with no back-up, she needed to pick and choose her battles that were the most critical. It seemed that almost everything was met with a battle.

Jacqueline did not give up on Charles; because, although she knew that teenagers bear responsibility for their own behavior, the dynamics that ensued here were way beyond just that of teenaged rebellion. This was the effect of a young person who deeply needed to believe in his father, being misled by a rebellious adult. Charles was being negatively influenced and manipulated by the very one who was supposed to guide, lead, and teach him how to be a man and a good citizen. Instead, by emotionally indoctrinating his son against the mother, Derek was pouring emotional poison into Charles, and it was damaging his soul. Jacqueline was committed to not allow its effects to prevail.

Sometime during this nightmare of years, Jacqueline was sitting in her office grieving over how her son had been led to have such contempt for her when she poured her whole heart into him. She had been the parent who dropped everything she was doing when he unexpectedly needed to go to the doctor and took him to all of his extracurricular lessons and activities and paid for everything. She covered all of his expensive musical equipment, lessons, medical treatment, school necessities, and vehicles. With very little income, she prioritized her responsibilities as a parent to their son and delayed completing her education in this process. She made sure that Charles' needs were provided for before her own.

With the backdrop of all of these sacrifices, she prayed to God, asking why and how her son could seem to reject her and her values so unfairly. Immediately an image came into her mind of Jesus, standing in the middle of the city, with all of the crowds who He was about to sacrifice himself for. They were yelling, "Crucify him! Crucify him!" This picture suddenly changed her whole outlook. If Jesus, the Son of God, could encounter such severe rejection by the very ones He loved enough to give His life for, how could she assume that she should be exempt from this comparably small rejection from only one person? In her mind, this immediately normalized and reduced the power of Derek's campaign against her. She emerged from this revelation, having a newfound strength that helped her to rise above the situation going forward. She suddenly realized that even God gets disrespected. So Derek's efforts lost their power to impact her.

This is an example of a dramatic reframe that can completely change the perceptual landscape of what is happening to you. One possible perspective to take when others are mistreating us is the scene when Jesus was about to be crucified. The whole Lord of Lords and Creator of the Universe was rejected and scoffed at by the very ones He Loved and for whom he was about to rescue. In this reframe compared against things that happen to us, who are we to be above experiencing rejection?

People who engage in hate are being misled, deceived, lied to, and manipulated by an enemy, whether it is a human enemy, a spiritual domain, or both. It is important to look at them as someone who is being grossly deceived and therefore victimized just as if they are being infected by a virus and need help.

When you use cognitive reframes, it allows you to take on a

higher perspective that transcends the immediate and tangible level of perception. There are often parts of an event, outside of our knowledge, that come into play. We are sometimes unknowingly spared from a worse outcome when things don't go our way. Using this type of cognitive reframe by shifting to a more hopeful perspective can spare you much precious time, emotional energy, and anguish.

Complicated Situations

There are cases where you may have been hurt by a person who you do not want to exclude from your life. This can involve a spouse, relative, or adult child, for example. Sometimes these loved ones may or may not be intentionally toxic or harmful. Review their positive efforts and remind yourself of the many, many more moments where they were perhaps making efforts to be kind to you and how those events may far outweigh (if true) the moments that they messed up. Emphasize in your mind the abundant weight of that person's good intentions and positive actions over their mistakes. Notice where their misguided actions may have had a constructive intention behind it. God looks at the heart (I Samuel 16:7 NKJV).

Consider whether they may still be in the midst of a growth process. Ask God to give you insight into their intentions, even though they may have totally botched the situation. We often expect young adults to be fully grown at 18 years of age when the brain does not complete its growth in maturity until at least the age of 25. It is okay to have expectations for our adult children but remember that they have not yet had the experiences that you have had. Remember what your perspective was when you were younger. They perhaps may not have grown at the same rate that you may have had to. Everyone's life journey is different, so don't be disappointed if they do not handle decisions exactly the same way that you do. They may have also had different events and setbacks to deal with that you did not have to endure. Ask God to help you see them through His eyes.

There are events that seem to go so far in the wrong direction that we cannot imagine to understand why. These events tend to stretch and expand us into more dimensions than what we could have imagined. When things happen that are so out of the scope of what makes sense, we may be in the process of a training ground designed to launch us into a higher destiny than we thought possible. Genesis Chapters 37-42 cover what would seem to be a treacherous story about Joseph being terribly betrayed over and over again, first by his own brothers, lied about unjustly, imprisoned, but ending up a ruler second in command with wealth and his family restored to him. His final promotion would not have happened without those significant hardships. When our life turns into one of these disasters, do we want to celebrate, jump up and down about it, or cheer? Of course not. Sometimes it takes a long time for us to see the purpose behind those unexplained twists and turns.

Shifting your perspective is designed to give you a peace that passes all understanding (Philippians 4:7 NKJV). When you know that you really *can* trust God, you can rest in the knowledge that He does have a bigger plan that we cannot yet see (Isaiah 55:8-9 NKJV). Experience in knowing Him has taught me that we *can* trust Him to make everything that went wrong turn out for good at the end (Romans 8:28 NKJV). One day we will see this (1Corinthians 13:12 NKJV). All of our perplexities and questions will be answered, and it will all fit together, making sense. Here on planet earth, we may certainly not jump up and down with glee when life takes strange twists and turns, but the more you personally get to know the Creator, the more you can have a peace and confidence that what happened to you, to your loved ones, to your dreams, will not get to have the final say. Your world can turn back to right-side-up again.

Tools, Resources., and Final Points in Preparation for Facing this Head-On

Below are some tools and exercises to help you retrain your brain and learn how to do the Cognitive Shift. As you tune in to your thoughts and emotions, you can glean information about what you are needing. Balancing this awareness with good judgment can help you to gain a better perspective on appropriate actions to take. Awareness of your thoughts and emotions, combined with wise decision-making, can transform your life.

Receive Support

While working through anything painful, it is important to reiterate, that you need to allow solid supports into your life. From the beginning of creation, God said, "It is not good that man should be alone" (Genesis 2:18 NKJV). Now, you may not have friends for one reason or another, or you may not know of trustworthy people at this time. If that is the case, seek out professional support. This is not only fruitful, but it is an important part of healing. You can learn how to select and screen out toxic people with the help of counseling. Human beings need people.

Receive Resources

There are three levels of resources from which you can seek to supply your needs. Notice the chart below, titled Three Resource Pathways. You can see that the left side panel represents YOU (the recipient) and three areas where you can choose to receive nurturance (physically, emotionally/intellectually, and spiritually). The horizontal row across the top shows three resource domains from which to receive support. These include yourself, others, and God.

This chart shows some examples of ways to take care of yourself from within, from others, and from the Creator. You may have even more helpful ideas to add to your own personal repertoire of taking good care of yourself, using all three resource domains.

Table 5
Three Resource Pathways

Needs	Three Domains From Which to Receive Need Fulfillment		
Within You	**From You**	**From Others**	**From God**
Physical Needs	Choose healthy meals & nutrition. Choose to get enough rest and sleep. Choose appropriate exercise.	Ask a friend for a hug. Get a massage. Seek the care of a physician or other medical professional.	Ask God for physical healing. Attend a healing service. Study scriptures on healing.
Emotional/ Intellectual Needs	Generate nurturing self-talk and thoughts. Acknowledge one's own feelings. Process emotions appropriately.	Confide in a close friend. Consult with an expert about your issue. Attend counseling/ Join a Support Group.	Cry out to God about your feelings. Spend quiet time with God. Engage in open and honest conversations with God about what is troubling you.
Spiritual Needs	Prayer & Meditation Study of Scripture Inspirational readings. Take time to rest in God's Arms.	Listen to sermons. Consult with a Pastor. Participate in corporate worship. Spend time with others who are supportive	Spiritual prayer and meditation Scriptural study on spiritual growth Baptism of water and of the Spirit. Take time to rest in God's arms.

*Dr. Joan Weathersbee Ellason, PhD, LPC, Oasis Workshops.

Notice that we tend to most often seek our support and validation from the middle column (Others). This is the social domain. Notice how we may tend to place such high personal meaning and power upon the social arena. For instance, we often place the greatest importance upon whether or not we have a significant other in our lives or a social life with many friends. This column is also labeled the general term Other because many of us seek our worth and value from wealth, prestige, money, or possessions. If we put all of our hope only in this one Resource, we are setting ourselves up for disappointment, because these external resources are sometimes not available. We sometimes encounter loss in this area.

We all need social connection. We just need to keep it within balance. Some people have co-dependent relationships and cling to a toxic partner due to fear of being alone. Alternatively, others may isolate themselves from people altogether, turning to things rather than people for their fulfillment. If we have been hurt by people, we may engage in excessive work or become driven and ambitious to the point that we almost never get to see our family. We might dive into addiction such as alcohol, drugs, shopping, overeating, gambling, or pornography. Healing old wounds can help us to balance the use of our resources.

Other people may have many, many great friends with healthy relationships, but that is their only selected resource. If they miss out on the third column, they may not *really* know God's personal side and how truly loved and cherished that they are. This column is, in my experience, the most powerful resource. The third column, God/Creator is the resource we can find constantly available and able to pervasively attend to all levels of our needs.

The most neglected column is the first one. Many people do not know how to have a connected, nurturing, loving, and healthy relationship with their own selves. Healthy self-love is different from selfishness. This resource involves conscious loving and supportive thoughts one generates in their own private mind, as well as choosing to physically, emotionally, and spiritually take care of themselves outwardly. We are expected, *and it is scriptural* for us to love ourselves, "Love your neighbor as yourself" (Mark 12:31 NIV). The more good emotional nutrients you pour into your soul, the more positive loving responses you have within yourself to pull from and to give to others. Having a soul filled with genuine love and positive perception makes it easier to forgive yourself, which makes it tremendously easier to extend mercy to others. You cannot give anything to anyone from an empty heart.

So, ask yourself, what are you doing to connect to the Creator, what are you doing to nurture yourself, and are you taking care to choose healthy external resources (Others)? How are you treating yourself on a daily basis? Have you considered the task of becoming a good parent to yourself?

When we tune into our thoughts and emotions, this gives us information about what we are needing. A good parent tunes into the person, hears their needs, discerns what resources are appropriate for them, and then supplies those resources. When we grow up, we all get to choose to become the parent that we need (whether we had good parents or not) by 1) tuning in to what we are needing (sometimes through awareness of our thoughts and feelings), and 2) discerning and deciding the best and wisest resources and options for us to take. What kind of parenting are you giving to yourself now? Do you comfort yourself when no one is there? You can. Do you set appropriate limits with yourself when tempted to cross the line into unwise behavior? In your thought-life, do you communicate with yourself nurturing and hopeful truths? Deciding to be good to yourself is crucial.

Cognitive Tools

Many of the exercises to follow will show you how to examine and rethink the thoughts you may have been thinking. Stephen Post and Jull Neimark, in their book *Why Good things Happen to Good People*,[lix] tell of account after account where positive attitudes have been associated with a healthier life, increased longevity, and a better quality of life. These authors found that the emotions and attitudes associated with these healthy life qualities are purpose-filled passion, love, celebration, generativity (helping others grow), courage (speaking up and speaking out), respect (deep processing to find the value), compassion, loyalty, listening to others with a deep presence, creativity (use your creativity and innovation), and forgiveness. These attitude states originate from positive thoughts and emotions.

How-to Exercise Tier II

How to do this is with simple practice and repetition. Start with one or two concepts that you want to use as a replacement. Choose thoughts that you can believe or at least know to be true, even if the believing part is still a bit challenging. *Make sure it is a healthy thought or healthy belief.* Then repeat it to yourself over and over again throughout the day and every day. It is like taking vitamin supplements – several times per day. Neuroscience has shown that those new thoughts will become stronger by repetition, and the old ones, if ignored, will weaken.[lx]

By learning to examine, take authority, and take charge of your cognitions, you can heal. You can also learn how to create a constant, ongoing barrier of protection around your heart and mind that the enemy cannot penetrate. Moreover, you can develop this skill to a point where you most often remain *un*fettered in the face of ongoing offense. There are, of course, times to leave a negative situation; however, for those ongoing situations where you need to remain for a time, the power of your cognitions combined with God and available resources can be limitless.

Shifting to Positive Cognitions Does Not Mean Avoiding Assertiveness

One of my favorite and to-the-point books by Joyce Meyer is *Do It Afraid*, which means that, when faced with a decision which is wise yet you feel fear, you don't have to wait until the fear goes away before you can do that wise action. You can proceed forward while feeling shy, scared, unconfident, and even trembling with fear. This step may be 1) speaking up and saying no to a bully, 2) taking action to call the police, or 3) making a decision to begin a recovery program, even though you do not feel like doing it. I once had to stand up to a person who had been harassing me for months, trying to get me to back down on a safety matter. I remember my legs almost feeling paralyzed as I began to put one foot in front of the other, almost wooden-legged, walking into the courtroom with my witness. With slow deep breaths, I was able to stand up to the offender. You can change your negative perceptions and beliefs into positive ones while still standing up to an adversary. Sometimes you just have to "Do it afraid."[lxi]

Continuing with Derek and Jacqueline

After the mediation process mentioned above and within one week after the judge signed the new agreement, Jacqueline learned that Derek was seen drinking and driving with a minor, who Jacqueline thought to be Charles, in his car. He also had reportedly almost caused a collision. Jacqueline was actually terrified to stand up to Derek about this because Derek had been so vengeful and threatened to take their son away from her if she came forward about it. She knew that Derek had a unique gift of persuasion. He could look you straight in the eyes with conviction, telling you his version of the truth, while it was completely false. He had charm and influence and she feared that he would use this in court. She also knew, however, that she could not just stand by and do nothing. Even if she failed in her stand against this, she could not just hold her breath every time Charles went to his father's house, hopeful that they would not get into a collision.

She scraped together all of the money that she had, which was less than $1,000, and took it to the only attorney she could afford and asked for help. She asked the attorney to file a motion to enforce the injunction as her first priority. When the attorney filed a motion to modify the parent-child relationship instead of the motion to enforce, she knew that this would lead to repercussions from Derrek; but, she had no idea of the storm that would follow. Derek was served with the same motion that he had previously served Jacqueline with just months before.

Often when standing up for what is right, it takes great courage. Here is where you need to apply cognitive thoughts and beliefs that bring you hope in the face of fear. The type of thoughts that you need to focus on will not necessarily take away the fear. The cognitions needed here are those that can broaden your perspective, examine an array of options, and lead to a reduction of the original fear.

For instance, in this story above, Jacqueline was well aware that taking a stand involved the risk of increased retaliation from Derek. However, this situation involved the choice between letting Derek continue to drink and drive with their son, which would allow her to remain in favor with Derek and his group, versus taking a stand to protect her son's life even if she were treated terribly. This was a no-brainer. She decided that she would rather have an ex who was angry at her <u>while their son remained alive and healthy than</u> the alternative. The fear of her son's harm significantly outweighed the fear of losing favor and popularity in his eyes. Taking appropriate action while still feeling the emotion of fear is the very definition of courage.

Constructive thoughts and perceptions can help to bolster your emotional strength without changing reality. There are many cases and situations, however, that are extremely difficult and may merit the addition of more resources, such as counselors and sometimes medication. If you find that shifting into constructive thoughts and emotions are too difficult, you are not alone. The need to consult a doctor about the possibility of including medication to help you through a rough spot should be no more shameful than taking an aspirin for a headache or a vitamin supplement for physical strength

Make use of Reasonable Resources

It is worth revisiting again the point that medications are often necessary tools and that there is nothing unscriptural about taking medication when appropriate. If you look out across the entire planet, you will not find very many people who are not on some form of medication, whether a supplement or even a vitamin. It may be aspirin for a headache, a pill for weight loss, or medication for hypertension. Medication is part of the human condition, and people from all walks of life have found help to function through this avenue. Also, don't be hard on yourself if you find it difficult to practice new thoughts. It takes practice and application of some of the tools and supports described in this book. Choose the tools and resources that work for you personally.

Spiritual Tools

Scripture is powerful, and I believe that there is nothing more powerful than speaking God's word over your life and against an offense. This is what Jesus did to get Satan to leave him alone (Matthew 4, Mark 1, and Luke 4). He responded with the Word of God. There is more on this in Chapter 7.

What Happens If You Relied Upon the Wrong Resource?

Derek and Jacqueline

Jacqueline had always believed that courts ruled justly. She came from a family system where the father was wise, patient, and kind. She believed that the court could finally be her refuge from all of Derek's bullying and disregard for their child's safety. In fact, everyone in her family believed that the courts would operate with wisdom and insight.

While Jacqueline had grown up trusting authority, she also feared that Derek could try to manipulate the courts, so she was still very afraid. She expressed this concern to her attorney, but he told her that the worst thing that would happen would be nothing. Jacqueline trusted this attorney because he was a professional and thought that he must know better than she did. At the advice of another previous attorney, it was a private investigator who had witnessed and reported Derek's drinking and driving very few days after their final signed agreement containing the injunction.

As mentioned above, this attorney filed a motion to modify the parent-child relationship on the stated grounds of Derek's witnessed driving under the influence of alcohol with their son as a passenger. Jacqueline wanted Derek to have equal time with their son as long as he would not drink and drive or abuse alcohol when with him.

When Derek was served with the motion to modify the parent-child relationship, everything hit the fan. Derek raged at Jacqueline and resumed his harassing messages, but this time he pulled Charles directly into the middle of the drama. Derek called Jacqueline on the phone and told her that he showed the motion to modify the parent-child relationship to their son, Charles, telling him that "your mother is trying to hurt 'us' and take you away from me." Ironically, this had been the exact same paperwork that Derek had filed against Jacqueline just months before. Derek then told Jacqueline that he also told their son that he was going to have to sign a piece of paper just like he allegedly 'had to do' for his first-born son, terminating his parental rights. This was a lie, and it stressed their son so much that when their son returned to his mother's house right after that, Charles yelled and cursed at his mother so severely that when 911 was called, the police had drawn their guns.

In the next counseling session that Derek had previously agreed to attend with Jacqueline for co-parenting, Derek had expected Jacqueline to bring a parental rights termination form with her for him to sign. It seemed like he planned to sign right in front of the counselor so that the counselor could see Jacqueline as a villain and see Derek as the victim and righteous martyr. None of Derek's fantasy was anywhere in Jacqueline's plan. She had asked for co-parenting sessions and had wanted Derek to be a good influence on their son.

There is a critical question here. Why would Derek just not agree for their son's safety? Even though Jacqueline was not trying to take their son from Derek, why would he have to sign over anything if he was just willing to refrain from putting their son in harm's way?

None of this drama had to have taken place. This could have been a simple agreement where Derek, from the very beginning, could have agreed to no driving while under the influence of alcohol when having their son in the car. If Jacqueline had been able to have peace of mind about their son's safety, this would have been easier for her since, at the time she was trying to finish her degree. School took a far backseat, however, since Derek seemed just to sign paper agreements but then proceed to do the same as before. Jacqueline believed that the problem needed the help of a wise authority that she thought she could find by going to court.

It did not make sense that Derek was stressed about going to court. He had persistently threatened to take Jacqueline to court over and over again during all of the previous dynamics, both before the finalization of their divorce and all during the mediation process. On the other hand, Jacqueline knew that she was in unchartered territory, never having sued anyone before, but believed that she had no other options.

Approaching the court date, Derek tried to talk Jacqueline into dropping the case repeatedly. Jacqueline believed that he would just lie again and put their son in danger if she made another simple written agreement without a person of authority to enforce it. Since Jacqueline was not going to back down about these concerns, Derek, at the eleventh hour – literally the night before the trial – filed his own counter-motion to change the custody of their son.

Naturally, Charles loved his father, and with all of the things said to him leading up to this point, Charles felt that he needed to protect his dad. Charles was a very compassionate and empathetic young man from as early as he could talk. During this drama, Charles was somehow led to believe that in order to prevent the calamity that might befall Derek and avoid a modification of their relationship, he would have to go in and tell the judge that his dad does not drink and drive and also tell the judge that he wanted to live with his dad.

Jacqueline did everything she could to try to keep him out of the adults' drama. Jacqueline knew that communicating with Charles about these issues would make him feel pulled in both directions, creating conflict inside his heart. For instance, when Charles came back from his father's house, he was enraged, thinking that Dad was going to have to sign him over to Jacqueline and give up his rights to Charles. What was she to say to this? If she said that was not true, then she feared that what her son would hear was, "Your dad is a liar." If she said, "Your dad signs agreements to not drink and drive with you but then turns around and violates that agreement," she feared Charles would hear the implication, 'Your dad is not trustworthy.' Charles did not need to hear the counter-arguments to his dad's assertions because it would make him feel pulled even more between both parents. Jacqueline addressed the disrespect as best she could single-handedly and outnumbered. She was a household of one against a group of several who seemed to believe that Derek's pattern of having several drinks before driving was acceptable. Charles already knew that Jacqueline disagreed with Derek's lifestyle. When Charles would come home angry at her, rather than pouring confusion into Charles by opposing arguments, she *simply placed an emotional shield over her heart as the torpedoes hit her chest. She realized that Charles was inappropriately burdened by his father's words, and she knew trying to tell Charles her side or matter would burden him even more. These were adult matters that needed to be settled between the adults, not through the child. This enormous pressure that Derek had poured into Charles and pulled him into was a form of emotional abuse. So, while Jacqueline did her best to restrain from saying anything to Charles that would come out sounding bad about his dad, it was a different story at Derek's house.*

Jacqueline had already set up counseling to buffer Charles from the impact of these dynamics, but Derek resisted the counseling. Jacqueline knew that counseling could help her son navigate these stressors. Plus, every time she tried to have a constructive conversation with Charles about anything stressful, it was next to impossible. Charles seemed to be strongly influenced by Derek and increasingly defensive toward Jacqueline. One day when they were getting ready to leave for a counseling appointment she had set up for their son, Charles got a call from his dad on the house phone line.

Since Charles acted so hateful toward her every time he returned from his father's house or spoke to him, Jacqueline felt like she needed to know what was causing such disrespect. So, on that day, for the first time, she went to the house fax phone and pressed the button to allow her to silently hear what Derek was saying to Charles. Derek was coaching Charles on how to act toward Mom in this trip to his appointment. She heard Derek say to Charles, "When you get there, you tell your Mom to go way out of the room and don't let her come into your session with you." Then Derek said to Charles referring to Jacqueline, "She's sicker than all her patients."

They got into the small truck that she had bought Charles, and he was in the driver's seat. He had his driver's permit, and she believed in offering him every chance possible to practice driving so that when he was fully licensed and driving on his own, he would have ample experience under his belt. Charles was already a good driver. Half-way there, going down the highway, Charles began telling his mother that she was not allowed in the counseling session (like he had just been coached to do). Jacqueline attempted to have a conversation with him about it and she mentioned to Charles that she had heard what Derek had said to him. She did not expect what happened next.

Charles immediately flew into a temper tantrum while behind the wheel amidst massive traffic. He started alternately revving up the engine and slamming on the breaks, trying to change lanes to turn the truck around. Charles started raging at her. Jacqueline knew not to get into an altercation on the highway with an angry teenager driving. Several times they almost ran into the back of the vehicle in front of them. It was a miracle that they did not have a wreck on that crowded highway. Charles managed to change lanes and turn the truck around to go back home. When they were finally a few blocks away from the house and now moving at a much slower speed, Charles began to repeatedly spit on his mother's face. This is an example of how toxicity from a parent can not only poison a child but lead them into behaviors that harm their soul. Derek was turning Charles into something that he was not.

At this moment, she closed her eyes and began moving her lips silently. To young Charles, she must have looked like she was quietly talking to herself or maybe responding to internal stimuli. Charles said in a loud voice, "What are you doing?" She calmly replied, "I'm praying." Suddenly, the shouting and spitting stopped. It was quiet and peaceful for the rest of the ride home. Derek had no idea that his words to Charles, that afternoon right before the appointment, could have gotten both his son and Jacqueline killed on the highway that day.

His mother was not going to give up on her son; she knew that this was not who he really was. From the earliest age, Charles had a caring and compassionate heart. At the age of seven, Charles had made a commitment to Christ and, by example, had led his own aging grandfather into baptism. At two years old, Charles tried to comfort his father after intuitively picking up on Derek's sadness when he had lost a job. Derek knew their son's compassionate nature, and now he was taking advantage of it.

Court Calamity

When the case went to trial, the judge did not allow into evidence the private investigator report that she had been advised to obtain. Even though the private investigator reported under oath that Derek had almost caused a collision after consuming alcohol and driving, the judge chose to believe Derek, who swore on the stand that he only drank two beers. The judge also did not factor in the home study report written by a judge, which recommended that Derek reduce his alcohol consumption while both parents share equal time with their son. The judge did not read this report, nor the private investigator's report, nor notice the fact that Derek's counter-motion had only been filed the night before. The attorney did not challenge any of these events, and the judge did not take any of Jacqueline's concerns seriously. The ruling did nothing to address the alcohol issue. The judge kept the joint custody in place but made Derek's house the primary residence, with Jacqueline now having standard visitation and now having to pay Derek child support. Derek wrote in the new decree for Jacqueline to have even less than standard time with Charles - less time with Charles than she had given to Derek. The judge signed Derek's written order without reading a word of the document. While still a student, Jacqueline was now to pay Derek, the airline pilot, child support. The reversal of child support rendered her a $1000.00 decrease per month and Derek and Lucy a $1000.00 monthly increase. Jacqueline now had to add on a third job.

Wouldn't it be nice if a giant sign would drop down out of the sky, telling us the exact steps to take in a challenge? In the intensity of fear or out of desperation, we may sometimes place our faith upon authorities who we thought to have the best interest at heart.

Sometimes the noise of the situation may drown out that still small voice that comes from intuition or discernment. Other times we hear advice from different opinions, each coming from those who love us and don't know what to do. If you find that the road that you thought would be the refuge turns out to be a disaster, pick yourself right back up immediately and continue pursuing victory. Choose to continue to heal.

Derek and Jacqueline – Who Paid the Biggest Price?

Since Charles knew that Derek regularly drank and drove whenever he wanted to, the result of the court proceedings made it look in this young person's eyes as if Derek was right all along, and his mom was the wrong one. It seemed to be a normal thing to his young eyes for adults to drive under the influence of alcohol and get away with it.

Within the first month after going to live with his dad, just blocks away and within the same school district –Charles' academic grades went from As and Bs to Fs. This was extremely out of character for him, who regularly had excellent grades. This semester, he almost failed the entire grade if it were not for the mercy of two teachers who rounded two of his grades upward, allowing him to pass on through.

Even though Jacqueline still maintained joint custody, Derek had cut her out of all Charles's school events. At the start of the following school semester, she discovered that Derek had written in Lucy's name as "Mother" on the enrollment paperwork, and Jacqueline was not listed anywhere on any of the forms - not even as an emergency contact. She was never notified of any of his school activities for a while until she was able to get it corrected.

For the next two semesters, it seemed that Charles was drunk every time Jacqueline saw him. Because she had stood firm against Derek's alcohol-related behavior, she was not allowed to go to any of their gatherings, which meant not seeing him at all on Thanksgiving. When she asked Charles if he could *just come over for the early part of the day and then spend the rest of Thanksgiving with his dad, Charles said he couldn't because everyone had already had too much to drink by then, and no one was able to leave. Given the pattern of shaming and out-casting that was placed upon anyone who stood up to impropriety in this group, Charles had been indoctrinated into what appeared to be an alcohol cult.*

In the second half of his senior year in high school, when it came time to order his cap and gown and high school ring for graduation, Jacqueline went to the school to purchase them. She had Charles called to the office area so he could pick out his ring, and Charles told her that he did not believe that he was going to be able to finish high school. Jacqueline looked at him and firmly assured him that he would graduate. So, Charles picked out the graduation ring he liked and went back to class.

Charles' academic performance had slid down so far that it derailed him from the college track that he had spoken of as a child and almost destroyed his chances of graduation. Charles was a very intelligent young man, but his self-esteem had been shot, and he had lost all hope in his future. Seeing this happening, Jacqueline stepped in to hire tutors and paid for everything required to help him redeem his grades. Derek was willing to let Charles spend time at Jacqueline's for all of the tutoring, but he did not help pay for any of it. With substantial expense for this, she got behind on her house payments. After helping Charles regain and fulfill the necessary academic requirements, Jacqueline received a letter from her bank threatening foreclosure. She took this letter over to Derek's house and showed it to him, asking if he would be willing to reimburse her for some of the tutoring so that she could catch up on her mortgage. Derek looked at her with a triumphant smirk on his face and shook his head no. He knew that she could not afford the house in that affluent neighborhood with her low income and no living parents remaining to help her. Was his former professed threat to make her lose the house about to come true? By her spending everything she had to get their son back on track, it meant that she could not pay the mortgage, but Charles's welfare was much more important to her than any house.

Charles did graduate from high school, and during the next years, he was working and succeeding in the area of his talent. He had moved out of state. However, the alcohol that he had become saturated with while living at Derek's had already taken hold of him. He began to fall deeper and deeper into a depression. Jacqueline was surprised when he told her that he felt trapped in a dark hole while in the midst of his success. She told him to come home. So, he drove halfway across the United States back to his home town. He got an apartment and went to work right away.

One day while Charles was sitting on the back porch with his mother after he had just spent the night with his Father, he told her that he had consumed an extreme amount of alcohol trying to overdose while at his dad's. This was the second time when her eyelids flew open. She got him into treatment immediately, and this involved a series of many treatments off and on in response to several further attempts of his to end his life. Jacqueline was now fighting something bigger than Derek. This battle took all of her might, and she was not backing down. She prayed harder than she had ever prayed before, spent more money than she had, and would not allow anyone to speak doubt over his chance at recovery. This went on for several years, with three different interventions. Jacqueline fought for him and prayed over him with cries and wails that can only come from a mother. By the grace of God and one inch at a time, Charles was gradually pulled from the jaws of hell and death.

Today he lives a very healthy and wholesome life with good Godly friends and enormous love surrounding him. He now looks back and appreciates and respects his mother. He continues to grow in wisdom and maturity, and his positive character and heart are no longer hidden in the dark.

Traumas that occur here on the earth are not simple. They can be complex, with many unforeseen twists and turns. You may need to use all of the tools in this book *during* and *through* your journey. The point is, don't give up. Don't give up on yourself nor your goals. Don't give up on those who you love and need to protect. And don't give up on God.

Examples of the Cognitive Shift

The following examples show how you can use some of the cognitive tools to change your thinking from a negative to a positive and reality-based mindset even in the midst of calamity. Traditional cognitive theory encourages us to replace negative thinking with positive thinking.[lxii] I believe that if you replace some of your negative thoughts with Scripture, this becomes even more powerful.

The following table contains some examples of situations in the first column, with Cognitive replacements in the second column, and Spiritual replacements (scriptures) in the third column. Use any of these that are helpful, and feel free to come up with a few of your own. These are only a small number of examples of the many types of positive cognitions that can be applied.

This table also includes thoughts and scriptures to help you forgive yourself. You may modify them to fit your needs as long as they remain loving and supportive toward you. Select any that you find helpful and begin to repeat them to yourself several times throughout the day. This may, at first, feel like you are lying to yourself. That is only because they are new thoughts and may feel foreign to you. Your neuronal pathways are yet to become strengthened, which occurs through repetition.

It is effective to do the repletion in more than one form. Speaking the new cognitions and/or scriptures out loud several times per day is even more effective than just thinking them silently, although I recommend doing both. It is also good to write them several times a day in perhaps a journal. You may also want to place some of the written new beliefs in visible places throughout your home or any place where you will see them frequently and be reminded of them. You can make them into art or write a song about them. When you are by yourself, look yourself in the mirror and tell yourself the new cognition or scripture, face-to-face and eye-to-eye. You can engage a trusted and supportive friend to tell the new positive thought to face-to-face, as well, and receive the validating nod that can come in return. I recommend using all of these forms of repetition that you can and as often as you can throughout the day.

The repetition can start to transform your old way of thinking into new ideas, perceptions, interpretations of events, and positive beliefs. The more you practice, the more automatic they can become. Positive thoughts and perceptions carry hope. Some of the experiential work that follows in the next chapter may also help you to move more fully into this new way of thinking, taking it from the head level of dutiful repetition (cerebral) to a deeper level that transforms your soul.

The next Table provides some examples of both cognitive and spiritual positive truths that can replace negative thoughts about yourself and negative perceptions in general. The work you do in Chapter 6 will require that you have a positive, loving, and supportive attitude toward yourself.

Please do not rush into the exercises in Chapter 6 until you have retrained your mind to think lovingly toward yourself.

Table 6
The Cognitive Shift

Situation	Cognitive Replacements	Spiritual Replacements (Paraphrased)
Rejection by Others	I am still loved and loveable.	God loves me. John 3:16, 1 John 3:1, Jeremiah 31:3
	That person does not get to decide my value.	God will never leave me nor forsake me. Matthew 28:20, Psalm 139:8
	I refuse to give my power over to that individual.	God is on the Throne and in charge of my destiny. 2 Chronicles 18:18 Isaiah 6:1, Jeremiah 29:11
	I am going to be my best friend; therefore, his/her rejection does not carry strong weight to hurt me.	It is scriptural to love yourself. Mark 12:31, Psalm 139:14
Mistakes Made by Me	Beyond the act of sincere repentance, I refuse to hold on to shame nor torture myself.	God is not mad at me. Psalms 86:15, Lamentations 3: 22 – 23
	I will CHOOSE to forgive myself.	It is scriptural to forgive yourself. Psalm 103:12
	It is not healthy for me to keep beating myself up.	If I dwell on my mistakes, I am doing nothing more than being a voice for the devil. I will not do that. Revelation 12:10
	I can choose to stop punishing myself and begin to step right back into the plan that God has for me NOW - giving my regrets to Him.	It is scriptural to leave the past behind and press forward to the prize that God has in our future. I will stop wasting energy and step into the God-ordained destiny for me. Philippians 3:12-14

*Dr. Joan Weathersbee Ellason, PhD, LPC, Oasis Workshops.

Table 6
The Cognitive Shift
(Continued)

Situation	Cognitive Replacements	Spiritual Replacements (Paraphrased)
Abandonment by a Loved One	I will need to take some time to grieve.	God is my comfort. Matthew 5:4
	I can reach out for support from friends and others.	God will never leave me nor forsake me. Deuteronomy 31:6
	I am never without a family. I will always have a place where I belong. I will create a new family and develop new friendships.	If my parents (or family) reject me God has adopted me as His own. I am not alone – God will not leave me. Psalm 27:10
Hatred, Abuse by Others	I can seek legal protection. I can cry for help. I can say no.	He is my shelter and my rock. Psalm 18:2, 2 Samuel 22:3
	Hurting people – hurt people. What they did to me is not really about me. They are cruel because of something that happened to them that they are not handling in the right way.	This person needs prayer. Matthew 5:44 – 45
	This person is impaired, misled, and or sickened by something. This is not my fault.	There may be more than meets the eye. This person may be being played by the enemy. We do not deal with flesh and blood, but with . . . a spiritual realm. Ephesians 6:12
	I know that good will come of this. I will rise up and overcome this.	God will pay back to me twice of what I lost. Zachariah 9:12
	I will refuse to wear that person's shame. What they did to me does not define me.	Instead of my former shame, God will give me a double blessing. He will give me beauty for ashes. Isaiah 61:7

*Dr. Joan Weathersbee Ellason, PhD, LPC, Oasis Workshops.

Chapter 6

Exercises: How to Turn Your Trauma into Triumph

*****First and Very Important: Before proceeding to these exercises,*
MAKE SURE TO TAKE CARE OF YOUR EMOTIONAL SAFETY

PREPARATION FOR THE EXERCISES

Safety is Paramount

The following pages contain exercises to help you do the cognitive shift and move from Tier I through Tier II and eventually to Tier III. It is imperative that you read the chapter on the necessary tools before embarking on these steps. If you find any of these exercises difficult or too emotionally painful, it is recommended for you to seek professional assistance to work further through the exercises in this chapter. Even if these exercises seem more detailed than what you are used to, it can also be a good idea to seek a therapist to assist you. Otherwise, after doing the preparatory work and choosing issues with no more than a moderate pain level for the exercises below, you can progress through the exercises by reading a small section of the steps at a time as you move through each step. Throughout these steps, I will be continuing to remind you to use any needed preparation and resources described in this book to encourage you to take good care of yourself through this work.

Before You Start: Preparing to Work Through Pain

The previous chapters build up to this one, so it is not recommended for you to just jump into this one without covering the previous ones. The tools described in earlier chapters involving self-awareness and support are important throughout this chapter to manage the severity of your emotional responses during these exercises and help you pull back into a calming place (Safe Oasis, next section) when necessary. I have never agreed with harsh methods in therapeutic work. Healing does not have to be grueling any more than open-heart surgery needs to be conducted without anesthesia. So, use good judgment and protect yourself by not embarking on any of these exercises prematurely or without the appropriate and needed supports.

Apply all of the preparatory tools described in Chapter 4 as you do this work.

It is imperative for you to take care of yourself while doing this work.

You will also need to have reviewed the specific examples of the cognitive shift before going into any emotional work. This is not a demolition project. Healing is to be a healthy process that often takes time. Be patient and remember that at any point within this work, you can invite the help of a trained professional, if needed, to guide you through these steps. ***It is imperative for you to take care of yourself while doing this work.***

First, Create a Safe Oasis

Remember when we discussed how God had us in a safe womb before we even entered the world? If we required approximately nine months of an initial safe oasis before entering the stresses of earth, it is not too much to require just a few minutes to first create an oasis before you embark on dealing with unpleasant emotional events. This will be a safe haven that you can retreat into if the work begins to feel too intense or when you need a break.

Your Own Personal Oasis

Therefore, imagine a soothing place that you find relaxing and safe emotionally and physically. This can be any place at all that is soothing to you personally, indoors or outdoors. Bring all of the scenery into view. Tune into the sights, sounds, textures, smells, and aromas, along with any movements and possibly include any pleasant tastes in this place.

I like to call this your Oasis because you can create any scenery here that you want. It does not have to make sense to anyone else. It is your oasis. For you, is it an ocean or a meadow? Perhaps it is a pleasant memory with loved ones, remembering a time with things were happy. Some people prefer their own room or favorite restaurant. Create this place that represents safety for you.

Now tune in to all that is pleasant that you see, hear, tangibly feel, smell, and possibly taste in this scene. The more you include your five senses in this personal place, the more effective you can be at pulling yourself away from the distressing thoughts and emotions when needed.

The oasis you create can also be used to help you self-regulate your emotions in your daily life. If you become stressed or panicked, you can move away from the stressor for a moment and regroup. At any point that you need to during these exercises, take a break and move back into your Oasis as often as you need.

Your imagination is a very powerful God-given tool to help you restore peace of mind. We already use our imagination when we worry or obsess. Can you recall a time when you were ruminating or imagining yourself taking revenge for an injustice? You may have noticed that your attention became so focused that your heart rate increased, or others had to call your name loudly to pull you back into the present moment. You are already creating places in your mind when you walk down memory lane or worry about something you fear. In creating an Oasis, you are using the same skill of imagery, but in a direction that leads to mental health instead of distress. Our imagination is intended to be used for good. More examples of using our mind constructively include prayer, meditation, and creating positive plans for the future. We can use this amazing and wonderful God-given faculty, known as our brain, to create solutions, soothe our emotions, and overcome obstacles.

Since we can choose what we put into our minds, let's begin using this powerful tool for the positive. Philippians 4:8 admonishes us to think of things that are pure, lovely, and excellent. Romans 12:2 states, be transformed by the renewing of your mind. So, let's start here with the renewal.

Now let's add more detail to your Oasis. Is it indoors or outdoors? Is there thick, rich green grass? A pond? Does it include a pleasant childhood place that you remember fondly? Bring in the detail. There are no rules, no limits to its beauty, elements, colors, aromas, or textures. It can be a combination of many places you have been, or somewhere you wish to be. Apply your five senses (sight, sound, touch, smell, taste) plus movement (kinesthetic) to increase your calmness and sense of safety.

A Way to Measure Your Level of Emotional Pain

Next, identify your pain level currently associated with the incident that you plan to process, using the Emotional Pain Scale shown below. What level of intensity do you perceive your own pain to be? Zero represents no pain at all, and 10 represents the highest level of pain, such as completely paralyzed emotionally, unable to get out of bed, or totally unable to function. A five on this scale represents your subjectively perceived level as moderate pain. For instance, this level may feel tolerable to you; the issue bothers you, but it does not overwhelm you or take over your life.

You may want to ask a licensed professional to help you determine whether your level of pain is higher than a five if you are uncertain. If you have been suppressing your emotions much of the time, it would be important to ask for this guidance. Sometimes we may think that an issue is not bothering us at all, but then we open it up to find it to be a volcano roaring back up with a vengeance. Please take care of yourself by accurately assessing the level of any hidden pain before taking on these experiential exercises independently.

It is strongly recommended that you do not embark on any of these exercises in this book if your emotional level of pain is above a five on this scale. For events that seem to be higher than a five on this scale, please utilize the help of a trained professional to walk with you through the steps in this book.

As you are working through your emotions, you will need to self-monitor your level of emotional intensity at points all along the way throughout this work. Each of us is different, and some have more trouble tolerating emotions and sensory input than others. A competent therapist may also be able to help guide your pacing of the work intensity by reminding you to retreat into your safe oasis periodically to manage your tolerance level.

Figure B
Emotional Pain Scale
(Subjective)

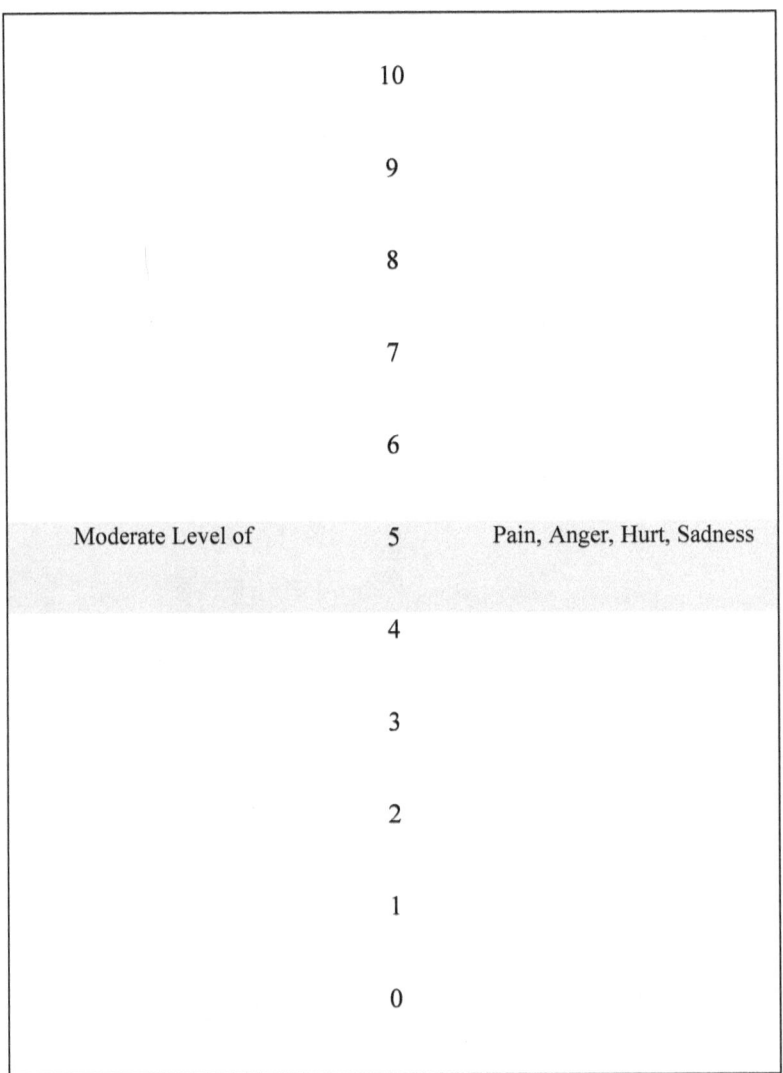

Managing Emotional Intensity During Your Processing

The next paragraphs guide you on what to do *while you are doing the processing of your pain.* The diagram below shows a construct from a spectrum of emotions that I first learned about from some highly respected colleagues who specialize in trauma work.[lxiii] This subjective scale is often used as a self-monitoring tool during trauma work. I refer to it here for our purposes as the Emotional Repair Dimension because it is helpful to remember that anger is energy designed to repair and also that anger turned inward can sometimes become a form of depression or deep-seated sadness.[lxiv] This sadness and depressive emotion can often be released through tears or the expression of anger itself. Accordingly, anger and sadness are two sides of the same coin or opposite ends of the same dimension, which can together comprise the full dimension of our emotional pain.

Anger turned inward is not the only cause of depression. Often it is chemical. Many people need the help of medication because of an inherited condition involving reduced serotonin and other necessary chemicals in the brain. In a significant number of cases, the use of medication is life-saving and very necessary. Often the combination of appropriately prescribed medication and therapeutic work flow beautifully together.

If you are on medication, always follow your doctor's guidelines and do not decrease or adjust medications on your own without your physician's guidance. These exercises in this book are not considered to be a replacement for medication.

How to Use the Emotional Repair Dimension

This diagram displayed below is designed to help you maintain a productive range of emotional intensity as you process your feelings. In your life, you may have been exposed to levels of anger or sadness that were unbalanced and also inappropriately demonstrated. These may have been in the form of rage, prolonged unproductive anger, misplaced anger, or inappropriate actions associated with unmanaged anger. Those examples are not healthy nor productive examples of anger. For sadness, you may have seen it demonstrated at an extreme as well, with debilitating despair, victim-related weakness, or sadness that leads to neglect of self or others. These are also not healthy examples. These forms of sadness and anger are not demonstrated here. The range of sadness and anger are to be processed as grief work (a healthy form of sadness) and empowering repair (a healthy form of anger).

Make sure you maintain balance in the intensity of your anger and sadness.

Do not allow yourself to become overwhelmed.

Here is how to maintain your emotional processing within a healthy balance. Notice in the chart below, anger is at one end of the continuum and sadness is at the other. When processing your anger and sadness, keep the intensity of both within a balanced range (approximately 20-80 on the scale). On this dimension (sadness – anger), a balanced, workable range is represented by a number above 20 for sadness and below 80 for anger. Any level of anger that is subjectively felt to be above 80 in intensity or sadness that is below 20 is not productive. If you find that your emotions are increasing in intensity in either direction (intensity above 80 or below 20), you need to immediately take a break, redirect your mind back into your oasis, and resume the safe place that you created prior to beginning this work. If you cannot maintain this balance in intensity, please stop the exercises altogether and consult a trained therapist or psychiatrist.

Furthermore, if you are dealing with any form of psychosis or mood disorder that is not being managed medically or psychiatrically, then it is imperative that you seek the proper medical help before embarking on these exercises, even if you perceive your pain level to be below a 5 on the Emotional Pain Scale. This does not mean that you cannot do these exercises. It simply means that they need to be conducted when the chemicals in your brain are properly adjusted to allow your processing to be successful.

Here are some further suggestions on how to think of the points between 20 – 80. In this dimension, the midpoint, 50, is considered to be neutral. This also represents calmness. As you move above 50, you are moving into increasing intensity on the dimension's anger side. Mild anger is represented by annoyance or irritation (51-60), and moderate to strong anger (61 – 79) represents balanced processing of emotional pain. Increasing to 80-100 represents rage, which is not healthy nor helpful to you at all. Rage is too intense and can lead to physiological distress.

Now, starting at the midpoint of 50 again and moving into the range below, this represents your range of sadness. As you feel your sadness progress toward zero, monitor it. As you move below the 50 mark, in your awareness, you may feel mildly somber or slightly mournful (40-49). Somewhere between 21 and 39 would be more intense but appropriate grief, sadness, and heartbrokenness. Sadness between 0 and 20 is too extreme and represents despair, where a person becomes devastated, hopeless, or self-punitive. Do not allow yourself to go into this level of intensity because it becomes self-abusive. This is the exact opposite of the intention of these exercises.

Healthy balanced processing of these emotions, sadness and anger, involves the expression of energy being directed outward (out of your body). We must direct this energy outwardly in an appropriate way to avoid allowing it to make us sick. The next steps ahead involve ways to release it by moving it out of your body by expressing it verbally and emotionally.

When you are processing your emotional pain, maintain awareness of your intensity in your feelings and body, and manage them responsibly. Remember, you can't heal if you do not take care of yourself. Whenever you need to, take a break (come up for air), pause, and take some slow deep breaths. Also, apply some of the cognitive tools and scriptures from the previous chapter as you work through your pain. Periodically throughout this work, use these strategies to pull yourself back to neutrality and calmness in between expression of anger and sadness. This process is an ebb and flow.

A good analogy is childbirth. Notice that labor pains come in waves followed by periods of respite? Can it be any clearer that there is a reason for an ebb and flow of pain work from the very beginning? How horrible would it be if the process of child labor and delivery involved one huge insurmountable pain all at once with only one gigantic push – no preparation, no gradual path of intensity? You do not need to process your emotional pain all in one large dose. *Pace yourself!*

Another important point in keeping yourself in balance as you work through unfinished emotion is to be aware of your most common emotional tendency. For instance, if you find it easier to be angry and you tend to avoid getting in touch with sadness, then you actually need to work a little bit more within the sadness dimension than you would likely want to. Remember to keep the intensity range here between 21-49. If you find it easier to shed tears, then you need to learn to safely get in touch with your anger, keeping the intensity range between 51-79, as you process your feelings in these exercises. We all tend to lean toward either sadness or anger at one end of the spectrum more than the other depending on our comfort zone, but it is important for all of us to work through our pain with balance, processing both the anger and the sadness.

Lock Box

You may reach a point where you feel like you have worked on enough for now. Any remaining and unfinished emotional pain can be set aside for a later time when you are rested or ready to work further. Using your imagination, create a box or vase of your own preference. Design it in whatever form you want and create a top with a lock on it. It can be ornate or made of heavy steel – it is up to you. Some trauma theories call it a Container,[lxv] and others have referenced the idea of a God Box.[lxvi] This is your box, to name and design as you wish.

At intervals, when you are ready to stop for a while, put all of the remaining pain into this box, close the lid, and set it aside . You can lock it away until you are ready to deal with it the next time.

Figure C
Emotional Repair Dimension
(Subjective)

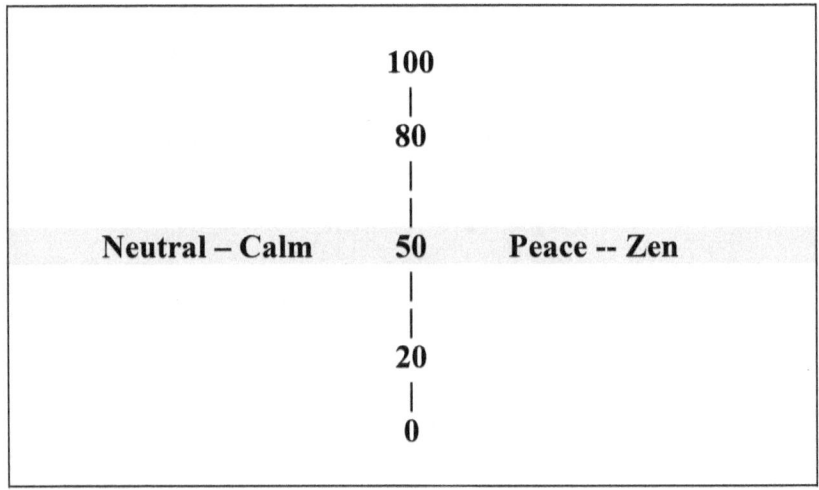

Instructions:

Do not let your emotions rise above 80 or fall below 20 in intensity on the Emotional Repair Dimension as you are processing emotional pain. If you feel overwhelmed, immediately move back to your Safe Oasis that you first created before starting these exercises. You do not have to get rid of all of the pain at once. Listen to your own sense of limit and respect it. Getting overwhelmed is not helpful. If necessary, put anything remaining into a box that you can create through imagery, secure it, and re-open at a later time.

Empowerment

After processing both sadness and anger, within the balanced intensity described above, you can begin to speak empowering statements out loud that help you to claim your victory over the situation. For instance, declare that the situation, loss, and/or person is not going to steal your life. State out loud and even shout if you need to that you are taking your power back. Say out loud that you are also taking back your health/freedom/dignity and that the situation or person no longer has any power over you. You can also claim out loud some of the promises in scripture, such as, 'No weapon forged against [me] shall prevail!' '[I am] sanctified and made whole!' 'He has removed [my mistakes] as far as the east is from the west!' as you reclaim and retake your God-given destiny.

The Rhythm of Pacing and Containing

In any of the work in this book, pace yourself. If you begin to feel tired or overwhelmed, you can also put the remainder of the pain in the box that you created to reserve for more work later. This is different from stuffing your emotions because you are conceptualizing it as outside of your body or soul and are planning to return to continue processing it at another appropriate time. This is known as Pacing and Containing. When you have a project to do at work, are you required to complete the entire thing all in one day without even taking a lunch break? No. Neither is healing work intended to be accomplished in a single sitting.

Next Steps

Before we embark on doing the exercises in this chapter, there an important task that I believe may enhance your healing further. It involves your spiritual perceptions and is an awareness task to help you clarify those perceptions. Some of this work invites you to assess and possibly re-examine your perceptions of yourself and others, as well as God, Christ, or Higher Power. Whether Christian or not, other religious affiliation or not, atheist or not, I invite you to examine the Spiritual Awareness Exercise ahead, as this awareness may translate over into *ALL* of your relationships.

SPIRITUAL AWARENESS EXERCISE/ASSESSMENT

Spiritual Perception

What is your concept of the Creator? If you have been hurt or misled by humans, you may have formed a slightly (or grossly) skewed vision of God. We have all been exposed to human foolishness and misguidance at one time or another. Some humans in authority and some religious leaders have exploited and abused their power throughout history. This can make it hard for a person to want to ever connect with a deity of any kind. Take a moment and walk through this first exercise to allow you the chance to reexamine any distortions that you may have been given or adopted along the way.

In recovery, the Creator is referred to as the Higher Power for a number of reasons. One reason is to respect the different understandings that people may have of this being who presides overall. This title is also used because some of the traditional labels for God have become triggering for some who may have experienced spiritual abuse. Sometimes misguided people have imposed inaccurate interpretations of God upon others, giving them a distorted impression. Having an untainted view of God/Creator/Higher Power can help you reach a higher level of safety, healing, and power. If you are not ready for this step, it is okay. I only mention it here because I would like for you to be able to heal spiritually as well as emotionally.

The exercise in the next paragraphs below, I refer to as the Spiritual Awareness Exercise, provides an opportunity for you to examine your perception of God. Notice the four questions below. Use a separate sheet of paper for each question. The first ones ask for you to list the features – both positive and negative about your parents and any caretakers to whom you were attached during childhood. Blend all your caretakers together as you do this exercise. The next questions ask for you to describe your positive and negative perceptions about God. Include your experiences encountered (prayers answered or not answered). These four items are shown below on one page; however, it is recommended for you to list all four of these features on four separate sheets of paper.

Spiritual Awareness Exercise

Feel free to do these exercises to sort out and remove any incorrect perceptions that you may have transferred to God, others, or yourself. Re-connecting to a Being much greater than ourselves serves as a great resource for recovery. Allowing positive resources of healthy peers, professionals, and therapeutic organizations into your life can lift you up and free you.

Use a separate sheet of paper for each question

1. Blending your Parents/Caretakers/Attachment figures:

A) Describe the **positive features** about them. Include all relevant interactions and experiences.

B) Describe the **negative features** of these caretakers

Include all relevant interactions and experiences.

C) Describe the **positive features of your early (or later) understanding of God or Higher Power**. Include your experiences and encounters (i.e., prayers answered, etc.).

D) Describe the **negative features of your early (or later) understanding of God or Higher Power.** Include your experiences and encounters (i.e., prayers unanswered, etc.).

Assessing Your Spiritual Awareness

Align the sheets of paper with caretakers side by side with the features of the Higher Power. Now examine all of the positive and negative features, comparing your caretakers with your perception of God or Higher Power.

Focus on your perceived experiences, knowing that the intention of the caretaker may or may not have deliberately been negative or hurtful. Alternatively, if the intention of that caretaker may have actually been negative, it is important for you to understand that the pain that they were spewing at you was coming from their own pain reservoir and was totally not mean for you.

Unfortunately, we are raised by humans with all their imperfections and flaws. What happened to you *was and is not* your fault. The only reason that you did not receive whatever it was you needed from that caretaker (love, respect, patience, value, safety) is *not* because of you. It was because that ingredient was simply *not there within that person*. You had nothing to do with it and are still worthy of those wonderful, loving ingredients.

After you have listed everything that you can think of, both positive and negative, about your parents/caretakers and about God on separate pages, now align the pages together. Look at the contrasts or similarities between your parents or caretakers with those of God. Do some of the positives match? More importantly, do some of these perceptions of negativity align between your early authorities and God? Do some of these features also seem to shape your own self-perception? Remember, these are *your* perceptions and interpretations. These do not necessarily reflect the actual intention of those in your life. As you go through some of this work, leave an open place in your mind for the possibility that any negative perceptions about God may have been transferred, from negative experiences that you had with parents or caretakers, and placed onto your mental picture of God.

We sometimes project our caretakers' face onto God. What contrasts or differences do you see? How may some of these perceptions between parent vs. God be separated? Do you see any negative perceptions and interpretations that you may have transferred onto the Creator or also onto yourself? Take time to get to know yourself better and also get to know your Higher Power. You may find a different picture by removing any of the negative narratives that may have pervaded your life.

Examples

As a child, when I wanted to talk to my mother, she was often rushing to get the meal ready, so her back was often turned to me; she was distracted and not listening. This was not intentionally negative. She was trying to cook for the family and was not aware of the mound of interpretations that I was forming in my young mind. *I must not be important. I am not worth listening to.* I projected all of these perceptions onto myself, others, and God. I used to be timid in public speaking and petrified to speak up in meetings most of the time. Throughout much of my young adult life, I assumed that God was too busy to listen to my prayers. I pictured Him busy, uninterested, and my prayers being too trivial for Him.

Another example is, throughout my mid-thirties, I was reluctant to yield or allow God to have full control over my life. I always wanted to hold back some of the control. I had goals and was determined that no one was going to obstruct them. I did not trust God completely because I thought that if I yielded my will to His, I would have to forfeit all of my goals and dreams to a life of meaninglessness. My religious instruction, while growing up, involved humility and self-denial to an extreme. When circumstances in my life changed dramatically and I decided to let go of that piece of control and allow Him to take over, life actually improved. I have reached my goals and dreams better *with* Him in driver's seat than without.

This belief that I had was unconscious partially. I just assumed God was that way because a number of the people in my life who represented Him had been that way. Many of the people I encountered who were religious were also controlling, so I thought *that* was what Christianity was. Although I had loving parents and faithfully attended and served in church most of my life, I had unconsciously blended my perception of God with the some of those people. In particular, a distant relative, whose perception of God was very skewed and who did not act like God, had been a brief but substantial influence in my life.

It was not until my late 40s and early 50s that I really got to know God more accurately. When life had swept the entire rug out from under me, the only thing left supporting me was the hand of God. This semi-conscious perception moved into my awareness, and I realized that he is not like many of the religious people I had encountered from the past. I discovered that 1) God is not a control freak, 2) God is not neurotic, and 3) God *really does* care about our plight here on earth.

So, What *IS* God Really Like?

If we are going to identify the many ways that God is different from our original caretakers (i.e. what God is *Not*), then Who is and What *IS* He Like? The Bible gives us several descriptions of God. God is Spirit (John 4:24). He is a Creator; thus, He has creativity (Genesis 1:1). He is strong (1 Chronicles 16:11) and immortal (1 Timothy 1:17). God is light and has no darkness in Him at all (1 John 1:5). The counsel He provides is so wise that it stands forever (Psalm 33:11) and proves to be perfect, true, and a shield for our protection (Psalm 18:30). He is everlasting, untiring, and profoundly intelligent (Isaiah 40:28).

He is Good. He is the provider of every good gift (James 1:17). His Holy Spirit is described as having love, joy, peace, patience, kindness, goodness, and faithfulness (Galatians 5:22). Hebrews 1:3 (NIV) states, "The Son (Jesus) is the radiance of God's glory and the exact representation of his being, sustaining all things by his powerful word. After he had provided purification for sins, he sat down at the right hand of the Majesty in heaven."

He is loving and merciful toward us. He is more interested in the state of our heart than surface, outer appearances (1 Samuel 16:7). He loves us deeply and generously (John 3:16). He is fair and reasonable in that when Jesus walked the earth, He was tempted in all ways that we are tempted; yet God provides us a way out of those temptations (1 Corinthians 10:13). He is not overbearing or burdensome in His requirements for us (1 John 5:3). When we do make mistakes, He is faithful and just to forgive us and He cleanses us completely from all our wrongs (1 John 1:9). In fact, God is merciful and forgiving to us before we can even measure up and before we have even earned it. Romans 5:7-8 (NIV) says, "Very rarely will anyone die for a righteous person, though for a good person someone might possibly dare to die. But God demonstrates his own love for us in this: While we were still sinners, Christ died for us." Forever He is faithful and loyal to us; He will not lie to us (Numbers 23:19), He does not change His mind (Numbers 23:19), and He will never leave us (Hebrews 13:5). God keeps His promises to us, is patient with us, and wants us to be restored (2 Peter 3:9). His word is truth (John 17:17).

He is fiercely protective of you and will come to your rescue as a strong and mighty refuge. It states in Deuteronomy 33:27 (NIV) "The eternal God is your refuge, and underneath are the everlasting arms. He will drive out your enemies before you, saying, 'Destroy them!'" He is Holy (Isaiah 6:3), everlasting (Psalm 90:2), and unchanging (Hebrews 13:8, Malachi 3:6).

Has your impression of God been misrepresented? Or has it been tainted by people who have a distorted view of Him, themselves? Religion is to be differentiated from relationship and it is important to realize that these religious misrepresentations come from people and not from God. These perceptions are different from the actual person and personality of God. I invite you to take some time to explore who He *really* is and what He is like. You can do that by reading the New Testament or by talking to people who seem to be emotionally and spiritually healthy in their relationship with God. You can also do this by beginning to talk to Him (or talk to Him more).

Further Assessment

Now, mentally compare all of these features with people in your life today. Do you see any parallels from your listed features of your original caretakers as compared to your perception of other people in your life today? Original interpretations such as these can have a pervasive impact on how we perceive and interpret God and how we perceive and interpret others in our life. We may misperceive the intentions of our partners, friends, or bosses when they, in fact, are actually not intending our harm. We tend to put the originator's face onto God, friends, spouses, etc., and rob ourselves from knowing the true person and relationship that exists right there in front of us.

This also applies internally as well. We often treat ourselves as we felt treated (i.e., self-neglect, harshness, etc.) and even sometimes select partners, friends, and work environments that recreate the same dynamic. These may be people who do have intent for harm, because of their own issues.

Taking this further, ask yourself if you have been treating yourself with the same neglect by ignoring your feelings and needs or selected abusive people in your life? From the upbringing of an absent parent, did you, perhaps form an opinion that God is also too busy for you? If abandoned by a parent or loved one early in life, did that absence translate over into a belief that no one is there or that God is not real? Perhaps your memory of your parent or caretaker was one of anger toward you, and therefore your perception of God is one of anger. God is not mad nor too busy for you.[lxvii] In fact, God has an overflowing river of love for you.

Why do we sometimes see God as negative? As human beings, we naturally tend to project whatever style of parenting we received onto the image of God in our minds to some degree or another. If we received great parenting, then we may see the Creator as loving. If our caretakers were too busy for us or abusive, we might see the Creator as unavailable or even scary. We often project an image onto the deity without really taking the time to learn who this deity as a person really is.

If your mother, father, or caretaker hurt you, I can assure you that God is not happy about that either. In Ephesians 6:4, God tells parents not to provoke their children to wrath. Have you ever had someone have a negative, false impression about you, and they would not even talk to you to find out that you are not like what they think you are? Do you recall how that felt? If you have a distorted image of God, I invite you to reexamine this perception.

Sometimes we are disappointed in God. We prayed so hard for that answer, and it did not come about or turn out as we wanted. This can be hard to understand. I have had prayers that were not answered in the direction that I yearned, and I have learned that there are more dimensions to life's circumstances than seen by the human eye. Often the justice is still on its way, but we do not yet see it.

Finally.......The How-To of Forgiveness

EXERCISES TO PROCESS YOUR PAIN

Safety Management

Before we begin, and yes, I will reiterate it here again: do not begin to work on your emotional pain without taking the steps outlined above to assess your pain level and review the sections involving preparation. These exercises are intended to be conducted with a mild and no more than a moderate level of emotional pain if no therapist is present. Chair Imagery Part One, in particular, requires this guideline due to the nature of the emotional processing.

If you do not have a professional available and want to get rid of intense pain (subjectively perceived as above a 5 on the 0 – 10 scale), it is possible to work safely on these issues by moving directly over to Chair Imagery Part Four, skipping the more intense work of Chair Imagery Part One. You may also find that as you successfully process mild to moderately intense pain through all of the exercises and are practicing the Cognitive Shift, your perspective may change, making it easier to process formerly intense events safely, because they are now perceived as less intense than before. Ideally, I hope for you to be able to free your soul from all levels of pain that may be stored inside. Stay encouraged. Even if you are only able to process part of the exercises that follow, God can take whatever amount that you do and work miracles.

Four-Part Process of Emoting: Chair Imagery

The exercises conducted here with the skills described throughout this book are intended to help ameliorate your perceptions and automatic approach to many life events. Do not rush through these exercises. Take plenty of breaks. Return to your Oasis as often as you need to and give yourself a pause, putting the remaining issues aside temporarily as often as needed.

Be honest with yourself in working at your own comfortable pace. You do not have to complete all of the exercises in this chapter to be considered complete in your own unique process with God as your healer. You also do not have to do everything described in these exercises to achieve the maximum benefit. Your pace, your comfort zone, and your timing are all the right pace, zone, and schedule. Also, as you work through any of these steps, you can simply just read a small part, apply that much, and then read the next step. The only requirement is that you keep yourself in a state of emotional safety throughout this entire process.

The exercises that follow stem from some traditional methods and include some additional procedures that I have developed and expanded with the use of guided imagery. It is recommended that you start with a mild hurt to process the forgiveness work first, and as you become accustomed to this way of perceiving and thinking, you can work on more challenging issues. These exercises may help you to experience a reduced impact from other painful experiences going forward.

Who Hurt You?

Pick a person for whom you have had difficulty forgiving. Choose an event with your pain intensity level that is no more than a five on the Emotional Pain Scale shown earlier.

Before you imagine the person sitting there, you may need to imagine a protective boundary between you and that person. This can be a hedge, a fence, a wall, or a host of angels. You can invite Jesus to accompany you. He already knows the depth of how you feel. Use all emotional images that you need to provide yourself with a sense of emotional safety. People also sometimes imagine having a powerful animal, their favorite pet, or a family member as a protective resource. You can choose a trusted friend in person and or a trusted therapist. Use what works best for you.

Remember to Pace yourself

Emote / Vent / Express / Release

In the exercises that follow, with any needed protection in place, you can begin to process your pain and unfinished feelings. I have outlined here some methods, all of which make use of your God-given imagination. Always do these with any and all protections that you need to be placed between you and that person (or situation).

<u>Chair Imagery (Part One)</u>

Imagine a chair in front of you at some comfortable distance across the room. Again, make sure that your pain level from this person does not exceed a five on the Emotional Pain Scale. Next, visualize that person sitting silently in the chair in front of you at a distance that feels safe. See that person sitting in the (empty) chair as silent and attentive, having no rebuttal nor backlash. In this imagery, they are not going to talk back, gaslight you, threaten you, nor abuse you in any way.

The benefits of using this method of getting rid of pain and anger are many. For one, you do not run the risk of having to deal with their retaliation, lame excuses, or false accusations that you might encounter if actually confronting them in person. Also,

God has created our brains to allow us to have the experience of relief without having to actually have the person right in front of us. Here, you can say whatever you have been wanting or needing to say to that person (via imagery) that you cannot say in person. Your brain can feel as if you really did get to have your say to that person. Through this exercise, your whole body can feel a release of emotional pain without having to change the person at all or even get them to hear you. They do not even have to know how you feel in real life for you to get rid of the pain and move past what they have done.

Remember to Pace yourself

Pace yourself by taking slow deep breaths, in between expressions of anger and sadness. Prevent yourself from hyperventilating or becoming overwhelmed and back away if you begin to feel panic. Retreat immediately into your Oasis that you created before beginning this work.

**Note: Chair Imagery Part One is not a practice session for a real-life confrontation.*

Sometimes it is wise not to allow the person actually to know what we have been feeling. In many cases, it could be dangerous actually to confront that perpetrator in real life. In other cases, it may not be useful, or it may unnecessarily burden them. Some people hurt us unintentionally, or they have an ongoing disorder creating significant challenges in their behavior.

Now, visualize that person sitting there in front of you. Notice everything about them. Make the features of this image as specific as possible. Notice their attire, appearance, and facial expression. Notice their apparel, their stature, and, if possible, bring in the memory of their smell. Here in this situation, they are all eyes and all ears. They cannot talk back but only will hear what you have to say. Make the features of this image as specific as possible and tolerable for you.

Process the Anger

Now, tell them everything that you are not able to say to them in person. Tell them in uncensored form. Don't hold back. Tell them off thoroughly. Process the anger that you have been holding onto in your heart (and in your body). Express whatever you have been holding on to. There is no shame in bringing up what has been kept in your heart when you are doing so in order to get rid of it. God already knows what is in there that you need to get rid of. Express, yell, holler, cry, sob - emote. Anger is designed to repair, and this is one form of repair- repair of you. Here is where you get rid of all of the pent-up pain. Medically when a wound is infected, it needs to be drained. Here is where you get to drain out all of the pain. Tell this image of them directly about what they did, didn't do, or should have done.

Process the Sadness

Expressing sadness is also important to balance your emotions by telling them what has you sad, hurt, or disappointed. Allow the tears to flow.

Balance Your Pacing

Continue to protect yourself. This may mean that you have a trusted friend present or, better yet, a trained professional. You can do this verbal exercise out loud or silently without speaking a word, using imagery, giving you more privacy in the presence of whoever is with you.

Process your pain until you feel relief or feel done for now. You may find yourself quite exhausted after this exercise, simultaneously with a nice sense of relief and a weight lifted off of your shoulders. Give yourself time to rest.

Is the Offender Really the Offender?

Take a moment to assess whether the person you are targeting with your anger is really the original offender. Does this recent person remind you of a parent, caretaker, or someone who hurt you long ago? Is part of your anger about something earlier? Who was the first person originally associated with this pain? If it originated from someone earlier or more powerful in your life, the remainder of this work may need to be processed with a professional present or may just need to be set aside for another day.

Sorting out the portion of the pain that is associated with the recent person as opposed to the original person can help prevent you from placing undue, past baggage onto the present individual in your life. It can help you narrow the scope appropriately while working on the more recent pain. If you elect to work on the original and earlier pain, it is much deeper and can provide you a greater benefit. Just remember that the deeper the work, the more the company of a trained therapist is recommended. Don't rush the process. Take care of yourself all the way through.

Chair Imagery (Part Two)

After dealing with the anger and sadness, to the point where you feel relief, now visualize that person in the chair again. This time allow yourself to imagine and see them at the younger age at which their own damage may have occurred. You do not have to know those details about them. You can also ask God to give you insight and perspective into what it was that may have caused them to be that way or was possibly going on within them. *This is the first introduction for you to learn how to perceive them and that situation through God's eyes.*

A Different Perspective

Much of this is through your imagination; however, it is a

reasonable certainty that this person, at some point, did not receive necessary components into their soul that would have led them to behave lovingly. Did they not receive healthy parents, were they traumatized by events, or perhaps do they have a chemical imbalance? Without dismissing their responsibility for their actions, they most likely, have a wounded soul.

Knowing the likelihood that a wounded child resides within them, visualize this part of them sitting right in front of you. You can still keep the boundaries intact that you used in Chair Imagery Part I. Allow yourself to visualize them at that younger age in a state of their woundedness. What do you see with your imagination? Are they five? Are they even younger, an infant alone in a crib? Are they a teen who was abused? Imagine what their spirit and soul look like in this condition. Are they tattered or gaunt? With their soul at this level of deficit, do they look small or frail? Ask God to give you spiritual eyes to see what is likely in their probable original pain and abuses from their own life story. Ask God to give you a glimpse of their soul.

Psychodynamic theory supports the understanding that it is a wounded soul who is running the show in situations that hurt others. Author and theologian John Bradshaw refers to this as a *wounded inner child*.[lxviii] People do not start out in this world intending to cause others pain. The infraction upon them can be at many levels and could originate from child abuse, neglect, or some other trauma during their own lifetime. There could also have been impact in utero, such as drug abuse, loss of oxygen, or lack of nutrients to the fetus.

Now, the purpose of this part of the exercise is not for you to give them a free pass. We are all still responsible for our actions. So, this task is not designed for you to feel guilty for your anger. That would simply be false guilt.

As you visualize them sitting there in that younger state, imagine some of the events that possibly happened to them to make them this hateful or cruel. You may have some idea from what you already know about them. See them sitting there in front of you, still at a safe distance, and with any boundary needed. Notice what you see. Imagine how frail, gaunt, scared, weak, or small they appear in comparison with that outer adult appearance that you encountered. Notice how they do not really have power but were acting out from their own woundedness and the toxicity that was poured into them. This is their wounded inner child.[lxix]

Perspective of Their World View

Again, without excusing their behavior, this is the stage where you can imagine their world view from their own eyes. There are different methods of doing this and you do not have to do all of the methods described in this section. You may do this from a safe distance. You can imagine that God is showing you a video of their past experiences that made them this way. If you are comfortable and depending on who the person is, you can imagine that you are able to stand behind them to see the world through their eyes. If you feel safe enough, you can imagine that you have full-body armor and temporarily slip into their own internal world for a moment, seeing how scared, cold, or empty their world may feel to them. Stay as distant as you need to and continue to keep any emotional, physical, and spiritual boundaries that you need.

Remember, do not do anything that is uncomfortable or feels too intense for you. This is a time to tune in to your feelings and respect them. If you do not want to imagine yourself anywhere near this person, then you can view the video of their world from far away, as if on a distant movie screen.

I do not mind repeatedly saying, **remember to take care of yourself emotionally as you do this work**. It is completely understandable to not want to slip into the psyche of a rapist or someone who hurt your loved one. So, **hear and respect your own feelings and needs.** It is still very revealing to view this information from across the room, while remaining sheltered by a strong boundary.

Now, for just a few moments, as you allow yourself to imagine the world from their own eyes, you may begin to see that they are (most likely) an empty vessel or someone carrying around significant pain (toxins). Children who are abused and mistreated typically internalize those events as evidence that they themselves are *bad*, and they, therefore, sometimes choose behaviors that reinforce their self-concept of *badness*. Imagine these likely deficits in their soul.

Perceiving Now at a Distance

Now move back across the room away from them where you can see them at a distance with all of that information. Notice how empty and baren their soul appears to be. How would that individual *ever* be able to give you what it was that you needed? Where is that love, respect, approval, loyalty, or positive ingredient that you needed to receive from them? Their internal world, soul, and psyche may be so damaged or empty that it is just like an empty vending machine. Would you ever repeatedly continue to put dollars into an empty vending machine, seeing clearly through the glass that there is nothing at all inside?

Continuing in your anger toward them (using your energy to attempt to repair them or the situation) is literally that futile. It becomes clear that you cannot repair this person or situation by continuing to churn that anger through your own soul. In our own power, we cannot get them to change, have remorse, repent, love us, or treat us well. What we were pursuing *is simply* NOT *in there*. Place the image of an empty vending machine superimposed over the image of that person, wounded inner child, or empty soul.

What is very important at this point for you to realize is how - what they did to you was *truly* not about you. It was about them and their distorted world view. You do not have to receive, internalize, nor take in an offense if it was not really about you in the first place. The insult, smear, betrayal, attack was not really targeted for you. You just happened to be the person in the crossfire. Their offense was really for something else or someone else in their own world.

Refuse to allow their offense to have any more room in your soul. Notice that s/he does not really get to have the power that was once claimed. Allow yourself to see that image in all of its weaknesses. It is not yours to fix, and you can hand it over to someone who can.

Ready to really get rid of all of this baggage? Don't stop here. The next step can be the restorative part for you.

Chair Imagery (Part Three)

There is good news found in 1 Peter 5:7 (AMP), "casting all your cares [all your anxieties, all your worries, and all your concerns, once and for all] on Him, for He cares about you [with deepest affection, and watches over you very carefully]." This is what leads us to the best part of this work. To do this next step in the traditional form, you will need a trustworthy perception of God. If you do not have that yet or do not believe in God, you can use an image of someone you trust and perceive as a refuge. If you feel more comfortable selecting a trusted human, it is okay. Just remember, however, that humans are not all-powerful and are sometimes fallible. You can choose a grandparent, a beloved pet, a friend, or your interpretation of a Higher Power. In this next exercise, I am going to use the Christian language; however, you may apply the image of a resource in which you feel comfortable and trust.

Now, visualize that trusted image. Allow yourself to go up into God's chair, His throne in a manner that feels safe and nurturing to you. You may picture yourself being cradled in His strong protective arms. Apply whatever picture and tangible experience that works best for you. See Him gazing into your eyes with a love that goes far beyond anything that you have ever seen before. Hear Him telling you the things you needed to hear from that person (the empty vending machine or wounded soul) who couldn't. Hear the Creator's words of how truly loved and precious you are. Hear the reassurance that your life matters and that you have a unique purpose here on this earth that no one has the power to take away. Hear from Roman 11:29, "For the gifts and calling of God are without repentance" (KJV). Hear Him say that He is with you and that you are never alone. In Deuteronomy 31:6, "Be strong and courageous. Do not be afraid or terrified because of them, for the Lord your God goes with you; he will never leave you nor forsake you" (NIV). Notice as the Creator gazes into your eyes as with a gushing river of love that is richer and deeper than anything you have experienced here on this earth. Notice this flow contains everything that you need as you experience His Respect, Love, Honor, Dignity, Safety, and Validation. Feel it pouring right into your heart and your soul. Here is where you can receive everything you need at any time without a moment's delay.

Sit with this image for as long as you need. This is a part of the exercise that can be repeated at any time at all, and revisited as often as you like. The reality is that this love *IS always present* and waiting for you to plug into, even in the midst of a busy day, a bad experience, or a screaming boss. Plug in and rest whenever you need and as often as you need.

Sometimes even best friends are not available or are carrying burdens themselves at the time we need them. God's Love is always there for you. It remains a constant, available resource, regardless of what images we project onto Him. If you feel that you hate Him, know that He still loves you regardless. In Lamentations 3:22-23, "The steadfast Love of the Lord never ceases. His mercies never come to an end. They are new every morning. Great is (his)faithfulness" (ESV). He waits ready, willing, and available to supply everything you need right there at the moment – right at the very second. He is there to provide us with unconditional love, respect, and dignity - even if we do not feel it. In Revelation 3:20, Jesus said, "Here I am! I stand at the door and knock. If anyone hears my voice and opens the door, I will come in and eat with that person, and they with me" (NIV). Earth is imperfect. The best of best friends, husbands, wives, bosses, or parents cannot always intuitively give us precisely what we need at times. God is a constant available resource where we can receive faithfully, continually, and reliably when we ask.

If you do not feel worthy of calling on Him to ask for what you need, remember that He has removed all of your transgressions from you as far as the east is from the west (Psalms 103:12 NKJV). Therefore, the guilt you may be carrying is *false guilt*. Jesus said in Matthew 23:37, "How often I have longed to gather your children together as a hen gathers her chicks under her wings, and you were not willing" (NIV).

Soak in this love and acceptance from God, your Higher Power, that He has been wanting to wrap you up in. He has patiently waited for you to ask. Allow yourself to see the beam of love in His eyes as His Love flows from His heart into yours and He gazes at your sweet face, sweetly reflected in His eyes. Take in as much as you need and for as long as you need. Repeat it as often as you need to. This may have been very long overdue.

Chair Imagery (Part Four)

After absorbing all that you need from the Creator, looking back down at the person in that chair at a distance from you, let's take care of the last step. While returning to the room and noticing the chair in front of you, lift that person, job, marriage, spouse, boss, child of yours, or enemy that you have been formerly hurt by and hand them over to God. Hand over to Him ALL of those things that you cannot control, fix, repair, or change. Take the person who was in the chair (that full-grown adult and wounded inner child) and all those hurts and send them directly up to God.

1 Peter 5:7 (KJV)

"Casting all your care upon him; for he careth for you."

Occasions to Bypass Chair Imagery One and Two

You may also be able to include, in Chair Imagery Part Four, some of those bigger hurts (with emotional pain ranging from 6-10), if you are not ready for the emotional intensity of the early phase in chair imagery part one. You don't necessarily have to process the anger and sadness before giving anything directly over to God. Sometimes if the pain is too intense and there is not a professional available, there is nothing wrong with just handing over those big hurts directly to God without going through Chair Imagery One and Two.

Hand over to Him all of those broken pieces of things that happened, disappointments, the broken marriage, the child that died, the broken trust. Allow Him to make a great exchange for you. Give over to Him the broken pieces and disappointments of your life and allow Him to take them and make them into something beyond what you could ever imagine. He will give you beauty for those ashes (Isaiah 61:3).

Reasons for Praying for those Who Hurt Us

These exercises may make it easier to understand praying for our enemies. When you *really* know 1) they are wounded, 2) what they did is NOT about you (but is about something wrong within them), and 3) you don't need for the recompense to come from them because 4) you can receive *everything you need* from God, this breaks their power over you. When we pray for our enemies, we are praying for God to give them what they truly need. Things they need are 1) to be made aware of the gravity of their deeds, 2) lessons taught with experiences that only God can give, and 3) removal of the toxicity that had poisoned their soul so that they may change.

It is not our job to fix them and what a relief that is. When you live in a place of freedom from having to worry about them or be the one to take revenge, you have peace and can rise higher into the level of forgiveness discussed in the next chapter, which I refer to as H.O.P.E. To do this, you must also learn self-forgiveness.

Self-Forgiveness

The Root Intention

Sometimes as Christians, we think that being punitive with ourselves is being humble and holy. It is not. It is actually a form of self-abuse and possibly arrogance. Self-forgiveness is not the same thing as giving yourself a free pass nor indulgence for wrong-doing. Self-forgiveness still includes accountability for one's actions and making amends when merited.

The self-forgiveness that I discuss here involves a deeper look that can help you gain understanding and direction toward healing. We are typically so much harder on ourselves than on others, and this robs us. We not only rob ourselves of the awareness that can help us to be healthier internally, but we also rob everybody else because we deplete our ability to help others effectively. So please, at least for the sake of others, decide to let go of your inappropriate self-punishment.

Just as the other person who hurt you was misguided by their own wounded inner child; your own mistakes are the result of similar misguidedness. If you look at the intention beneath your actions, you can often trace it to a basic root that can be understood through the eyes of mercy – through God's eyes.

What are your intentions underlying the action? For instance, if your action was rooted in fear, this is not to be judged as cowardice. It could easily have been self-preservation, which is a natural survival instinct. Perhaps you were afraid of being alone or rejected, yet your action on the surface appeared selfish. Your actions may have been rooted in an attempt for survival (emotionally, physically, spiritually). God instilled within us an instinct to survive, because He wants us to live. If you just remain focused on the surface action, judging and condemning yourself, you will never get to the root beneath the action.

Why should I pay attention to myself? Wouldn't that be selfish? The Webster definition of selfishness involves an excessive concern for oneself <u>at the exclusion of others</u>. This is not at all what I am talking about here. If you are unwilling to tune into awareness of your own feelings, needs, and wounds your radar will be distorted. This can lead to poor decision-making. You can miss out on intuitive wisdom because part of that wisdom comes from divine alignment and intuition. You may fail to accurately interpret the guidance of the Holy Spirit because self-condemnation may cloud your judgment and block this connection. Without awareness of the needs, intentions, and hurts inside of us, we set up blinders and limits on our ability to help others. If you are accustomed to ignoring your daily needs, this can also translate into you also squelching your own children and loved ones' spoken needs.

I believe that every misguided action is rooted in a wound or a need that is buried beneath the surface. Continuing to just beat yourself up for this only perpetuates the problem. By ignoring your own buried pain or need, you are doing nothing but self-neglect. This not only robs you of relationships, but it also robs the other person from the blessing that you can be to them. It steals from you *and* them.

Learn to tune to your needs, intentions, fears, and emotions for the purpose of choosing a healthy action. We do not need to act directly on our emotions or let them govern us, but we need to weigh this information in the process of balanced decision-making. Through deeper awareness in this form, one can discover more effective responses and choices, which can benefit everyone.

Repair

As you soul-search for the root of your regret, you may find an area of repair that is needing to be addressed. This can be an important step in self-forgiveness. The 12 steps in recovery programs recognize the need for awareness of issues within oneself, yet this is done with acceptance rather than condemnation. Considering the passage, "Therefore, there is now no condemnation for those who are in Christ Jesus" (Romans 8:1, NIV). Making amends in this manner is constructive repair. As a major step in recovery is to make amends, this may be a part of your own self-forgiveness process, as well.

There are a number of ways to make these amends. One method can be in person; however, consult with a trusted professional before you attempt to interface with someone who may meet your attempt with hostility or harm. Sometimes it is not safe for you to emotionally or physically make amends face-to-face. You do not always have to do this in person.

For some situations, it may be too painful to the recipient to have the memory brought back up to them in person. You can use one of the chair exercises described below to make amends without the person having to be present. The other person may not want to forgive you and may become very abusive if you mention the incident. Nevertheless, know that you do not have to depend upon their forgiveness of you, for you to heal and forgive yourself.

Sometimes, the situation does not seem repairable. In these

cases, you can ask God to do the repair that you could not do. You can be amazed at the miraculous things that God can do. In the chair exercises, you can deliberately give over to God those areas that you cannot fix.

Decision

Much of self-forgiveness begins with a deliberate act of decision. You begin to refuse to abuse yourself by beating yourself up or replaying past mistakes. You replace these old thoughts with new realistic and self-forgiving ones.

Before you do the exercises on self-forgiveness, please make a firm decision to refuse to abuse, abandon, or punish yourself in any way. Realize how loved and cherished you truly are by God. Also, consider the fact that you would *never* want a child or loved one of yours to be berating themselves in the way that you are berating yourself. Forgiveness of yourself frees up a wealth of energy for you to heal, grow, and help others around you as well.

Exercise in Self-Forgiveness

Again, remember to include supportive and or professional help for any work that may be painful. Now, let's imagine a different chair. Visualize yourself sitting in that new chair in front of you. Pick your disappointment (level 0-5 intensity). Take time to apply all relevant senses to this imagery, such as sight, sound, smell, kinesthetics. What do you see? How old are you in this chair?

You will not vent toward yourself in this exercise, as in Chair Imagery One described above, because it is likely that you have been doing that in your mind already if you need this exercise. We will proceed with gentleness, insight, and mercy in the exercises on self-forgiveness.

Next, as you visualize yourself in the chair across from you, ask yourself about the first time that you ever felt this way or made this type of mistake. Examine the underlying motive or intention beneath your action that you regret having done. In asking yourself when the first time (earlier in your life) was that you ever felt this same way, notice what was going on during that time in your life. Did this earlier time contribute to your recent mistake? See if you can connect with that early memory or feeling state involving the first time that you made this mistake. What was happening in the context of that earlier time? Were you misled? Were you intimidated or abused? Were you confused?

Now, reduce that image of your adult self to that child you once were at that earlier age. Examine the first time it all started. **You _must_ address yourself from the standpoint of compassion and nurturance in this exercise.** If you cannot do this exercise with emotional safety or if you find yourself becoming harsh with yourself, stop the exercise immediately and only continue this work with a seasoned professional present.

With this image of your wounded child in front of you, tune in to the original feelings from the standpoint of a child's thought process. You may have acted out of fear, desperation, or hurt. Identify the root of your mistake. This is most likely to come from a very well-intentioned foundation originally. Recognize this child's (your) positive, well-meaning intention and give that part of you the nurturance and mercy that is long overdue. Spend enough time telling that child part of you (telling yourself) the loving, supportive messages that you needed at that time.

Recognize that your intentions were not wrong. Self-preservation and safety are God-given instincts. Tell yourself some of these statements below:

- I know you were scared. I will begin to learn how to take care of you now.
- I know that you did not want to do harm but just wanted that person to understand how much they hurt you. I will now provide you with the constructive

things that you needed and did not get then.
- I am making a decision to stop being mad at, harsh with, and critical toward you.
- You are a good girl/boy/person.
- I love you.
- I am willing to learn how to love and be kind to you.
- I will learn how to help you make better decisions and will be patient with you.

Recognize in the original scene any adult who may have been responsible, yet you have perceived the event as all your fault. Take time to review and re-interpret the original situation correctly. Children are not powerful yet tend to absorb blame for events that they could not stop or prevent. Examples of these dialogues could be:

- It is not your fault that your sister got hurt.

- You were a child who was placed in the position of an adult, and this was not fair to you nor realistic.

- I will stop expecting you to do what you cannot do.

- I will begin to show you and learn how to make more realistic choices.

Next, allow yourself to imagine that you and this part of you are floating up toward Heaven, where you see the throne of God. If this image is difficult, you can also imagine yourself approaching whatever you perceive as a trusted resource. This can be your older, wiser self in the distance or a trusted friend. Whether your imagery involves God, some other form of Higher Power, or an older, wiser version of yourself, ***the dialogue MUST be nurturing.*** See yourself wrapped in their arms. If this is too intense, see yourself sitting near or in front of them. Allow yourself to receive the love, support, and encouragement that you missed during this stage of your childhood. Take as much time as you need to constructively re-parent yourself in the areas of woundedness and unfinished nurturing that you need. Parenting yourself involves two components: 1) nurturing (forgiveness) and 2) edification (education about how to behave more constructively in the future). This is all conducted within a spirit of love and support toward yourself (and that wounded inner child of yours). It is never too late to decide to take charge of the unfinished business and receive what you needed, that the parent or care-taker was not equipped to give you at the time.

Internal emotional security can be increased through the next phase of this exercise. To the degree that is comfortable for you, imagine being held, cradled, and cherished by God for the very one that you are. Feel His mighty strong arms protectively around you and see His river of Love flowing from His eyes into your heart. You can also visualize that you are receiving this unconditional love from your older, wiser self, a loving grandparent, or another trustworthy one. Appendix A has further guided imagery on self-forgiveness.

Healing Examples

More about Monique

Remember Monique? One day when she attended a support group for eating disorders, she began to hear story after story of girls who had been in similar situations. Suddenly, her greatest healing and clarity began as she discovered that she was not alone. This was the start of her journey out of the clutches of dark clouds of abuse and oppression.

Before this revelation, she had resorted to other healthy escapes during the meantime. When younger, during the middle of the night, she would walk down to a nearby pond in their neighborhood, where it was quiet, and she felt safe. At times Jesus would give her the sweetest image in her mind, showing her that all of her loving pets (that had mysteriously gone missing at the hands of her father) were safe and protected under the hand of Jesus. She had created coping tools by her own resourcefulness and with Christ, but she had one missing component. It was the needed connection of others who had walked where she had walked. She needed people for support. Her first experience in joining group support provided the additional solace that she had been missing.

Derek and Jacqueline

Jacqueline experienced reoccurring pain from Derek over and over again for a number of years. As one issue seemed to get resolved, a new one emerged. Since the events involved a threat to their son's safety, life, and the mother-and-son relationship, the emotional stress was very strong. The level of your emotional intensity has a direct relationship to the level of the personal importance of that issue.

Jacqueline had learned early to process her pain and to get rid of anger as soon as she had the opportunity to do so outside of work and family time. When she found a private moment, she would go into the garage where they had a bat and a punching bag. She would pick up the bat and voice phrases to help her overcome fear, as she released her anger energy onto the bag. This allowed her to get that emotion out of her body and discharge it onto a neutral object without harming property and without taking it out on another human being. While doing this activity, she would voice proclamations out loud, laying claim to her determination to protect her son and prevent Derek from getting under her skin.

Jacqueline also made a point to make sure that she continually kept her cup full from God, others, and herself. She began every morning having time with God. She frequently scheduled nurturing and recharge time for herself. She also regularly reached out to friends and family for support throughout the years of this tribulation. She was eternally grateful for the friends who courageously attended court with her, stood by her, and helped her face him.

Dayle

For a while, even though Dayle was a believer in God, He was not a part of her life. This stemmed from the distance and rejection she had felt from her mother, which was transferred onto God as she unconsciously assumed that God must feel the same way about her that her mother did. Dayle did the above work and began to see her mother as an empty vessel. She learned that her mother's mother had been jealous of her also when she was born and mistreated her mother throughout the years. Therefore, Dayle's mother did not know how to relate to a female. The likely reason that Dayle's mother had wanted a boy was that her mother possibly feared the same rejection that might come from a female child, just like it came from her own mother. It was in this area that Dayle's mother had been empty – the unconditional love had not been poured into Dayle's mother, making it difficult for her to give Dayle the unconditional love that she lacked.

She also began to learn that her experiences she received from her mother were different from those that come from God. She began to separate her earthly parent from her perception of the Spiritual Parent, knowing that she <u>can</u> receive everything she needs from God. Both therapy and support groups showed her how to trust God and to know Him personally.

Although her mother has since passed away, she has forgiven her. Once she began to receive love from God and take on the responsibility to give love to herself (through her inner positive thought life and healthy choices for herself), she became strengthened. Through imagery, she was able to imagine her own mother as the newborn infant that did not receive love from her own mother (Dayle's grandmother). Now she understood how her mother had been so deeply deprived and empty, seeing her own mother as the vulnerable and *helpless infant devoid of unconditional love. It became clear that there was no way that her (empty) mother could have provided that type of love for her, deprived during her own childhood. During a guided imagery, Dayle visualized her mother that infant right in front of her, and began to pour the needed compassion and love into her own mother as she saw her in this vulnerable helpless state.*

By doing this, Dayle became empowered. She moved herself from a position of deficit, lacking, and need to a position of abundance, giving, and power. Before making this transition, Dayle's ability to give and receive love had been blocked. As her heart opened in this way, she became able to begin mending her relationship with her own child. This is how doing a deep forgiveness process, not only frees you, but it also gives you back more than what you lost.

This work can impact a change in your life going forward as you clear out old pain from the past and maintain wholeness in the present. It is our responsibility as adults to be a healthy parental figure for ourselves, and that can include re-parenting our self if needed. This is accomplished by two forms of self-parenting: 1) pouring kindness and love into our own soul (nurturance) and 2) self-directed limit-setting guidance (management of behavioral choices), just as you would when raising a child. When you begin to love and appropriately parent yourself, this can domino forward preventing skewed perceptions, misinterpretations, and poor choices in your life. You get to take over the task of what you may have missed out on from your childhood. You can then begin to handle life's events from an emotional and spiritual place of strength instead of weakness. It is our own responsibility to make sure our cup remains full. When you realize that God has given you a reservoir from which to supply everything you need; you can approach difficulties and injustices from a place of wholeness and strength. This happens more and more as we continue to grow. Let's take a look at what this can look like, going forward.

Chapter 7

Tier III:
A Higher Order Perspective Existence (H.O.P.E.)
Bullet Proof, Powerful, and Beyond
(Tier III Level of Forgiveness)

Psalm 91:1,2 (AMP)

"He who dwells in the secret place of the Most High shall remain stable and fixed under

The shadow of the Almighty [Whose power no foe can withstand].

I will say of the Lord, He is my Refuge and my Fortress, My God; on Him I lean and rely,

and in Him I [confidently] trust!"

Luke 10:19 (NKJV)

Behold, I give you the authority to trample on serpents and scorpions, and over all the power of the enemy, and nothing shall by any means hurt you.

Psalm 112:7-8 (ESV)

⁶For the righteous will never be moved; he will be remembered forever.

⁷ He is not afraid of bad news; his heart is firm, trusting in the LORD.

⁸His heart is steady; he will not be afraid, until he looks in triumph on his adversaries.

Imagine that you are in a movie called your life. You have now learned to see everything through God's eyes. Everything that happens to you, you can see from a higher and multidimensional perspective. Faith-based thinking is now automatic and second nature for you. As you walk on the pathway of your life, you are entirely focused, eyes forward, totally committed to your purpose in this life, and unimpressed by the futile distractions that attempt to pull you aside. You are virtually unshakeable. You briefly notice but are unfettered by the bullets, darts, and spears that are bouncing off your chest and shoulders. You are fully focused on more important things within your sights in front of you - your calling here on this earth, your mission, your purpose - and you are virtually impenetrable emotionally and spiritually.

Fiction? No. Possible? Yes. As we grow spiritually, we learn to see a much bigger picture than the tiny detail of what is happening to us at the moment. Jesus exemplified this way of dealing with the world, and the closer you become to Christ and develop a relationship with the one who made you, the better you can rise to this ultimate level of existence. Can we do this perfectly? No, because we are human. This chapter is designed to show you how to make this level of perceiving, thinking, and functioning an increasingly automatic emotional place of existence. This level involves thinking beyond the here and now, beyond yourself, and beyond the current dimension. This perspective creates a place of ultimate peace.

Tier III is the level of forgiveness that I believe many Christians strive to do on a regular basis. It is forgiving immediately – *truly* forgiving quickly. The difference is that you now can immediately filter things that happen to you through what you have learned. You filter your surroundings through the eyes of the Holy Spirit so that most events do not even reach the initial point of personal offense. With few exceptions, emotional pain does not develop in the first place and is, therefore, not stuffed in your body. There is no anger to go underground. In these cases, invitations for anger, offense, and hurt bounce off you before even having a chance to penetrate your heart or soul. This does not mean that you are not moved emotionally or responsive to humane issues; you just no longer give the enemy a foothold into your soul.

You can develop to the point that many offenses, other than substantial traumas, do not impact you. Although the substantial trauma may still need to be processed with grieving and healing, it may lay less claim to your life, have a shorter period of pain, and inflict less impact than before. The following is designed to show you how to achieve this level of forgiveness.

What is a Higher Order Perspective Existence (H.O.P.E.)?

I have called this emotional and spiritual place a Higher Order Perspective Existence because it involves an existence on an emotional and spiritual plain, where you rise above what is happening to you in the present moment. Your perception expands beyond the situation to see the bigger picture from a higher and multidimensional perspective. This happens through growth and maturity. The closer you get to the Creator personally, the more readily you begin to see events through the eyes of God. This chapter goes beyond the cognitive tools in this book and into the Spiritual to help you develop a multidimensional approach to experiencing life events.

This level does not negate the reality that on earth, sometimes things happen that require a grieving process. As you recall, Jesus wept (John 11:35). There are legitimate times where you must grieve before moving back into a place of H.O.P.E. For such events, I refer you back to the chapter on grief work and also remind you that Jesus did not negate emotion (John 11:35). Therefore, remember that Tier III does not involve an instruction for you to avoid your emotions, as they can provide you with information and intuition. This level of functioning does not involve a detachment of your feelings (remember God gave you feelings for a reason) nor a blind eye to what is happening around you. You can be keenly aware of the events in your surroundings yet have an awareness that expands beyond merely the single dimension seen by the human eye.

This perspective also does not omit our responsibility in our interactions. While it is true that we do not have the power to cause that person's emotions or angry response, we do have a responsibility to manage our own actions constructively. Therefore, this perspective does not mean that you walk around insensitive to the plight of others. We are still to walk in love (Ephesians 5:2, Colossians 3:14 NKJV).

When you begin to see things through spiritual eyes, you *will* begin to tune in to a bigger picture of plausible issues that are likely to have influenced the offender's behavior. Thus, this is a lifestyle of thinking and perceiving in such a way that provides you protection emotionally and spiritually, with H.O.P.E. throughout your life.

You still have the full range of choices in your response depending on the situation. If you look closely at the life of Jesus, you will see that he felt and expressed emotions at times. He also made decisions about responses to attacks from others, depending upon the situation. In some instances, He provided an answer, and in others, he denied the accusers a response. In another situation, He ducked out of the crowd to avoid violence against Himself, and while in the Garden of Gethsemane, He yielded himself to save the world. There are times to be open and responsive, and there are times to set boundaries. The Higher Order Perspective Existence is an emotional place in which we can assess the situation through spiritual eyes, maintain emotional stability through a healthy cognitive perspective, and exercise a response guided by spiritual wisdom.

This approach to life involves several dimensions within your interpretation of events and multifaceted resources from which to draw strength. For instance, your level of thinking, perceiving, and responding includes the factual, the physical, the emotional, the social, the historical, the practical, and the spiritual. Suppose Cognitive Shift (Chapter 5) has now become automatic and second nature for you. In that case, you will be able to choose an interpretation of the present event that is not only plausible from a reality standpoint but is also helpful rather than hurtful. This guides your emotions toward peace and confidence. As you grow closer in relationship with God, He equips you further in your relationship with His own Spirit that dwells within you, giving you a peace that surpasses all understanding (Philippians 4:7) and power to override fear and conquers obstacles (Acts 1:8). The Holy Spirit brings comfort in trials and strength within disaster.

John 14:26 (AMP)

"But the Helper (Comforter, Advocate, Intercessor—Counselor, Strengthener, Standby), the Holy Spirit, whom the Father will send in My name

[in My place, to represent Me and act on My behalf],

He will teach you all things.

And He will help you remember everything that I have told you."

At this level, you can see beyond just that angry person or that bad situation in front of you. In this higher level of this emotional and spiritual perspective, your cognitions (thoughts, perceptions, beliefs, and interpretations) generate emotional strength, and your walk with God lifting your sense of security and courage. This becomes a more automatic and day-to-day experience increasingly to the point that it becomes the place in which you live. Hence, this becomes your new existence: confident, brave, at peace, and unshakeable.

Wouldn't it be nice to walk with a degree of invincibility, as if you are 10 feet tall and bullet-proof? The more you grow into this level of emotional independence, the more you can become increasingly unstoppable in pursuing your dreams, mission, and purpose that you were put here on this earth to fulfill.

So, how does this work?

The following will show ways to look deeper and higher with a multidimensional approach. Here are some examples of how these dimensions may apply when encountering mistreatment.

1. Individual Dimension – What is possibly happening inside that person's mind currently leading them to react this way?

2. Historical Dimension – What may have happened to them to set them up to make these bad choices?

3. Spiritual Dimension – What may be happening behind the scenes spiritually right now?

4. Behavioral Dimension – Do I need to respond?

5. All Dimensions – What is the best, most appropriate response for this situation and to this individual right now?

When you train yourself to rise above and beyond what the eyes and ears merely see and hear, you move into a place where you are no longer easily offended because you know that there is a bigger picture, and it is not necessarily about you. If you are not easily offended in the first place, there is less pain to heal and less damage control needed for your forgiveness process. If you choose to live in this higher-order perceptual plain, you will begin to see every hateful act as rooted in woundedness and misguidedness.

So, let's play out a couple of scenarios. One example may be considered mild and the other more severe. Mild versus severe pain are perceptually in the eye of the beholder. What is significantly painful to one person is not necessarily as painful to another.

Let's say that you are doing some needed shopping and another customer is blatantly rude to you. They raise their voice and tell you to get out of their way and even slightly knock you off balance as they brush past you. If your perceptions are confined to the basic human level, you may perceive the situation with the following limited perspective:

1. Individual Dimension – That person is a jerk, is mean, horrible, scary, etc.

2. Historical Dimension – S/he was rude to me just now,

and that was uncalled for.

3. Spiritual Dimension – They must be incorrigible, bad, evil, etc.

4. Behavioral Dimension – Do I need to respond? I must retaliate to protect my dignity.

5. All Dimensions – What response? I should yell back at them, punch them, or have them arrested for assault because they brushed up against me, and I almost fell over.

If you choose to rise above this situation, you may make the following perceptual interpretations shown below.

Perceiving with a higher-order perspective (H.O.P.E.) may look like this:

1. Individual Dimension – What happened to that person? Are they having a terrible day, emotionally disturbed, or experiencing something terrible in their life right now?

2. Historical Dimension – Did they not get to learn how to treat others? Were they abused as a child or treated in the same way? Do they lack the emotional sustenance needed to respond appropriately?

3. Spiritual Dimension – Have they missed out on knowing what life can be like if they reach out for help or use God-given resources? Do they know how much God loves them and who Christ is?

4. Behavioral Dimension – Do I need to respond? I do not have the power to make them behave the right way. Would it be helpful if I say something, or are they just not in a good place to receive it right now?

5. All Dimensions – What response? I can pray, "God, will you please help them with whatever it is that is going on with them (Mercy and Compassion) & Thank You that

they did not knock me over and were not allowed to harm me (gratitude) physically."

The responses are case by case and involve discernment. The next situation is an example of an event that could be considered difficult. This one involves criminal behavior, such as robbery.

1. Individual Dimension –

   a. About the offender – What a terrible person. They are evil, dangerous sociopaths.
   b. About yourself – I am not safe, am helpless, defenseless, and stupid for letting this happen.

2. Historical (past and future) Dimension – I am not safe; these things always happen to me, I may never be safe again.

3. Spiritual Dimension –

   c. About the offender – They are evil, etc.
   d. About yourself - I must be cursed

4. Behavioral Dimension – Do I need to respond? Fight, Flight, or Freeze: Yes, I should make them pay (Fight). No, I need to stop going out or move away from this town forever (Flight). I am paralyzed with fear (Freeze).

5. All Dimensions – What response? Fight or Flight: Yes, I should hunt them down and retaliate (Fight). No, I must hide, never go out again, isolate to avoid the risk (Flight, Freeze).

Responding with a higher-order perspective (H.O.P.E.) may look like this:

1. Individual Dimension –

   a. About the offender – What a sad world

view/life/existence that person may have. They may be emotionally or spiritually impoverished to think that they must steal from others?

b. About yourself – God protects me. Thank heavens that I am safe and unharmed physically. Those things are replaceable - or - Those sentimental things taken cannot remove the experiences, memories, and meaning of the relationships that I had.

2. Historical (past and future) Dimension –

c. About the offender – Something must have happened to them to make them this way. They may be struggling with a drug problem, emotional problem, or a spiritual problem.
d. About yourself – I will not let what they did have the power to define my life or lead me to a life or future filled with fear.

3. Spiritual Dimension –

e. About the offender - Is this person wounded emotionally or spiritually?
f. About self – God is continually with me and is my shield.

4. Behavioral Dimension – Do I need to respond? Yes, or No, depending on the situation.

5. All Dimensions – What is the wise response to choose?

g. I can take legal action, make a police report, have an investigation launched, and press charges to prevent them from harming others.
h. I can install locks and other safety precautions.
i. I can grieve, some of those items involved sentimental attachments, or I can grieve the loss of time and effort it took for me to save up to

purchase those things.
j. I can pray for my protection, restoration, and healing.
k. I will place that person in God's hands, praying for God to deal with/ help/or heal them.

Examining the situations above involving the example of a person who tries to hurt us, we can know that more is going on than what meets the eye without knowing what that is. The event did not just happen at that moment in a vacuum all by itself. It has been in the making for several years beforehand, where the offender was perhaps robbed of needed emotional and spiritual components themselves. If so, they are currently reacting through a limited lens, clouded by their own barren beginnings and current misperceptions.

To some extent, you and I may have some vulnerabilities that incline us toward misperception and skewed interpretation as well, since none of us escape childhood nor life on this planet unscathed. The lack of our own growth can set us up for these vulnerabilities. We are not always immune from being blindsighted when life throws us a curve. Our woundedness can leave us open for a scheme of the enemy to hurl a wrench in our path, temporarily undermining our strength or confidence and possibly throwing us off our route to our purpose. While we are not entirely invincible toward the things that happen, the more we endeavor to heal and grow emotionally and spiritually, the more impervious we can become.

There is an impact when something terrible happens, such as robbery, and we will likely need some time to grieve. Applying the level of forgiveness in this chapter helps you see beyond the immediate surface level of the event. You know that what happened likely has nothing to do with you but has far deeper dimensions that extend beyond you. Furthermore, living in this higher order of perspective prevents the event from having the power to define you or knock you off of your path. At this level of thinking, feeling, and perceiving (H.O.P.E.), nothing can ultimately penetrate your soul, and you can emerge heroically.

A scriptural example is found in the New Testament. In Matthew 8:23-27, here, a storm suddenly erupted, and waves were rising over the boat. Jesus remained sound asleep through all of the commotion. His disciples were very afraid and woke him. Jesus arose and said to the winds and the waves, "Peace – Be still." Jesus was not phased in the slightest by the storm. While remaining in a place of peace, Jesus took appropriate action.

Our choice of appropriate action may look different from the above example. The more we grow, the more we can discern the most appropriate steps to take in the face of adversity.

You can grow and develop to the point of being virtually unphased by many of the emotional storms in your life. When the offense is hurled at you, you immediately see beyond the person and know that they are acting from a place of woundedness, which has very little or nothing to do with you. Imagine yourself developing to the point that most infractions only take a few minutes of your time. You stop, pray for God's help, protection, and guidance. You also pray for the offender and then keep moving straight ahead, right on toward your destiny.

Why are we told to pray for our enemies? This might be answered in looking at how to pray for them. We know clearly that people do not do wrong unless *something* is wrong somewhere. The type of prayers that you can pray for them can include praying for God to open their eyes to what they are doing. You can pray for them to become healed and delivered so that they do not continue in that behavior. You can pray for their correction. You can just simply lift them up to God, off of your plate and out of your hair, without anything specific. What would it be like to walk in peace emotionally, mentally, and spiritually on a continual basis? This involves a cognitive-emotional-experiential way of interpreting and approaching the world that maintains your internal peacefulness and creates hope. This way of functioning can become increasingly automatic, the more you practice it and the closer you move toward God. The closer you move toward God, the more you realize that you are protected, deeply loved, safe, and at peace. The more you walk in a place of peace, the more you can have emotional stability and overcome the stressors and adverse events that life can bring.

Can We Do This Perfectly?

The answer is no. So, make a decision right away to refuse to be hard on yourself for the times that you do not achieve this perspective. Only one person on earth achieved this perfectly, and that was Jesus Christ. We are to strive to be like Him, with the knowledge that we cannot be perfect. As human beings, we will often have initial emotional reactions within the first spit seconds of an occurrence. This is normal. However, we can train ourselves to develop a mindset that quickly goes to thoughts that rise above the situation and eventually become the norm for us as time goes on. This perspective can grow to become deeply woven within the fabric of our thinking, awareness, and personality, transcending the situation.

Beyond Mindfulness

Psychology teaches us to live and be mindful in the present moment. The method of thinking described in this chapter does not negate the usefulness of mindfulness; rather, it invites us to reach beyond mindfulness. It includes being anchored in reality (here-and-now) while also tuning in to the additional dimensions involved. This approach asks what is happening right here-and-now with the actions that you perceive with your five senses (mindfulness), and what dimensions may also be intersecting the here-and-now events at this moment (H.O.P.E.)? H.O.P.E. asks what might be happening in that person's mind (distorted thought process/misinterpretation), spirit (negative influence), or historical pattern (a possible tsunami of traumas or a lack of positive training during childhood) that could be tainting that person's own interpretation of you and the event? You do not have to know what these are. This is not a time to attempt to do psychoanalysis with the offender or a form of counseling. You do not have to fix that person. You can, however, know that these factors *do* have interplay in the situation and respond accordingly.

The H.O.P.E. perceptual place of existence allows you to be fully grounded while also transcending beyond the dimension of your senses. You get to live in a higher place of perception at the same time while your feet remain firmly on the ground, perceiving the moment with a much bigger multidimensional perspective. Some people intuitively do this to some extent more than others. However, if you are not one of them, it can be learned and developed. Moreover, a direct pathway to this level is by becoming closer and closer to God and filled with His Holy Spirit.

When we believe that we are prompted by the Holy Spirit to choose a specific action, we always want to make sure these decisions align with scripture. This is a litmus test to make sure that we are not misinterpreting our own biases and perceptions.

As H.O.P.E. expands beyond mindfulness, it branches into the mindset of God. Rising above into the mindset of God takes you to a much higher and more powerful place than just the here-and-now. This is a level of discernment that goes deeper, wider, and broader than the immediate and allows you to have a perception that can shrink the impact of current events within a bigger perspective. We can draw strength and peace with this level of existence. The next sections discuss how to develop this more fully.

What is the Mindset of God?

Take a look at Scripture:

Isaiah 55:8-9 (NIV)

"For my thoughts are not your thoughts,

neither are your ways my ways,"

declares the LORD.

Hebrews 4:12 (NIV)

"As the heavens are higher than the earth,

so are my ways higher than your ways

and my thoughts than your thoughts.

"For the word of God is alive and active.

Sharper than any double-edged sword,

it penetrates even to dividing soul and spirit, joints and marrow;

it judges the thoughts and attitudes of the heart."

The mind of God goes higher than the Cognitive Shift (described above), higher than any famous cognitive theories, and higher than any concept that we can muster. A perspective of H.O.P.E. is developed by walking closer to God, meditating on His Word, and spending time with Him personally. The more you do this, the more that He can change you from the inside out, giving you amazing peace and wisdom.

I was raised in a good Christian upbringing, and it was not until my adulthood that I realized that God is not like some of the humans I knew as Christians. God is not pushy, controlling, nor self-absorbed. He is not like those intrusive boyfriends (ex-husbands or wives, girlfriends, etc.) who stalk you or try to lure you back when you want to break up. You may not have thought about it much for that very reason because He has not been pushing you. You may have encountered a gentle reminder or a loving invite. People can be pushy. God is not. If you ask Him to help you and guide you, He will. If you ask Him to live in your heart, He will – without being forceful. "Behold, I stand at the door and knock. If anyone hears my voice and opens the door, I will come in" (Revelation 3:20 NIV). He gently waits patiently at the door of our heart just politely knocking and waiting.

Allowing ourselves to grow closer to God opens our eyes. If you become receptive to the depth and wisdom of the Holy Spirit, revealing the perspective of God to you, you will begin to see the veracity that there are many more dimensions in events than what meets the human eye. A stronger relationship with Him makes it much easier to see those who hurt us through His eyes and the eyes of compassion.

Another advancement of knowing your Creator personally is that God can equip us to go beyond what we think we can do. We become empowered.

Acts 1:8 (ESV)

"But you will receive power when the Holy Spirit has come upon you;

and you will be my witnesses in Jerusalem,

and in all Judea and Samaria, and to the end of the earth."

John 14:26 (AMP)

"But the [a]Helper (Comforter, Advocate, Intercessor—Counselor, Strengthener, Standby), the Holy Spirit, whom the Father will send in My name [in My place, to represent Me and act on My behalf], He will teach you all things. And He will help you remember everything that I have told you."

The spiritual relationship with God is the most powerful; because the closer we draw near to Him in a personal walk, the more we discover coping abilities that transcend beyond our own ideas alone. We learn to see things in a way that surpasses and rise above the worst situations. This does not mean that we skip over grieving when disaster strikes. There are still events that require a grieving process; however, within those times, this perspective gives us hope.

It is my hope that, if you have not already, you will explore the idea of seeing the Creator through a clear perspective that is not tainted by human error and in a fresh perspective of relationship. There have been plenty of misguided examples of religion in the world. Because of those misguided examples, many people have turned away from trying to get to know who the Creator really is. In the New Testament, Jesus himself was rejected by many of the religious leaders because he confronted them for their hypocrisy. If you set aside all of the bad examples from religiosity and check out who the Creator *really is*, you can learn that you are *immensely loved and cherished*. You can have a confidant, best friend, advocate, and an ideal parent who will surpass all limits of what you have previously experienced.

God sees the heart (1 Samuel 16:7) behind the person's action and He knows the background story of that individual. God knows every single hurt that s/he has experienced, leading them to choose wrongly. He fully sees every misperception, fear, lie, and torment that they allow to take over their life. The person victimizing others is coming from a place of enormous detriment. God sees all and still judges fairly.

How to Apply the Mindset of God

We will take another example here. This example may be modest in the level of stress or risk; however, it provides a good starting place.

Let us first use mindfulness. Imagine that a neighbor yells at you for leaving your belongings too close to their property. Perhaps they swear and curse at you and this is not the first time. Every time you see them, they are irritable, rude, condescending, and generally hard to get along with. The helpful aspect of mindfulness allows you to use your awareness for protection. Here are some options:

- Notice the distance they are from you and that they are not holding a weapon.
- Tune into your initial feeling of fear or offense and make a constructive choice on how to respond. Mindfully you notice your options to either walk away, use an assertive message telling them that it is not OK to speak that way to you. These options are available at your disposal. You also get to discern whether no response is wise, depending on the person and situation.

Beyond mindfulness, in a place of H.O.P.E., you rise above the tangible here-and-now that is seen by the human eyes and choose to operate from a place of higher insight. You are aware of several things psychologically and spiritually:

- This person's rant is not ultimately about you because you have seen them irritable many times before.
- Instead of seeing this situation as personal, you see with laser spiritual eyes into the pain that is possible within them.
- You know that this person's wounds likely came from somewhere else (childhood or current stressors).
- You consider the possibility that they may be tormented emotionally or misguided spiritually.
- You assess this situation from a multidimensional perspective, asking God to show you the best response from the bigger picture and through His Eyes.

One way of thinking about how to deal with a difficult person is to compare it to a medical situation. When dealing with an abusive person, you can treat the situation as if this is someone who has the flu. You keep firm boundaries and protect yourself. You likely keep a safe distance. If there is something healing to administer, you may inform them about it maintaining healthy boundaries, and then move on.

This behavior does not render you wimpy. When you learn to walk in a place of H.O.P.E., you maintain situational awareness. You are fully aware that a negative or potentially dangerous person is present. You maintain strong boundaries by refraining from negative engagement with them or even possibly distancing from them completely. You also exercise spiritual insight, remembering Ephesians 6:12, that we wrestle not with flesh and blood but with principalities of the air. With these boundaries and emotional and spiritual insights in place, you remain unaffected by that person's behavior. You realize that this is not about you and that they need God's intervention – hence, prayer.

Ephesians 6:12 (NIV)

"For our struggle is not against flesh and blood, but against the rulers, against the authorities, against the powers of this dark world and against the spiritual forces of evil in the heavenly realms."

It is worth reiterating that boundaries go both ways. Furthermore, while it is likely that something is leading this person to behave in this manner, you do not have to know what it is if they do not want to share it. It is not your business; it is God's. This can spare you a lot of energy if it not really yours to repair. So, by praying for them, you have fulfilled your obligation.

Knowing that the degree of their behavioral intensity is most likely equal to the degree of their pain, it should follow that the greater their intensity, the greater your compassion. When you can see a perpetrator as a wounded soul, it reduces their power and increases your own power in your eyes. It also implies that they need help from somewhere. I believe that this is the bottom line of why God wants us to pray for our enemies.

For all you know, this person may have a loved one diagnosed with cancer and be terrified, or they may have endured a life full of hardship and trauma for which they feel robbed. Their anger is energy designed to repair something that they do not know how to fix. Therefore, it is misdirected. Their anger is also likely rooted in fear, hurt, despair, and hopelessness. You are the Light of God that may be the only light that they will see. As you choose to see them through the eyes of God, you become a healing vessel of mercy and love that surpasses all understanding (Ephesians 3:19), just by the way you respond and the way you also apply your boundaries in the situation.

So, by using H.O.P.E. as your perspective, you tune in to the following avenues of interpretation:

- It is not all about you.
- Something must clearly be hurting them.
- You don't really have to know the cause of their issue.
- Their level of vitriol is likely equal and proportional to their level of pain.
- Therefore, this event does not have to penetrate your emotional world, infect your soul, nor steal one single ounce of your energy, time, and purpose.

One quick second to ask God to help them with whatever it is that they are truly needing is a brief use of your time that is exponentially powerful and effective. It goes beyond anything you or I could do to try to fix it ourselves. God knows *exactly* what it is that this person needs. We consider and take care of our part in the matter (do the part that you can do, i.e., constructive action) and allow God to do what He can do through prayer (Matthew 5:43 – 48).

Now, to be clear, this does not mean that you necessarily continue to stand there with the attitude of mercy, expecting your compassion to just immediately melt their heart. Many adversaries have a long journey to endure before they can reach a place of understanding. Always maintain your safety. There are some events that are extremely dangerous and the person has gone too far into the darkness for our empathy to dissuade them. These are situations where we may need the ultimate of boundaries. We may need to run first, then pray. Some people have been so badly burned emotionally or their brains so severely changed by drugs that they will need an act of God. Discernment can determine whether it is time to apply mercy from a distance and leave the situation, letting God take over.

What Do You See?

When a negative event occurs, what do you see – *really*? When you are badly treated or falsely accused, do you believe that the fiery dart is actually meant for you, or would you like to divert that dart? Do you assume that the abuser has the ultimate power over your life, or do you want to rely on resources that God has given you?

The Armor of God

God has equipped you and me with everything we need to overcome what life throws at us. You do not have to face anything alone. We are given both power *and* authority over evil. While sometimes God's intervention seems to take longer than we wish, often, the main reason that evil seems to prevail is that many Christians will not stand up and take hold of the resources and tools that God has given to us. He has given us armor to protect, defend, and prevail, yet many of us do not really understand how to use them.

Luke 10:19 (KJV)

"Behold, I give unto you power to tread on serpents and scorpions, and over all the power of the enemy: and nothing shall by any means hurt you."

To walk in a place of H.O.P.E., it is necessary to take on the full armor of God described in Ephesians 6:10–18. The following pages describe these in detail. For further application, the middle columns in Table 7 show specific examples of each element of armor, eloquently described by David Jeremiah with biblical applications. [lxx] In the last column, I have added practical, cognitive tools that you can apply to your circumstances to help you apply the armor and rise to a level of H.O.P.E. You can also come up with many applications of your own.

Ephesians 6:10- 13 (NIV)

"Finally, be strong in the Lord and in his mighty power.

Put on the full armor of God, so that you can take your stand against the devil's schemes. For our struggle is not against flesh and blood, but against the rulers, against the authorities, against the powers of this dark world and against the spiritual forces of evil in the heavenly realms.

Therefore put on the full armor of God, so that when the day of evil comes, you may be able to stand your ground, and after you have done everything, to stand."

This spiritual armor includes the **belt of truth** buckled around your waist, the **breastplate of righteousness**, the **shoes of peace**, the **shield of faith**, the **helmet of salvation**, and the **sword of the Spirit**, which is the **Word of God**. For a more detailed description, see *The Book of Signs* by David Jeremiah.[lxxi] His description gives explicit detail of the meaning and use of each of these elements. From that writing, I will summarize.

Understanding the tools that God has given us is very important. You cannot use armor if you do not know how to wear it and what to do with it.

Applying the Armor of God

The Belt of Truth

The **Belt of Truth** represents a belt that the soldiers would secure around their waist. The soldier would hang each of their weapons on this belt so that each weapon was made immediately accessible for their use. Why does the Scripture identify this **belt as truth**? Every spiritual (and emotional) weapon or tool that we use to fight an offense needs to hang firmly upon the foundation of truth.

This makes logical sense. If you need to find the best response to a negative encounter, the weapon you select will not be effective if it comes from a false perception, misinterpretation, or a lie. For instance, if a person attempts to humiliate me in public. I can respond from a premise that is false (i.e. believing what the abuser is telling me), but it will not have the best effect on the situation. Specifically, here are some Untruths: If I believe that the attacker is correct (that I am indeed worthless or stupid), my response may be to shrink, fill up with shame, and retreat. I have selected a weapon founded upon a lie (a self-perception of worthlessness or stupidity). Therefore, my response was not anchored in truth at all, and thus, was rendered ineffective.

These negative self-perceptions are lies because we are all deeply valued by God, valued enough for the ultimate sacrifice made on our behalf. We are also valuable because we all have been given gifts to use, which contain inherent intelligence within them. I can still select another weapon not founded upon truth. I can choose the interpretation that the attacker is a horrible person. From this false premise, I may then respond with hostility, judgment, or even more fear. If your weapon is not founded upon truth, it will not be the right tool, and it not give you power. If I select my weapons from the premise and foundation of truth, the result can have a multidimensional impact for good.

If I am wearing the **Belt of Truth**, I will know that:

- This person is likely misguided.
- Their escalated anger is not necessarily all about the current situation and nor completely about me.
- God knows what they need.

- God is my protector.
- No weapon forged against me will prevail (Isaiah 54:17).

Wearing truth around my waist produces a strength that solidifies my core, and my weapon selections can be right on target, effective, and powerful.

My response choices anchored upon truth can be:

- I will consider what the person might be going through and extend mercy.
- I will discern what part I may have played in the situation and address this appropriately.
- I will ask God to help them with whatever it is that they are going (or have gone) through.
- I will ask for God's protection, and if they are dangerous, I will get myself away from them, call the police if necessary.
- I will do what is appropriate within my power and give the rest to God.

Maltreatment of another human being begins with the introduction of a negative idea that originates from the enemy in the spiritual domain (Ephesians 6:12 NKJV). This negative suggestion is selectively whispered to a person who might be a likely target for such a suggestion.

We make ourselves into targets, vulnerable to negative suggestions when we do not take action to grow spiritually and emotionally. Without growth, we may just allow ourselves to believe whatever is handed to us without questioning its validity. A person who is open to negative suggestions may have unchecked emotional wounds or unresolved negative experiences.

In Genesis, when Satan was making the first strategic attempt of entry of evil into the world, he chose a target (Eve) who he saw as having small vulnerabilities, just big enough to allow a porthole of entry. This had nothing to do with the fact that she was a woman. In Genesis 3:5-7, he told Eve that if she ate the forbidden fruit, she would be like God and know good and evil. The fruit was also pleasing to the eye. The first vulnerability in Eve may have been a lack of trust. The **Belt of Truth** here would have been the sound belief that God is trustworthy. If God forbade something, it is for a good reason. The second vulnerability was that the fruit was appealing to her. The **Belt of Truth** for this temptation would have been in knowing that God abundantly supplies all of our needs, including those we taste and touch. Adam also fell prey to his vulnerability, which led to his compliance. Did he lack confidence or assertiveness? This root of vulnerability, possibly from failing to realize the truth of how truly cherished, loved, and valued they were, may have caused them to be misled and subsequently, hiding in fear.

On and on it goes; the fear and shame are passed down from event to event, human to human, and generation to generation. There is an architecture of dynamics behind the scenes of human interaction. When people hurt you, they are being influenced from somewhere, whether spiritually or humanly. Remember the example involving the marionette, whose strings are being pulled and manipulated by the hidden operator? The person attacking you can be thought of as merely a puppet who is being manipulated by spiritual influences (1 Peter 5:8 NKJV). If the person accepts those lies of manipulation, they are downloaded, infiltrating their thinking and influencing emotions and actions. You may just be witnessing the aftermath of what has happened behind the scenes.

Your weapons (tools) represent your responses that you have ready access to (hanging on your **belt of truth** around your waist). The most natural responses (cower in shame, accept negative words, or alternatively abuse that person back) do not hang upon the truth. Those natural actions allow ourselves to be manipulated by the manipulator as well. So, to anchor your tools (responses) on the **Belt of Truth**, you immediately discard what they just said, look deeper, and respond with wisdom. Sometimes this calls for being assertive and standing up against the violation of your rights, or sometimes it entails diverting to a different direction. The closer you grow in relationship to God, the easier it is to hear wisdom. In this regard, we are all at different points along this pathway in our growth process.

You cannot effectively stand up against evil if you are not operating from a basis of truth. You cannot accurately nor powerfully respond if you are misinterpreting the other person's intent. Everything must hang on the truth. Perhaps that is the reason that this piece of armor is mentioned first by the Apostle Paul. Wearing the **Belt of Truth** gives you discernment, and from accurate discernment, the most effective and powerful tools can be selected.

The Breastplate of Righteousness

This breastplate was used to protect the soldier's vital organs, especially the heart. The application here is that when you walk in righteousness, you are protected in vital areas. It does not take much to agree that righteous behavior can help preserve and protect your relationships, your career, and your dreams. When you walk with integrity, no one can accuse you of wrongdoing without it, ultimately becoming exposed as a fraudulent accusation. Research has shown that employees are more likely to get fired for contentious behavior than for errors. More often, marriages end because of someone's unrighteous choices, whether cheating, lying, or some form of selfishness. Choosing righteous behavior protects everything that is vital to having a good life.

When you do err, as we all do, you realize that the behavior is not right, repent, and ask for God's help continuing to grow in moral stature. He removes our sins from us as far as the east is from the west (Psalms 103:12), allowing us to start all over again. Here, we can straighten our path and continue wearing righteousness that protects our hearts and breath of life.

I wonder what would have happened if Adam and Eve had gone straight to God and repented, rather than tried to hide their guilt. Guilt does not save you – Jesus does. I wonder if the future, theirs and ours, might have unfolded differently. Think of how one act of repentance can mend the course of a relationship, a career, and a future in today's world. We have Jesus who turned everything right side up again, forever. Repenting from our own wrongdoings restores our **breastplate of righteousness** and protects what is vital to our lives.

This spiritual shield of making righteous choices in your life has a broad spectrum to protect you not only spiritually but also physically and emotionally. The way that righteousness protects your life physically is by reducing stress. When you make good moral choices, you don't have to worry about the repercussion or getting caught. You minimize the impact of health-threatening stress hormones that plague your body and decrease your immune system.

Continuing with the example above of the abusive person, let's suppose that you are not putting on this **breastplate of righteousness**. For instance, you choose unrighteousness. You decided to hit the person. Now, you could end up with an assault charge on your record, or they could retaliate with more violence. Perhaps you decide to give them a dose of their own medicine, and you verbally attack them with hateful, sharply cutting words. They, in turn, are motivated to up the ante by retaliating further. Now, you are hit with more emotional pain. Perhaps they are passive-aggressive, and you find your tires slashed the next day, or they escalate the viciousness by threatening your family. Operating in unrighteousness leaves you open and vulnerable for more attack – more pain. Your heart (the things you care about in life) and vital organs (legal security, personal safety) are unprotected.

Alternatively, you put on the **breastplate of righteousness** by taking the high road and refusing to return the hostility. This gives you several options. You may choose to respond with a soft yet firm tone of voice (Proverbs 15:1, KJV "A soft answer turneth away wrath"). On the other hand, you may decide to say nothing and walk away. This can be a form of setting a strong boundary by not allowing that person any further opportunity to abuse you. Other forms of boundary setting might involve shutting the door, hanging up the phone, calling the police, or pressing charges if they committed a crime. Righteousness does not allow the person to walk all over you. The wise response may involve taking a stand to prevent them from inflicting pain further.

When you walk in righteousness, you are less likely to get arrested, sued, or retaliated against through payback. There are some cases that are complicated since we live in a very wounded world. Choosing to do what is right does help you avoid more stressful and negative consequences. The righteous responses described above relate to the next section involving peace.

The Shoes of Peace

Why would **peace** be represented by **shoes**? If I were a soldier, I would want steel-toed boots in case I needed to kick someone – right? Wrong. This is one of the more counterintuitive pieces of armor. In fact, according to David Jeremiah, these shoes even had opened toes.[lxxii] The **shoes of peace** are represented by shoes with iron-studded soles, which went deep into the ground to keep the soldier anchored firmly. The closest thing we may have like that in today's time would resemble football cleats. I believe these steel soles were much stronger than what one would use for football. This piece of armor kept the soldier stable, firmly planted, grounded, and immovable from being thrown off of their position.

Our family used to have a cat who lived to be over 21 years

old. Most cats do not make it beyond 16 years. She could come indoors and outdoors at will. One day to my amazement, when I was standing with her in the front yard, I watched a dog four times her size come charging at her full speed. She just remained in her sitting position, unmoved, staring at him. When the dog reached her, he was forced to stop right in his tracks to avoid running right into her. She did not budge nor look scared at all. She sat there in her same position, unphased, with an unimpressed look on her face. The dog did nothing further and left her alone. For her wearing the **shoes of peace** was a game-changer. Is it any wonder that she lived 30% longer than expected?

Think of how powerful peace really is. The abusive person described above comes at you screaming and ranting, hurling despicable words at you. You stand firm, unflappable, and are not swayed nor manipulated emotionally. This spiritual armor gives you strength and power to remain stable and calm so that you can think clearly. When nothing throws you off balance, it can interrupt the game plan of your enemy.

If we could re-write the account of Adam and Eve, depicting them to have the **shoes of peace**, that moment of temptation may have played out differently. With the **shoes of peace**, I am at peace with the here and now. I am content and at peace with everything I have and everything I do not have. No matter how appealing that fruit seems, look at all that I *DO* have in this beautiful garden and it is wonderful. I am satisfied and content with the fruits supplied to me. I do not need to search for more. When the serpent came to tempt Eve, she might have said, "Oh, no, thank you. I'm good," and walked away. When you have peace, you have strength and do not need to find things to medicate distress, such as too much food, wine, spending, gambling, nor other substances. Think of all the sales and bad business deals that we would avoid with the application of peace.

As with all of the tools, for this piece of armor to work

effectively, it needs to be anchored on truth as well. When you are wearing the **shoes of peace**, you stand firm, anchored in the truth that since God is for you, no one can really be against you (Romans 8:31). This belief ties into the element of faith.

The Shield of Faith

According to David Jeremiah (2019), the shield of a soldier was immense. This piece of equipment was four feet tall and two-and-a-half feet wide. The soldier was able to protect the whole body from a barrage of fiery darts that were hurled. The whole essence of this part of armor involves having a boundary for protection that is founded upon faith.

Faith can give you mental, emotional, and spiritual boundaries. This is not blind faith or foolishness. You still take practical and reasonable steps to protect yourself or mitigate the situation. This form of faith keeps you grounded and calm. You realize that no weapon forged against you will prevail (Isiah 54:17 NKJV). You don't have to be concerned about vengeance because, by faith, you know that the failing of the wicked has already been set in motion (Psalms 37 NKJV). You hold to the faith that, because God is on your side, no one can irreparably harm you (Romans 8:31 NKJV). You maintain faith in God's love for you, and this faith protects you from tricks, threats, and offenses.

The application of this tool used physically, emotionally, and spiritually involves saying "*NO*" when necessary, knowing that God will give you what you need in a healthier way. You exercise this faith by declining to engage in a hostile conversation and by closing the door to continued exploitation or abuse, knowing that God is your protector.

Setting a boundary is not always met with acquiescence. Let's say that you decide to stop interacting with the abusive person in the example above. I have rarely seen an abuser jump with joy when the door is shut on them. They may threaten to damage your reputation or worse. There are cases requiring reasonable and legal methods of protecting yourself. Pray for wisdom and discernment if you are unsure and consult wise legal counsel. The next piece of armor directly relates to cognition, decision-making, and perception.

The Helmet of Salvation

The helmet of that day had a hard outer surface that would not allow the enemy to penetrate it. In pragmatic terms, this is the armor that protects your sanity. When you have been mistreated, the removal of unhealthy thoughts cannot be stressed strongly enough. It is very important to be continually aware of our thoughts and perceptions. In 1Peter 5:8, we are told to be sober and alert. Because the enemy roams around seeking whom he may devour. We need to continually examine, discard, and replace unhealthy thoughts with positive, healthy truth. You can ask God to help you see what is really going in the spiritual realm, as in the example below.

Derek and Jacqueline

During the midst of their storms and court battles, Jacqueline sat at her desk in her home, sobbing and praying. In the midst of it, she got an image in her mind. It was the child's version of a man that looked like the side of a child's face where his head was tilted at an angle. The focus centered on his ear. She noticed that his ear was tender, vulnerable, and naive. She realized that this was an image of Derek, so she began to pray for him. After fervent emotional prayer and more tears, she got up, washed her face, and looked in the mirror. Her eyes had a light and a sparkle shining from them that she had never noticed before.

The interpretation she made from this is that Derek was being whispered lies in his spirit. The ear in the picture was that of a tender young child, meaning that Derek was being deceived like a child and those lies were targeted toward his vulnerability (hence, the ear appeared like that of a child's ear). Derek was believing lies, such as, "You cannot trust women - they are all controlling." "Jacqueline is trying to take Charles away from you." "You are 50 years old and have the right to do anything you want to do." Some of the whispers may have come from darkness and been filtered through Lucy, who may have been vulnerable to such lies herself, such as "Jacqueline does not need your child support. Look, she just spent money on house repairs."

Take hold of the cognitive tools that God wants you to utilize. God has not given us a spirit of fear, but of power, love, and a sound mind (2Timothy 1:7 KJV). Sound thoughts are also anchored in truth. When you have trained yourself to automatically turn a negative thought or belief into a healthy one, you can increasingly reach a point where you virtually walk with invincibility. If an abuser throws a negative insult toward you, the more you are conditioned to believe in hope and walk in love, the more those darts just bounce right off of you. This is the **Helmet of Salvation**. Believing and thinking healthy truths saves your sanity. It saves you from much-unwanted strife, stress, and hurt. You remain free to make sound decisions and do not waste your time in turmoil. You keep looking forward and continue marching right ahead toward your destiny

The Sword of the Spirit

During biblical times, the sword was a dagger that was six to eighteen inches long designed for specific and incisive aim. I have been a Christian all of my life but did not ever learn about the power that is present in speaking God's Word out loud until much later in my life. You can speak and proclaim the Word of God deliberately in the face of trouble. When Jesus was led into the wilderness to be tempted by the devil, He responded by speaking the Word of God out loud back to the tempter (Matthew 4). This is the reason for meditating on scripture daily so that you have

God's Word right at your fingertips. Words tend to have power, but God's Word has the most powerful of all.

You can use the Word of God to claim His promises over your life. For instance, if someone threatens to abandon you, you can say out loud that God promises you that He "will never leave you nor forsake you" (Deuteronomy 31:16, NIV). If someone threatens to devastate you in any manner, you can speak out loud, the 23rd Psalm. Some situations call for more silence. In these cases, you can resolutely, in the privacy of your mind, tell yourself those promises in your thoughts. Post Scriptures in various visible places in your home to remind you that you are not alone and that God has good plans for you.

Jeremiah 29:11 (NIV)

"For I know the plans I have for you," declares the LORD, "plans to prosper you and not to harm you, plans to give you hope and a future."

Zechariah 9:12 (NIV)

"Return to your fortress, you prisoners of hope; even now I announce that I will restore twice as much to you."

Ephesians 6:18 also commands us to "pray in the Spirit on all occasions with all kinds of prayers and requests. With this in mind, be alert and always keep on praying for all the Lord's people" (NIV).

Derek and Jacqueline

Time passed, and Jacqueline grew. She was no longer the same person as before. While the events that followed rendered any restoration of their former relationship an impossibility, she no longer tensed up over the things that Derek did. She was able to interact with him constructively when a situation called for it without resentment or impact because she had moved beyond the past. Their relationship never was the same as before, where she, in the past, had expected a reasonable response from Derek but was disappointed. She now had no expectations from him and had learned to remain neutral in response to his actions.

On one occasion, when it was time to take Charles back home after a month in an addiction treatment facility, Jacqueline was ready to drive him back in the vehicle that she had rented. While Charles was now old enough to drive independently, he was not old enough to drive a rented vehicle. The rental company had strict rules against anyone under the age of 21 driving their vehicles. Jacqueline intended to abide by those rules.

As they got ready to get into the vehicle Derek, who was going to drive back in a separate vehicle with Lucy, announced to Jacqueline and Charles that Charles really could drive the rented vehicle as he rode back with Jacqueline. Jacqueline reiterated the rules again, but Derek proceeded to disagree in front of Charles, imposing his view into their situation. Jacqueline had explicitly signed the contract when she had paid. This may have been a continuation of Derek's pattern of leverage in previous manipulations, setting up Charles to be frustrated with his mother, promoting a false theme of 'Your mom tries to baby you and overprotects you.'

Derek was not going to let go of his assertion even though it was not valid. This had the potential of 1) undermining Jacqueline in their son's eyes, and 2) setting up a dynamic based on a sensitive subject so that Jacqueline and Charles would argue throughout the four-hour drive home, 3) reinforcing myths about Jacqueline that promoted or continued to drive a wedge between her and their son while making Derek the hero, and 4) undoing any peacefulness and hope that their son had just now gained from this wonderful and life-changing time in the treatment experience. Nevertheless, Jacqueline was not going to give in because it would have made her liable if anything were to happen and she was not going to lie about it. She also knew that if anything did go wrong from breaking that rule, Derek would not be present to pick up the pieces or to help her pay for the damage.

Instead of taking the bait from Derek, trying to fix him, change his mind, give him a lesson on insight, or prove a point in front of their son, Jacqueline interrupted the whole dynamic midstream. In the middle of Derek's argument, she suddenly dropped her shoulders, lifted her arms, placing them loosely around his neck with a casual hug, and said, "I love ya" in the tone of okay-whatever. Derek froze for a minute as if he did not know what to do, then he suddenly dropped the argument and said, "I gotta go," retreating to his own vehicle.

What happened at that moment on the practical level was that her response bypassed Derek's argument altogether. What happened on the spiritual level is that the enemy who had been whispering deceit into Derek's ear, just like the marionette manipulating the puppet, immediately fled. It appeared that the devil tucked his tail and ran. The enemy gives people deceit, and off they run with it, into the same toxic dynamic. Jacqueline cut off the enemy's arm that day by responding from a higher place and applying the armor of God:

The **belt of truth** (not giving in to the lie).

The **breastplate of righteousness** (refusing to break the rules and legal contract that she had signed).

The **shoes of peace** (standing her ground and refusing to argue).

*The **shield of faith** (knowing that God will protect her).*

*The **helmet of salvation** (refusing to give in to the fear-based thoughts that she needed to please Derek or their son, but standing firm on what was right).*

*The **sword of the Spirit** (she spoke the words that she felt that the Holy Spirit had led her to speak).*

When Jacqueline and Charles got into the rented car, Charles was also confused. He raised his voice, saying, "That's stupid!" Jacqueline said nothing more than, "I can either do the positive or the negative, and I am not going to do the negative." From then on, the trip was calm, solid silence at first, then a peaceful conversation for the remainder of the trip home.

Jacqueline had learned to rise above all the chaos. If Derek tried to manipulate or not, she chose not to be pulled into it. Derek had a consistent pattern of only paying for approximately a 10th of the expenses of their child's recovery needs, yet Jacqueline did not focus on that. Instead, Jacqueline was so thrilled that God had supplied her with the means to help their son not only survive but also thrive. She was grateful for God helping them rise above the storm that had plagued them for more than a decade.

Jacqueline did not end up losing the house nor her son. God continued to give her more jobs and opportunities. Even though Derek refused to help Jacqueline with their son's tutoring and the expenses for addiction treatment and recovery, God supplied those funds through Jacqueline's hand, and she was thankful. Moreover, the house became a haven for Charles to return to during part of his time of recovery. She was grateful that she was able to provide a comforting and soothing place for him. The house also later became a place where she was able to help others who had been devastated by events in life.

Jacqueline finished her doctorate, and God restored her income tenfold. She came to realize how personally God cared *for her as his own daughter, who He protects and abundantly strengthens. She learned that no matter who was against her, and even if it felt like her own son disregarded her, she remained immensely loved and cherished by God. No matter what, she was never alone. Jacqueline realized the power in the awareness that God has a plan for all of us and that it may be bigger and better than anyone can ever imagine.*

These are examples of using the Armor of God to rise above the chaos that is happening in the world. This involves a growth process that takes time, leads to maturation and internal emotional healing, and includes the power of God's Holy Spirit. Therefore, do not be impatient with yourself. Permit this to take time and diligence. Learning to claim God's promises over your life and practice these resources will strengthen your sense of hope.

How does the full armor of God fit into this higher level of forgiveness? Specifically, with all of your responses anchored in truth (**belted** around your waist – your core), all of your other tools are mounted upon truth. Your **faith** can **shield** you from the attacks and threats of the enemy (believing that God is with you and is reliable). Your emotional **peace** can make you immoveable (**shoes of peace** firmly anchored in the ground with solid standing). Your choice of righteous actions can protect you in the long run (**breastplate**). Your mental (**helmet**) cognitions (thoughts, perceptions, and interpretations) can save you from losing your sanity. All of your spiritual tools culminate with the Word of God (**Sword of the Spirit**), spoken over you and by you. This third level of forgiveness means remaining in an emotional place of peace and faith that protects and shields you as you choose wiser and higher actions. By maintaining the **Helmet of Salvation**, you mentally meditate upon God's Word and His promises for you while boldly and confidently speaking the (**Sword**) Word of God out loud over your situation.

Your cognitive, emotional, and spiritual life will be virtually impenetrable for most of the common offenses. The more you grow into this level, you won't have time to even flinch at the darts hurled at you because you are firmly grounded in the faith that God has got the situation in His Hands, He loves you, and He has a good plan for your life that no one can overpower. Living in this perspective gives you a spiritual insight to override the limits of the surface, as you begin to see events through the eyes of God. I believe that you can achieve every one of these skills to reach a life position involving a higher-order perspective of existence, H.O.P.E.

Table 7
Walking Invincibly:
Higher Order Perspective Existence (H.O.P.E.)

Element of Armor	Purpose	Biblical Meaning	Examples
Belt of Truth	Central function – Everything the soldier needed for hand to hand combat was hung on this belt – the sword, rope, ration sack, money sack, and darts. The belt made it easier for the soldier to run by tucking his tunic into his belt, thereby freeing up his legs for speed and movement.	Truth holds everything together, equips you to fight lies spoken to you and manipulations. Choosing tools that hang upon truth rather than untruths make you an effective warrior. It enables you the means to be free to run with confidence.	I gird myself in truth so that every action I take is based on a solid principle of truth. Whenever I take action, I first consult with God and wise counsel. When I step forward to take action, my choices are based on sound truth. This guides my interpretation and perception of people and the battles in which I chose to engage. I run with confidence.

Table 7
Walking Invincibly:
Higher Order Perspective Existence (H.O.P.E.)

(continued)

Element of Armor	Purpose	Biblical Meaning	Examples
Breastplate of Righteousness	Central function – This was a solid plate to protect the soldier's vital organs, including organs that are central to life – particularly the heart.	We put on Christ's Righteousness, which protects our hearts. Putting on righteousness protects everything vital to us: our relationships, our financial livelihood, and our security.	I walk in God's Will. I follow His plan for my life. I apologize to Him when I make a mistake and get right back on track. Making wise choices protects me Physically, Emotionally, and Spiritually.

Table 7
Walking Invincibly:
Higher Order Perspective Existence (H.O.P.E.)

(continued)

Element of Armor	Purpose	Biblical Meaning	Examples
Shoes of Peace	Central function – These shoes had open toes but had iron-studded soles designed to grip the ground and maintain a firm, immovable position during a fight, allowing the soldier to have stability and stand strong	While standing firm in Peace, you are stable, immoveable - nothing moves you nor throws you off balance.	If I am confronted by someone who is hostile, I remain grounded, firm, and unmoveable – knowing that God is with me. As I choose to keep my perceptions rooted in Love, I can keep my peace and not be manipulated or intimidated.
Shield of Faith	Central function – The Shield was four feet tall and two-and-a-half feet wide – Used to protect their whole bodies and to shield against fiery darts of the enemy.	Faith leads us to repel false messages from the enemy. We reject curses, verbal attacks, and all forms of negative offense. We put our faith in God instead of the perpetrator.	Though a person yells insults at me, I remain grounded in faith that God loves me, and He accepts me as I am while I am growing. If someone tries to scare or discourage me, I remember that God is faithful and He is with me.

Table 7

Walking Invincibly:
Higher Order Perspective Existence (H.O.P.E.)

(continued)

Element of Armor	Purpose	Biblical Meaning	Examples
Helmet of Salvation	Central function – Protect the head and skull from blows by the enemy – Keeps the soldier from being taken out.	The Hope of Salvation protects your mind from the lies, corrupt philosophies, and confusion of the deceiver. The helmet is a metaphor for the Mind of Christ. When you put on the Mind of Christ, you put on wisdom. You wear protection for your mental health.	I maintain thoughts of Hope and the Knowledge that God is faithful to provide for me no matter what anyone tries to do to me. I chose to see events through the eyes of God, which transcends the present moment and is multidimensional.
Sword of the Spirit	Central function – This dagger was six to eighteen inches long for specific, incisive aim for a vulnerable target.	Speaking the Word of God out loud and in thought is spiritual warfare. Speak God's Promises over your life, over the life of those you love, and repeat scripture in your thoughts frequently. Hebrews 4:12 "The Word of God is alive and active. Sharper than any double-edged sword, it penetrates even to diving soul and spirit" (NIV).	I meditate on Scripture regularly. I keep God's Word close inside my heart, and I remind myself and others about the Promises He has made for us. If tempted, discouraged, hurt, or afraid, I speak the Word of God out loud just like Jesus did when He was in the wilderness.

* Column 1 from Ephesians 6:10-18; Information listed in Column 2 and much of the information listed in Column 3 are adapted from *The Book of Signs: 31 Undeniable Prophecies of the Apocalypse*, 2019 by Dr. David Jeremiah, pp 125-138.[lxxiii]

Tragedies and Multi-Tier Processing

This perspective is not a naïve perspective and it does not negate the validity of needing to walk through the emotions of grief when tragedy occurs. Horrors sometimes happen. Terrorist attacks and crimes are reported in our own country. The news is replete with terrible accounts of tragedy. In the face of an attack, the natural human response is fear and a state of fight or flight. This is a normal response for survival. These are events that are inflicted by someone with a horrifically damaged soul. Some individuals chose to allow themselves to be terribly misled by evil.

The Lincoln Family

There was a very faithful, devout Christian family. The parents poured everything into their children. They made sure that each of them knew that they were loved. These parents worked hard to provide for them a good education and authentically modeled their faith by example in their private day-to-day home life.

While life was going along, raising their two older children, they discovered that they were going to be blessed with another child who arrived as a pleasant and welcomed gift. She was unique in her own right. As she grew, it became apparent that she had a gentle and special spirit within her. Everywhere she went, others were touched by her kind heart. Her name was Precious.

Precious filled the world with innocence, joy, and laughter. She was raised with good, trustworthy people in her family, neighborhood, and her church. She never knew a stranger. Her grades were good as her parents devoted their time and energy to all of their children's academic needs. Her morals were high, and she had never seen the dark side of the world.

When she was eleven years old, one summer, she attended a church camp with some of her Sunday school friends. The leaders of the camp thought they had thoroughly screened all of their workers. Yet there appeared to be a wolf in sheep's clothing that had gone undetected that year. He had gotten himself a position within the camp counselor team. Appearing to be upstanding during the day's activities, behind the scenes, he invaded the safety and privacy of the girls' cabin. On one of these occasions, he caught her while she was alone. Although this happened within a short week's period to a number of the young girls there that summer, it went unreported for the next several years.

All at once, her pristine, sweet, innocent world and psyche were shattered. Complicating this further was the paradox of this perpetrator presenting himself as ostensibly holy, yet engaging her in things that she had never fathomed before. This left her feeling permanently tarnished and damaged. Shame roared through her soul. She was afraid to tell anyone that this had happened to her. How could she tell her parents? They were so proud of her. Now would they look at her differently? Her thoughts raced with fear. How could this not be her fault? Did she not say no clear enough – loud enough? Did she do something to cause this? She dare not tell her parents. She felt covered with shame like a clingy garment that she could not shower off. She idolized her parents and could not bring herself to tell them what happened. Therefore, she locked it away deep inside, pushing it down further and further, as if never to surface again.

Life went on after this camp, and she still loved the Lord and was faithful in her church activities, along with her parents. The guy was never seen again. Yet little by little, the barricade of pain began chipping away at her soul. She had received Christ at a very young age and was sealed by the Holy Spirit (Ephesians 1:13), but she continued to turn the shame inward. Gradually she began hanging out with the wrong crowd. Nobody could understand why. As her pain and shame ran further underground, her sense of self-rejection grew more pronounced. Relationships with her Sunday school friends receded more and more into the background as she wondered how she could deserve these good people in her life. She felt different from everyone and undeserving.

As the hidden secret became more entrenched, she began to get into drugs. Initially, the exhilarating chemical high gave her a temporary respite from the darkness that kept trying to pry itself into her mind. Before she knew it, it had a stronghold on her life. She found herself forever trying to chase that first initial emotional high – that first oasis of relief – but could never find it again. The situation got worse and worse, and her bewildered parents did not know what to do.

Her parents sought resource after resource until finally, the secret came out. Precious finally began getting help to address her trauma directly. The drugs by then had begun to latch onto her brain chemistry with relentless intensity. She worked hard in recovery and emerged clean, diligently following her aftercare plan.

No one can really understand how utterly difficult and challenging addiction recovery is unless they have walked through it themselves. Her parents poured their hard-earned money into each treatment center after subsequent relapses, never giving up hope. In her parents' minds, money was no object. Whatever it took would be worth it. Think of all the parents who put their children through prestigious Ivy-league college educations. They vowed that this was the education that their daughter needed at this time.

Some treatment centers can also be wolves in sheep's clothing, taking advantage of families who desperately want to save their loved ones. Discernment applies here as well. Her parents carefully researched the treatment quality of the facilities they considered. They were actively involved in the family sessions and visits as well. Her parents and siblings provided loyal support for her and followed all recommendations for her care. Precious did well in recovery. Her loving spirit could not be snuffed out as she created healthy new relationships with others along the way, often pointing them toward Christ.

Precious had periods of success in recovery that were encouraging. Each time she would get a part-time job and begin to step back out into the world. She had plans to go all the way through college to complete a doctorate.

After a period, unexpectedly, something would lure her back out at night to be with the wrong crowd, but she would get back on track and back into recovery again each time. This went on for a while, and each time her exhausted yet faithful parents would help her get back into treatment. Some had advised them to cut her off and give her tough love. This advice had seemed to make sense at some level, but her parents could not in their heart of hearts give up on her. It is important to know that each individual's situation is different, and one person's advice does not necessarily apply to the situation for another person's specific ordeal. No one can tell you really what to do. A wise counselor can only offer options and choices, with pros and cons for each; but the actual decision needs to be made between you and God.

With each relapse, the part of her brain designed to restrain urges became incrementally more impacted. Each time she would get back into recovery, remorseful at her mistake, and even more remorseful at having worried her parents and family yet again and caused them more expense. Each time, multitudes of people from her church and abroad would pray for her to heal. In the final recovery period, Precious had maintained sobriety longer than she ever had before. She had also written healing amends and appreciation letters to all of her family and friends. Her heart remained sincere.

One day a police officer appeared at the front door of her parents' home. Her mother answered the door. When she saw him, she asked, "What is it this time, officer? Is she in the ER again? Arrested?" "No," he said. She had been found alone in a hotel room, where someone had given her a lethal dose of opioids. Her mother dropped to the floor.

What do you do with that?! This kind of trauma takes all three levels of Tier I, II, and III over and over again and intertwined. The grieving alone involves anger at a multidimensional level. There is anger at God, anger at the treatment centers who didn't seem to mind taking her parents' money, anger at all parties involved, and of course, anger at the perpetrator. This type of trauma leads to a very complex response involving an emotional overload of anger, guilt, and shame with an ambivalence that involves some paradoxical feelings of relief, which, in my observation, would create a spiral back into more guilt.[lxxiv] The cognitions often involve a sense of self-stigmatization. The authors who researched this type of complex response found that in these situations, parents who lost a child through drugs tended to stigmatize themselves with thoughts of having failed as a parent. As mentioned above, negative thoughts and cognitions are often associated with many forms of trauma, and cognitive healing will need to take place as the emotional pain is processed. This level of pain requires supernatural intervention.

Therefore, the cognitive shift must be preceded by grieving and requires transcendence beyond the present dimension.[lxxv] Eternity thinking, which transcends the mere here-and-now dimension of time and extends into the hope of eternity where we can reunite with loved ones, often cannot be reached before much grief has been processed. This grief needs to be given ample time. Christians have hope in knowing that there is eternal life and that we will *truly* indeed see our loved ones again. Still, it is insensitive to expect the survivors to obtain an eternity perspective before walking through the stages of grief at their own pace.

The grief process in trauma work and healing often involves the need to grieve the dream that was planned for that loved one. It will take time to begin to even wrap your brain around the idea of what life could be like without that person present. Giving yourself time is very important. Allow yourself to process your emotions in small, tolerable intervals. It is essential to be patient with your recovery. After a traumatic experience of this level, the mind and body can become hypersensitive and easily triggered by reminders of the event or the person. This is a normal, human response to trauma. Often professionals can be a valuable part of this healing process, either through medication, counseling, or both. It is natural to want to avoid revisiting the pain. Counseling should be gently paced to help you take back your life and heal. While it is hard to see at first, you still have a purpose here on this earth. No wretched perpetrator should ever have any ability to steal one single ounce of your emotional life nor your destiny.

In my experience of witnessing the pain that families go through with a loved one in recovery, I have come to believe that God heals people either while in this life or by bringing them on to the other side where there is no more pain. Whether it is cancer, addiction, or another calamity, God does hear and respond, but sometimes differently from how we wanted Him to. So, whatever you have gone through, give yourself time to process the emotions. Allow yourself sadness to grieve the dream and a safe place for constructively expressed anger (energy designed to repair). As you drain off much of the pain, you may begin to be able to see a glimpse of dimensions beyond just the present, practical, here-and-now.

Eternity Thinking

The Lincoln Family

Had Precious, in those last dark moments of despair, felt struck by the fact that once again, she was about to take her parents through yet another round of worry and the financial roller coaster? Drugs spike your brain with mood-elevating chemicals, and then they abruptly drop you into despair that is irrational and lower than you were before. Is it possible that in those moments, Precious asked God for a way to stop this insane merry-go-round? Each time she returned to her family after being tricked again by this spiritual enemy, the malevolent peers, or her struggling brain chemistry, she felt more shame *and guilt than before. We don't know what happened in those last few moments, but we know that police investigation indicated that Precious did not deliberately take her own life. She wanted more than ever to make her parents proud, and she loved her family with all her heart. No level of darkness could succeed in snuffing out the fact that she was one innocent life meant for greater things.*

As the parents engaged in their healing journey, in and out of tidal waves of emotional pain, they were able to also latch onto glimmers of hope despite this horrible storm. They know that she is in the arms of Jesus. They have the relief of knowing that she is no longer struggling with the horrible addiction. They know with confidence that they will see her again one day and have her back for the rest of eternity.

As for the perpetrators? Consequences do come to the instigator of foul play (Galatians 6 NIV). Even writings that are not traditionally Christian-based report accounts of unrepented souls who were briefly deceased but were resuscitated. They reportedly go through something called a life review, where they feel the full pain and effect that they had caused their victim, plus the ripple effect of everyone and everything impacted by their actions. The Christian writer of *Seven Lessons from Heaven* also reports an emotional experience that she also calls a *life review*.[lxxvi] If we attempted vengeance in our human limitations, we could not come anywhere near inflicting that much impact and awareness upon our perpetrators, as in the experience of such a life review, no matter how much influence and power we may own.

The Higher Order Perspective Existence (H.O.P.E.) to help you rise above the situation is a process that takes time and growth. Sometimes we find that the trauma experienced is the very training ground to make you utterly undefeated and ready for a higher destiny and purpose than you ever imagined. I once had a situation that, to me, was a horrendous trauma in my family. After going through what I considered to be the worst thing that could ever happen to anyone, I emerged stronger, wiser, and virtually impenetrable. Nothing was able to scare me anymore. Nothing could have an effect on me after that. Every threat paled in comparison to the traumatic ordeal that I had survived. Furthermore, I also realized that I had developed an acute and specific knowledge of how to deal with that situation and could now help others. I had acquired profoundly more in-depth insight, wisdom, and decision-making skill than I would have had before.

The most effective helpers of humankind are those who have walked through and survived painful pathways. A prime example is Alcoholics Anonymous. Once, while I was a counselor working in a psychiatric hospital, I was asked to lead their intensive outpatient addiction groups in the evening. The patients intuitively could detect that I had not gone through what they had. It is true, I was clueless. No matter how many years of counseling training, experience, book learning, and academic degrees I had obtained, there was no comparison to the insight and understanding that a recovering alcoholic could bring. Generally, people going through addiction recovery truly respect the personal experience of someone who has lived inside the skin of an addict and has emerged with maintained sobriety. What you may be going through may surpass years of expensive education. No amount of doctoral degrees can outweigh the substance gained from going through and mastering difficulty.

Receive the help you need to recover from abuse, addiction, sexual trauma, divorce, cancer, or terrorist attack. It may turn out to be the very training ground of effectiveness and impact that launches you into the stratosphere of your highest purpose and farther than you ever believed you could go. Reach forward and take hold of your life and your God-given destiny.

Summary

H.O.P.E. can be learned and developed in anyone willing to begin to think with a perspective that goes beyond the mere surface. The more solidly you become anchored in this higher level of thinking and perceiving, the more invincible you can become to the world's insults and offenses.

H.O.P.E. can be a way of perceiving events in life, from a higher plain, that becomes second nature to you. This is why I chose to use the term *existence* because it involves a continual place in which to exist emotionally and spiritually, resting on the hand of God. You can rest on the hand of God.

I call this perspective a higher order perspective, because it rises above emotional entanglements that could weigh you down. H.O.P.E. results from changing your thoughts, growing into Christ-like mindedness, relying on Him for all of your burdens, and wearing the armor of God. The view from this perspective is spectacular as we learn to see things through the eyes of God.

John 8:36 (NIV)

"So, if the Son sets you free

you will be free indeed."

Appendix A
Additional Exercises and Guided Imageries

Spiritual Awareness Exercise

(How do you perceive God?)

Feel free to do these exercises to sort out and remove any incorrect perceptions that you may have transferred to God, others, or yourself. Re-connecting to a Being much greater than ourselves serves as a great resource for recovery. Allowing positive resources of healthy peers, professionals, and therapeutic organizations into your life can lift you up and free you.

Use a separate sheet of paper for each question

1. Blending your Parents/Caretakers/Attachment figures:

A) Describe the **positive features** about them. Include all relevant interactions and experiences.

B) Describe the **negative features** of these caretakers

Include all relevant interactions and experiences.

C) Describe the **positive features** of your early (or later) understanding of God or Higher Power. Include your experiences and encounters (i.e., prayers answered, etc.).

D) Describe the **negative features** of your early (or later) understanding of God or Higher Power. Include your experiences and encounters (i.e., prayers unanswered, etc.)

Assessing Your Spiritual Awareness

Align the sheets of paper with caretakers side by side with the features of the Higher Power. Now examine all of the positive and negative features, comparing your caretakers with your perception of God or Higher Power.

Focus on your perceived experiences, knowing that the intention of the caretaker may or may not have deliberately been negative or hurtful. Alternatively, if the intention of that caretaker may have actually been negative, it is important for you to understand that the pain that they were spewing at you was coming from their own pain reservoir and was totally not mean for you.

Unfortunately, we are raised by humans with all their imperfections and flaws. What happened to you *was and is not* your fault. The only reason that you did not receive whatever it was you needed from that caretaker (love, respect, patience, value, safety) is *not* because of you. It was because that ingredient was simply *not there within that person*. You had nothing to do with it and are still worthy of those wonderful, loving ingredients.

After you have listed everything that you can think of, both positive and negative, about your parents/caretakers and about God on separate pages, now align the pages together. Look at the contrasts or similarities between your parents or caretakers with those of God. Do some of the positives match? More importantly, do some of these perceptions of negativity align between your early authorities and God? Do some of these features also seem to shape your own self-perception? Remember, these are *your* perceptions and interpretations. These do not necessarily reflect the actual intention of those in your life. As you go through some of this work, leave an open place in your mind for the possibility that any negative perceptions about God may have been transferred, from negative experiences that you had with parents or caretakers, and placed onto your mental picture of God.

If we project the negative experiences of people in our life onto our perception of God, we are limiting our ability to heal. We perceive the situation through an untrue lens leading to a warped perception that can only produce inadequate solutions. It is often natural to place the image and impressions of fallible humans onto the face of God because of our experiences with others in authority who were not accurate images of who God really is. God surpasses the parents or caretakers who raised us, even at their best.

GUIDED IMAGERY TO COPE WITH STRESS

Tips on Using Guided Imagery

There are a number of scenes that you can use to soothe stress and pain. You can imagine yourself walking through a forest or a meadow, sitting by a peaceful ocean, or at your favorite indoor spot. When imagining any of these places, make sure that it is only associated with safe images and pleasant surroundings.

Use all of your senses to increase the calming effect of this environment. Apply your favorite scenery (visual), sounds – such as music or a water stream (auditory), soft green grass (tactile), movement – such as walking or floating (kinesthetic), taste possibly (gustatory), and very important smells and aromas (olfactory). The more senses you apply, the stronger the concentration and focus you will have away from the stressor and onto the soothing image. It is okay if you are not particularly visual. Many people are not. Simply use the senses that work for you. You do not have to use all of them.

Pick your favorite scene. You may imagine being cradled in the arms of your Creator, being gently rocked with the aroma of lavender (or other calming aromas), and hear words of unconditional love being spoken to you. You may want to imagine yourself getting rid of burdens by imagining yourself floating up in a hot air balloon, becoming lighter and freer as you label each of the sandbags at your feet with the title of a burden. You then, one by one, throw each one out of the balloon, watching it become smaller and smaller and further away as it lands in a tiny puff on the ground where you leave it behind. Examples of these stressors could be debts, situations, or conflict, naming the noun but not the individual person, as you can use the exercises in Chapters four through seven to deal with difficult people.

Use calming imagery whenever you need to have a healthy escape from daily stress. This can last from a brief few minutes to as long as you need.

GUIDED IMAGERY FOR SELF-FORGIVENESS

Sample of Imagery from Oasis Workshops
by Dr. Joan Weathersbee Ellason

You are suddenly transported back in time to 2000 years ago. You look down to find your scantly clothed feet covered in dust with tattered sandals. The road is long.

Your attention is captured by a massive commotion up ahead. You hear the noise of cries and wails, screams, and calamity. What is going on? You must see what this is. So, you make your way closer until you reach the crowd. Now, much closer, the noise reverberates in your ears like nothing you have ever heard before. It is almost overwhelming.

Nevertheless, you press your way through that crowd, elbow to elbow, ignoring the grungy smell of sweat and stench from the people. You've got to see what this is! Suddenly you notice a unique scent of dogwood and you see a tall, massive structure towering above your head. It appears as if someone is struggling beneath its weight. Now, as you get even closer, you see tall soldiers surrounding something, or . . . someone?. Who is this?

The crowd now almost engulfs you, tightly squeezing you within. You ignore it, as you make your way through the soldiers, the noise, and the chaos. You finally break through and see what is at the center of this horrific commotion.

There in the midst, you see the back of someone covered with dirt, bruises, and lacerations who is leaning forward and struggling beneath the weight of the tall wooden structure. Who *is* this person, and what has he done to deserve any of this?

You are within arm's reach of him now. As you stretch out your hand and touch his moist shoulder, you feel his sweat and blood now on your fingertips. All at once he stops suddenly and spins around, face-to-face and eye-to-eye with you. So close that you feel his breath on your face. A pure light shines from Jesus' kind, loving eyes, that sooths your heart and soul like nothing that you have ever encountered before here on this earth. Now, in a soft voice so clear, Jesus says directly to you, "I forgive you this much. I FORGIVE YOU ***THIS MUCH!***"

He goes on to say to you tenderly, "Please let go of all of that anger toward yourself. You are innocent in my eyes. Can you fathom how precious you are to me? I am paying dearly for you, paying a price to cover all of your mistakes and regrets, so that you can live the fruitful life that I have planned for you. I can handle what you cannot bear. Will you allow me to save you from the broken pieces of your life? Hand them all over to me now, all your regrets and past mistakes... all of your fears. I can take them all and make them into an amazing new beginning."

"I love you with a love that goes beyond anything that you have ever known. I love you, eternally."

REFERENCES

Aaron T. Beck, John Rush, Brian F. Shaw, and Gary Emery, Cognitive Therapy of Depression, Edited by Michael J Mahoney (The Guilford Clinical Psychology and Psychotherapy Series, The Pennsylvania State University, New York, NY: The Guilford Press, 1979).

Albert Ellis, Raymond Chip Tafrate, How to Control your Anger Before it Controls You, (New York, NY: Citadel Press Kensington Publishing Corp, 1997, 2016).

American Psychiatric Association, Diagnostic and Statistical Manual of Mental Disorders. Fifth Edition (DSM-5), American Psychiatric Association, Washington DC 2013.

Centers for Disease Control and Prevention (CDC) https://www.cdc.gov.

Caroline Leaf, Who Switched Off My Brain: Controlling Toxic Thoughts and Emotions, (Grand Rapids, MI: Baker Books 2006, 2007, 2009).

Caroline Leaf, Switch on Your Brain: The Keys to Peak Happiness, Thinking, and Health (Grand Rapids, MI: Baker Books 2013).

Colin A Ross. The Trauma Model: A Solution to the Problem of Comorbidity in Psychiatry, Richardson, TX: Manitou Communications, 2000.

Colin A. Ross, Joan W. Ellason. (2001). Acute Stabilization in an Inpatient Trauma Program.

Journal of Trauma and Dissociation, Vol. 2, 83-87.

Colin Tipping, Radical Forgiveness: A Revolutionary Five-Stage Process to Heal Relationships,

Let Go of Anger and Blame, Find Peace in Any Situation, (Boulder, CO, Sounds True, 2009).

David Jeremiah, The Book of Signs: 31 Undeniable Prophesies of the Apocalypse. (W Publishing Group an Imprint of Thomas Nelson: Nashville TN, 2019), 125-138.

Don Piper with Cecil Murphey, 90 Minutes in Heaven: A True Story of Death and Life, (Revell a division of Baker Publishing Group, Grand Rapids, MI, 2014).

Divorce Corp, DVD directed by Joseph Sorge, released January 10, 2014

Eben Alexander III, 2012 Proof of Heaven: A Neurosurgeon's Journey into the Afterlife. Simon and Schuster New Your, NY 2012.

Ed Young, Seven Blind Mice (Scholastic Inc, 730 Broadway, NY, NY.10003, by arrangement with Philomel Books, a division of the Putnam & Cosset Book Group, First scholastic printing April 1993,1992).

Edmond Burke quote –

http://www.openculture.com/2016/03/edmund-burkeon-in-action.html

Erika J. Wolf, Ph.D. and Filomene G. Morrison, Ph.D. Traumatic Stress and Accelerated Cellular Aging: From Epigenetics to Cardiometabolic Disease.

HHS Public Access, NCBI PMC US National Library of Medicine, National Institute of Health

Traumatic Stress and Accelerated Cellular Aging: From Epigenetics to Cardiometabolic Disease (2017) Published online 2017 Aug 29. doi: 10.1007/s11920-017-0823-5

https://www.ncbi.nlm.nih.gov/pmc/articles/PMC5588711.

Francine Shapiro EYE Movement Desensitization and Reprocessing (EMDR): Basic Principles, Protocols, and Procedures. Second Edition. New York: The Guilford Press, 2001.

Frederick S. Perls, Gestalt Therapy Verbatim Edited by Joe Wysong, originally published in 1969, this edition by arrangement with the Estate of Federick Perls MD, Gestalt Journal Press, Gouldsboro, ME 1992.

Graham Cooke The Life-Changing Power of Rest. Living Free and Staying Free, Living Free, and Staying Free: Discover and Understand Your Favor, Videos Brilliant Perspectives, Aug 22, 2018, https://brilliantperspectives.com/the-life-changing-power-of-rest.

Henry Cloud and John Townsend, Boundaries: When to Say Yes, How to Say No to Take Control of Your Life, (Zondervan: Grand Rapids Michigan, 1992, 2017).

Jay Shetty, https://jayshettygenius.com.

Joan W. Ellason, Colin A. Ross, H.D. Day. (2003). Spirituality and Ego Strength, (Master's Thesis) Published in the American Journal of Pastoral Counseling, Vol. 6(4), 43-49.

Joan W. Ellason, Colin A. Ross. (1997). Two Year Follow-up of Inpatients With

Dissociative Identity Disorder. American Journal of Psychiatry, Vol.154, 832-839.

John Bradshaw On Homecoming: Reclaiming and Championing/Healing Your Inner Child (Bantam Books New York, 1990).

John Paul Jackson, an audio CD, Keys to Receiving God's Justice. www.streamsministries.com, January 1, 2005.

Joyce Meyer web site www.joycemeyer.org.

Joyce Meyer. Knowing Who I Am in Christ. In Everyday Answers, (date unknown)

https://joycemeyer.org/en/everydayanswers/ea-teachings/knowing-who-i-am-in-christ.

Joyce Meyer God Is Not Mad at You: You Can Experience Real Love, Acceptance & Guilt-free Living. New York, NY, Faith Words, Hachette Book Group, (2013).

Joyce Meyer Do It Afraid: Embracing Courage in the Face of Fear New York, NY, Faith Words, Hachette Book Group Inc. (2020).

Joyce Meyer Do Yourself a Favor and Forgive: Learn How to Take Control of Your Life Through Forgiveness. (New York, NY, Faith Words, Hachette Book Group, 2012).

Judith Wilkins Ph.D., LMFT, LPC Personal Communication 1978; 10,6,2020

Kristine Berg Titlestad, Sonja Mellingen, Margaret Stroebe & Kari Dyregrov (2020): Sounds of silence. The "special grief" of drug-death bereaved parents: a qualitative study, Addiction Research & Theory, pages 1476-7392. Published Online: 20 Apr 2020,

DOI: 10.1080/16066359.2020.1751827.

https://doi.org/10.1080/16066359.2020.1751827.

Larry Dossey website http://larrydosseymd.com.

Linda Marten (Licensed Professional Counselor-Supervisor) in discussion with the author, November 1991, October 15, 2020.

Lisa Firestone Ph.D. ANGER: The Role of Anger in Depression: Turning anger on ourselves contributes to the severity of depression. (Psychology Today, Posted Oct 09, 2017)

https://www.psychologytoday.com/us/blog/compassion-matters/201710/the-role-anger-in-depression.

Louis Walter Weathersbee (My beloved father, 1924 - 1967) in discussion with the author, throughout my life.

Mark Felber, LPC, LCDC In Loving Memory

(https://www.linkedin.com/in/markfelber

Maryanne Watson, Ph.D., ABPP (Licensed Psychologist) inquiry response to the author, January 18, 2018.

Mary C. Neal M.D. (Author) 7 Lessons from Heaven: How Dying Taught Me to Live a Joy-Filled Life (Convergent Books an imprint of the Crown Publishing Group, a division of Penguin Random House LLC New York (2017).

Melissa Caldwell Engle, LPC, ATR, Clinical Director and Co-founder of Healing Springs Ranch and Executive Clinical Director at the Ross Institute for Psychological Trauma for 20 years) personal communication 10/29/2020.

Open University www.openuniversity.edu.

Oxford Dictionary

https://www.lexico.com/definition/cognition.

Paul Meier, M.D.

(https://www.psychologytoday.com/us/psychiatrists/paul-d-meier-richardson-tx/59332)

Physiopedia contributors, "Numeric Pain Rating Scale," Physiopedia,

https://www.physiopedia.com/index.php?title=Numeric_Pain_Rating_Scale&oldid=238203 (accessed October 26, 2020),

https://www.physio-pedia.com/Numeric_Pain_Rating_Scale).

R. Morgan Griffin 10 Health Problems Related to Stress That You Can Fix. WebMD. (2018).

https://www.webmd.com/balance/stress-management/features/10-fixable-stress-related-health-problems#1.

RT Kendall, Total Forgiveness: When Everything in You Wants to Hold a Grudge, Point a Finger, and Remember the Pain – God Wants You to Lay it All Aside (Lake Mary, Florida: Charisma House, A Strang Company, 2002, 2007), Chapter 2.

Shane Pruitt, CP Op-Ed Contributor, "7 Myths About Forgiveness," The Christian Post, CP CURRENT PAGE: OPINION | THURSDAY, APRIL 28, 2016.

https://www.christianpost.com/news/myths-about-forgiveness.html.

Stephen Post and Jull Neimark, Why Good Things Happen to Good People: How to Live a Longer, Healthier, Happier Life by the Simple Act of Giving, (Broadway Books, an imprint of the Doubleday Broadway Publishing Group, a division of Random House, New York, NY 2007).

Webster's Encyclopedic Unabridged Dictionary of the English Language (Gramercy Books, a division of Random House Value Publishing, New York, NY 1993).

Dr. Joan Weathersbee Ellason

SUGGESTED READINGS AND RESOURCES

BOOKS

Spiritual Growth

The Power of the Holy Spirit in You (to be released in 2021)
By Pat Robertson (Author) https://www1.cbn.com/700club.

Shelter in God: Your Refuge in Times of Trouble. (2020)
By David Jeremiah (Author) W Publishing, an imprint of Thomas Nelson, Nashville, TN.

The Jesus You May Not Know: Take the Journey from Knowing About Jesus to Knowing Jesus (2020)
by Dr. David Jeremiah (Author) W Publishing, an imprint of Thomas Nelson, Nashville, TN.

God Is Not Mad at You: You Can Experience Real Love, Acceptance & Guilt-free Living (2013)
By Joyce Meyer (Author) Faith Words, Hachette Book Group, New York, NY.

Unshakeable Trust: Find the Joy of Trusting God at All Times in All Things (2017)
By Joyce Meyer (Author) Faith Words, Hachette Book Group, New York, NY.

Emotional Growth

Born to Win: Transactional Analysis with Gestalt Experiments (1971, 1996)
by Muriel James and Dorothy Jongeward (Authors) Addison-Wesley Publishing, Boston MA.

Home Coming: Reclaiming and Championing Your Inner Child (1990)
By John Bradshaw (Author) Bantam Books, New York, NY.

Battlefield of the Mind (1995)
By Joyce Meyer (Author) Life in the Word, Inc Fenton, Missouri; Warner Books Inc. New York, NY.

Beauty for Ashes: Receiving Emotional Healing (2003
by Joyce Meyer (Author) Time Warner Book Group, New York, NY.

Healing the Soul of a Woman: How to Overcome Your Emotional Wounds (2018)
By Joyce Meyer (Author) Hachette Book Group. New York, NY.

Boundaries: When to Say Yes How to Say No to Take Control of Your Life (1992, 2017)
By Henry Cloud and John Townsend (Authors), Zondervan, Grand Rapids Michigan,
1992, Expanded Version 2017.

Perfect Daughters (1989, 2002)
By Robert J. Akerman (Author) Health Communications, Inc. Deerfield Beach, FL.

Who Switched Off My Brain: Controlling Toxic Thoughts and Emotions (2006, 2007, 2009)
Caroline Leaf, (Author) Baker Books, Grand Rapids, MI.

Switch on Your Brain: The Keys to Peak Happiness, Thinking, and Health, (2013)
Caroline Leaf, (Author) Baker Books, Grand Rapids, MI.

Do It Afraid: Embracing Courage in the Face of Fear (2020)
By Joyce Meyer (Author) Faith Words, Hachette Book Group Inc., New York, NY.

Hinds Feet in High Places (2010)
By Hannah Hurnard (Author) Wilder Publications, Blacksburg, VA

Seven Blind Mice (1992, 1993)
By Ed Young. by arrangement with Philomel Books, a division of the Putnam & Cosset Book Group, First scholastic printing Scholastic Inc, NY, NY.

Forgiveness

Do Yourself a Favor and Forgive: Learn How to Take Control of Your Life Through Forgiveness (2012)
By Joyce Meyer (Author) Faith Words, Hachette Book Group, New York, NY.

Radical Forgiveness: A Revolutionary Five-Stage Process to Heal Relationships, Let Go of Anger and Blame, and Find Peace in Any Situation (2009)
By Colin Tipping (Author) Sounds True, a Trademark of Sounds True Inc., Boulder, CO.

Total Forgiveness: When Everything in You Wants to Hold a Grudge, Point a Finger, and Remember the Pain – God Wants You to Lay it All Aside (2002, 2007)
By RT Kendall (Author): Charisma House, A Strang Company, Lake Mary, FL.

Self-Forgiveness

You Can Begin Again: No Matter What, It's Never Too Late (2014)
by Joyce Meyer (Author) Faith Words New, York, NY.

Radical Self Forgiveness: The Direct Path to True Self-Acceptance (2011)
By Colin Tipping (Author) Sounds True, a Trademark of Sounds True Inc., Boulder, CO.

Grieving

Bearing the Unbearable: Love, Loss, and the Heartbreaking Path of Grief (2017)
by Joanne Cacciatore and Jeffrey Rubin, Wisdom Publications Somerville, MA.

The Sudden Loss Survival Guide: Seven Essential Practices for Healing Grief (Bereavement, Suicide, for Readers of Together) (2020)
by Chelsea Hanson, Marty Tousley, Mango Publishing Group, a division of Mango Media, Inc, Coral Gables, FL.

It's OK That You're Not OK: Meeting Grief and Loss in a Culture That Doesn't Understand (2017)
by Megan Devine and Mark Nepo, Sounds True, Boulder CO.

The Other Side of Sadness: What the New Science of Bereavement Tells Us About Life After Loss (2010)
by George A. Bonanno Ph.D. (Author) Basic Books, New York, NY.

Inspirational lectures and Teachings

Your Move by Andy Stanley
https://yourmove.is/

Joyce Meyer Ministries
www.joycemeyerministries.org

Dr. Charles Stanley
https://www.intouch.org/

Dr. David Jeremiah
https://www.davidjeremiah.org/

Streams Ministries International
https://streamsministries.com/

Graham Cooke
https://brilliantperspectives.com/

Finally…….The How-To of Forgiveness

ACKNOWLEDGMENTS

Peer Reviewers:

Stephen Weathersbee, LMFT

Kathy Ives, LPC

Ron Killough, PhD

N. B.-Baghdadi, B.A.

Kathy Williams

Yvonne Kilburn-Mazzone

Front and back cover design

by Pro_design37

Scenic back cover photo

by Chad Weathersbee Ellason

Personal Stories for this Book

Other Unidentified contributors

[i] Tipping, Colin C. *Radical Forgiveness: A Revolutionary Five-stage Process To: Heal Relationships, Let Go of Anger and Blame, Find Peace in Any Situation.* Boulder, CO: Sounds True, 2009.

[ii] Meyer, Joyce Meyer. *Do Yourself a Favor and Forgive: Learn How to Take Control of Your Life Through Forgiveness.* New York, NY: Faith Words, Hachette Book Group, 2012.

[iii] Leaf, Caroline. *Switch on Your Brain: The Keys to Peak Happiness, Thinking, and Health.* Grand Rapids, MI: Baker Books 2013.

[iv] Physiopedia contributors, "Numeric Pain Rating Scale," *Physiopedia*, https://www.physio-pedia.com/index.php?title=Numeric_Pain_Rating_Scale&oldid=238203 (accessed October 26, 2020), https://www.physio-pedia.com/Numeric_Pain_Rating_Scale.

[v] Shapiro, Francine. *EYE Movement Desensitization and Reprocessing (EMDR): Basic Principles, Protocols, and Procedures. Second Edition.* New York: The Guilford Press, 2001.

[vi] Perls, Frederick S., and Joe Wysong. *Gestalt Therapy Verbatim.* Highland, NY: Center for Gestalt Development, 1992.

[vii] Bradshaw, John. *On Homecoming: Reclaiming and Championing/Healing Your Inner Child.* Bantam Books New York, 1990.

[viii] Beck, Aaron T., A. John. Rush, Brian F. Shaw, and Gary Emery. *Cognitive Therapy of Depression.* New York: Guilford Press, 1983. Edited by Michael J Mahoney (The Guilford Clinical Psychology and Psychotherapy Series, The Pennsylvania State University, New York, NY: The Guilford Press, 1979) (Aaron T. Beck, Cognitive Therapy and the Emotional Disorders (59 Boston Post Rd, Madison, CT International: Universities Press, Inc., 1976, 1979).

[ix] https://www.linkedin.com/in/markfelber

[x] Cloud, Henry, and John Townsend. *Boundaries: When to Say Yes, When to Say No to Take Control of You.* Grand Rapids: Zondervan, 1992.

[xi] Leaf, Caroline. *Who Switched off My Brain?: Controlling Toxic Thoughts and Emotions*. Baker Books, Grand Rapids, MI., 2006, 2007, 2009.

[xii] Leaf, Caroline. *Switch on Your Brain: The Keys to Peak Happiness, Thinking, and Health*. Baker Books, Grand Rapids, MI., , 2013.

[xiii] Griffin, R. Morgan. "10 Stress-Related Health Problems That You Can Fix." WebMD. April 01, 2014. Accessed November 17, 2020. https://www.webmd.com/balance/stress-management/features/10-fixable-stress-related-health-problems.

[xiv] Wolf, Erika J., PhD and Morrison, Filomene G., PhD. *Traumatic Stress and Accelerated Cellular Aging: From Epigenetics to Cardiometabolic Disease*. HHS Public Access, NCBI PMC US National Library of Medicaine, National Institute of Health. Traumatic Stress and Accelerated Cellular Aging: From Epigenetics to Cardiometabolic Disease (2017) Published online 2017 Aug 29. doi: 10.1007/s11920-017-0823-5 https://www.ncbi.nlm.nih.gov/pmc/articles/PMC5588711.

[xv] *Diagnostic and Statistical Manual of Mental Disorders (Fifth Edition): DSM-5*. Arlington, VA: American Psychiatric Association, 2013.

[xvi] Ross, Colin A. *The Trauma Model: A Solution to the Problem of Comorbidity in Psychiatry*. Richardson, TX: Manitou Communications, 2007.

[xvii] www.joycemeyer.org.

[xviii] These were my own observations from experience - generalized to the reading audience.

[xix] Kendall, R. T. *Total Forgiveness: When Everything in You Wants to Hold a Grudge, Point a Finger and Remember the Pain, God Wants You to Lay It All Aside*. Lake Mary, FL: Charisma House, 2002.

[xx] Kendall, R. T. *Total Forgiveness: When Everything in You Wants to Hold a Grudge, Point a Finger and Remember the Pain, God Wants You to Lay It All Aside*. Lake Mary, FL: Charisma House, 2002.

xxi Meyer, Joyce. *Do Yourself a Favor and Forgive: Learn How to Take Control of Your Life Through Forgiveness*. New York, NY, Faith Words, Hachette Book Group, 2012.

xxii http://www.joycemeyer.org.

xxiii *Webster's Encyclopedic Unabridged Dictionary of the English Language*, Gramercy Books, a division of Random House Value Publishing, New York, NY 1993.

xxiv Personal Communication 1991, 10/15/2020.

xxv www.andystanley.com. Also https://yourmove.is/.

xxvi Shane Pruitt, CP Op-Ed Contributor. "7 Myths About Forgiveness." The Christian Post, CP Current Page: Opinion. April 28, 2016. https://www.christianpost.com/news/myths-about-forgiveness.html.

xxvii Jackson, Paul John. *Keys to Receiving God's Justice*. www.streamsministries.com, January 1, 2005.

xxviii www.openuniversity.edu.

xxix http://www.openculture.com/2016/03/edmund-burkeon-in-action.html.

xxx "Some STDs, like **HIV**, can be fatal if left untreated." https://www.ncbi.nlm.nih.gov/books/NBK232551/.

xxxi "Sexually Transmitted Infections (STIs)." University of Rochester Medical Center. Health Encyclopedia. https://www.urmc.rochester.edu/encyclopedia/content.aspx?contenttypeid=85&contentid=p00651.

xxxii Cloud, Henry, and John Townsend. *Boundaries: When to Say Yes, When to Say No to Take Control of You*. Grand Rapids: Zondervan, 1992.

xxxiii https://www.cdc.gov

xxxiv Young, Ed. *Seven Blind Mice*. Scholastic Inc NY, NY.10003, by arrangement with Philomel Books, a division of the Putnam & Cosset Book Group, First scholastic printing April 1993,1992.

xxxv Beck, Aaron T., A. John. Rush, Brian F. Shaw, and Gary Emery. *Cognitive Therapy of Depression*. New York: Guilford Press, 1983. Edited by Michael J Mahoney (The Guilford Clinical Psychology and Psychotherapy Series, The Pennsylvania State University, New York, NY: The Guilford Press, 1979).

xxxvi Leaf, Caroline. *Switch on Your Brain: The Keys to Peak Happiness, Thinking, and Health*. Grand Rapids, MI: Baker Books 2013.

xxxvii Personal Communication Judith Wilkins PhD, LMFT, LPC, 1978, 10/6/2020.

xxxviii CBN. https://www1.cbn.com.

xxxix Keller, Carrie, *Thomas Raphael Verny (1936–)*. Embryo Project Encyclopedia (2019-07-31). ISSN: 1940-5030. http://embryo.asu.edu/handle/10776/13116.

xl Verny, Thomas, Kelly, John. *The Secret Life of the Unborn Child*. Dell Publishing: New York, NY, 1981.

xli Greenspan, Stanley and Thorndike, Nancy. *First Feelings*. Penguin Books, New York, NY, 1986.

xlii Bradshaw, John. *On Homecoming: Reclaiming and Championing/Healing Your Inner Child*. Bantam Books New York, 1990.

xliii Alexander III, Eben. *Proof of Heaven: A Neurosurgeon's Journey into the Afterlife*. Simon and Schuster New York, NY 2012.

xliv Piper, Don with Murphey, Cecil. *90 Minutes in Heaven: A True Story of Death and Life*. Baker Publishing Group, Grand Rapids, MI, 2014.

xlv Larry Dossey website. http://larrydosseymd.com/.

xlvi *The Bible*. Matthew Chapters 26 & 27. New King James Version®. Copyright © 1982 by Thomas Nelson. Used by permission. All rights reserved.

xlvii Ellis, Albert, Tafrate, Raymond Chip. *How to Control Your Anger Before It Controls You*. New York, NY: Citadel Press Kensington Publishing Corp, 1997, 2016.

xlviii Cooke, Graham. *The Life-Changing Power of Rest. Living Free and Staying Free, Living Free and Staying Free: Discover and Understand Your Favor.* Videos Brilliant Perspectives, Aug 22, 2018.| https://brilliantperspectives.com/the-life-changing-power-of-rest.

xlix Paul D Meier, Psychiatrist, MD. https://www.psychologytoday.com/us/psychiatrists/paul-d-meier-richardson-tx/59332.

l Meyer, Joyce. *Knowing Who I Am in Christ. In Everyday Answers*. Date unknown. https://joycemeyer.org/en/everydayanswers/ea-teachings/knowing-who-i-am-in-christ

li Perls, Frederick S. *Gestalt Therapy Verbatim*. Edited by Joe Wysong, originally published in 1969, this edition by arrangement with the Estate of Federick Perls MD, Gestalt Journal Press, Gouldsboro, ME 1992.

lii Ellis, Albert, Tafrate, Raymond Chip. *How to Control your Anger Before it Controls You*. New York, NY: Citadel Press Kensington Publishing Corp, 1997, 2016.

liii Beck, Aaron T., Rush, John, Shaw, Brian F., and Gary Emery. *Cognitive Therapy of Depression*. Edited by Michael J Mahoney. The Guilford Clinical Psychology and Psychotherapy Series, The Pennsylvania State University, New York, NY: The Guilford Press, 1979.

liv Leaf, Caroline. *Switch on Your Brain: The Keys to Peak Happiness, Thinking, and Health*. Grand Rapids, MI: Baker Books 2013. Leaf, Caroline. *Who Switched Off My Brain: Controlling Toxic Thoughts and Emotions*. Grand Rapids, MI: Baker Books 2006,2007, 2009.

lv https://www.lexico.com/definition/cognition.

lvi "Five Stages of Grief." Wikipedia. November 17, 2020. Accessed November 17, 2020. https://en.wikipedia.org/wiki/Five_stages_of_grief.

lvii Judith Wilkins PhD, LMFT, LPC Personal Communication 1978; 10,6,2020.

lviii https://jayshetty.me.

lix Post, Stephen Garrard, Neimark, Jill. *Why Good Things Happen to Good People: How to Live a Longer, Healthier, Happier Life by the Simple Act of Giving.* New York: Broadway Books, 2007.

lx Leaf, Caroline. *Switch on Your Brain: The Keys to Peak Happiness, Thinking, and Health.* Grand Rapids, MI: Baker Books 2013.

lxi www.joycemeyer.org.

lxii Ellis, Albert, Tafrate, Raymond Chip. *How to Control your Anger Before it Controls You.* New York, NY: Citadel Press Kensington Publishing Corp, 1997, 2016.

lxiii Personal communication 10/29/2020, Melissa Caldwell Engle, LPC, ATR, Clinical Director and Co-founder of Healing Springs Ranch and Executive Clinical Director at the Ross Institute for Psychological Trauma for 20 years.

lxiv Psychology Today, 2017, Lisa Firestone, The Role of Anger in Depression.

lxv Shapiro, Francine. *EYE Movement Desensitization and Reprocessing (EMDR): Basic Principles, Protocols, and Procedures.* Second Edition. New York: The Guilford Press, 2001.

lxvi http://www.dailyword.com/what-god-box

lxvii Meyer, Joyce. *God Is Not Mad at You: You Can Experience Real Love, Acceptance & Guilt-free Living.* New York, NY, Faith Words, Hachette Book Group, 2003.

lxviii Bradshaw, John. *On Homecoming: Reclaiming and Championing/Healing Your Inner Child.* Bantam Books New York, 1990.

lxix Diamond, Stephen A. Ph.D. *Evil Deeds, Psychology Today, Essential Secrets of Psychotherapy: The Inner Child: Has your adult self spent time with your inner child today?* Jun 07, 2008.

lxx Jeremiah, David. *The Book of Signs: 31 Undeniable Prophesies of the Apocalypse*. W Publishing Group an Imprint of Thomas Nelson: Nashville TN, 2019, pp 125-138.

lxxi Jeremiah, David. *The Book of Signs: 31 Undeniable Prophesies of the Apocalypse*. W Publishing Group an Imprint of Thomas Nelson: Nashville TN, 2019, pp 125-138.

lxxii Jeremiah, David. *The Book of Signs: 31 Undeniable Prophesies of the Apocalypse*. W Publishing Group an Imprint of Thomas Nelson: Nashville TN, 2019, pp 125-138.

lxxiii Jeremiah, David. *The Book of Signs: 31 Undeniable Prophesies of the Apocalypse*. W Publishing Group an Imprint of Thomas Nelson: Nashville TN, 2019, pp 125-138.

lxxiv Titlestad, Kristine Berg, Mellingen, Sonja, Stroebe, Margaret, and Dyregrov, Kari. *A Book Report*. Year Unknown.

lxxv Ellason, J.W., Ross, C.A., & Day, H.D. (2003).

lxxvi Neal, Mary C. M.D. (Author) *7 Lessons from Heaven: How Dying Taught Me to Live a Joy-Filled Life*. Convergent Books an imprint of the Crown Publishing Group, a division of Penguin Random House LLC New York, 2017.

www.ingramcontent.com/pod-product-compliance
Lightning Source LLC
Chambersburg PA
CBHW030902080526
44589CB00010B/111